The development of sociology in the Soviet Union

International Library of Sociology

Founded by Karl Mannheim

Editor: John Rex, University of Warwick

A catalogue of the books available in the **International Library of Sociology** and other series of Social Science books published by Routledge & Kegan Paul will be found at the end of this volume.

The development of sociology in the Soviet Union

Elizabeth Ann Weinberg

Department of Sociology,
London School of Economics

Routledge & Kegan Paul

London and Boston

First published in 1974
by Routledge & Kegan Paul Ltd
Broadway House, 68-74 Carter Lane,
London EC4V 5EL and
9 Park Street,
Boston, Mass. 02108, USA

Printed in Great Britain by
Willmer Brothers Limited, Birkenhead

ISBN 0 7100 7876 5
Library of Congress Catalog Card No. 73-93639

For My Family
With Love and Gratitude

Contents

Figures and tables

Acknowledgments

I wish to thank Suzanne Keller for initially stimulating my interest in the sociology of knowledge. Ithiel deSola Pool and Celia Heller helped in directing my early attempts to understand Soviet sociology. Special thanks go to Gayle Durham Hollander for initiating me into the world of Soviet source materials. I owe special debts of gratitude to the late Merle Fainsod who guided my master's dissertation on Soviet public opinion research and to Leonard Schapiro for his valuable assistance as my graduate supervisor. Eleanora Gottlieb helped me in many ways, not least in grappling with the complexities of the Russian language. Finally, my thanks to Angus Stewart for his advice and encouragement.

Introductory note

The origins of the present study lie in the intersection of two areas of interest, the historical and social circumstances surrounding the development of sociology (or rather, sociologies) in different societies, and a specific 'area' concern with the social structure and dynamics of the Soviet Union. My initial exposure to the issues and problems raised by a sociological analysis of Soviet society took place very much at the same time that the first post-'thaw' products of a reviving sociology in the Soviet Union were beginning to emerge. In addition to an interest in research findings in particular areas, there emerged a general concern with the obstacles to and the mechanisms of the acceptance of sociological enquiry in a society formally founded on the principle of planned social change through the agency of a centralised political apparatus.

Within this context, therefore, the following is a case study in the institutionalisation of a discipline in a particular society. As it happened, the historical period with which the study is broadly concerned – that of the 1960s – was characterised by a developing interest in the problematic, contingent nature of sociological enquiry in Western societies and in the social uses which that enquiry was meant to serve.* In general, the consequence has been to make clear that the 'unique' situation of Soviet sociology was more apparent than real. However, given the historical significance of the Soviet Union, an interest in the manner in which sociological enquiry has been legitimated there has continuing relevance.

Given its central focus on the problem of legitimation, the present study does not attempt a systematic assessment of the findings of

*See, for example, in general, A. W. Gouldner, *The Coming Crisis of Western Sociology*, London, 1971, and R. W. Friedrichs, *A Sociology of Sociology*, London, 1970. For a specific study of the controversy surrounding social science at the service of government, see I. L. Horowitz, *The Rise and Fall of Project Camelot*, Cambridge, Mass., 1967.

Soviet sociologists. Further, it is recognised that much work, either directly sociological or relevant to sociologists, has been and was produced in the Soviet Union by individuals and groups not calling themselves sociologists, but operating within the context of other disciplines. The assumption is made, however, that such work did not contribute directly to the institutionalisation of sociology as a separate discipline. Because the focus is on the emergence of a discipline within an institutional context, the criterion for sociology is that those who produce it call themselves sociologists.

Chapter 1 puts sociology in historical perspective, tracing its development from pre-Revolutionary times to the 1956 Twentieth Congress of the Communist Party of the Soviet Union. Chapter 2 describes how the sociological aspects of Soviet Marxism, dormant during the years of the 'cult of personality', were revived and how 'Marxist sociology' was advanced as a legitimate discipline. The second half of the chapter deals with this exercise in self-definition as it arises from the Soviet critique of 'bourgeois sociology'. Chapter 3 similarly deals with questions of the theoretical assumptions underlying research methodology, principally in so far as these relate to the process of institutionalisation. The next chapter is concerned first with the institutional framework in which the sociologists work, then with the sociologists themselves, that is, their education, regional ties, age, and specialities, and finally with their journals. Chapter 5 surveys the areas of research that contemporary Soviet sociologists are investigating and in particular highlights the purported relation between these research areas and wider aspects of Soviet society. This includes work on: time budget research; labour; social stratification; marriage, the family, divorce, and the woman's role; urban development, city planning, and urban-rural relations; criminology and juvenile delinquency; and religion. Chapter 6 traces in depth the development of an area of particular significance in Soviet sociology, public opinion research. Since its initiation in 1960, the expansion and improvement of such research in a period of liberalisation has reflected the increasingly pragmatic trend in sociology, the growing belief among decision-makers in the functional value of such research and the greater acceptance of sociological research by the country at large. At the same time, such research affords an excellent opportunity of chronologically tracing changes in the presentation, the research methods and the approach to this type of research. The final chapter discusses the general question of the institutionalisation of knowledge by detailing sociology's current role within the Soviet Union and indicating the obstacles the discipline faces.*

*An earlier formulation of the present work was submitted as my doctoral dissertation: The development of sociological studies in communist states – the case of the USSR, University of London, 1970.

A few words seem necessary about some technicalities. A glossary of Russian terms appears at the end of the text. All of the words in it follow Russian spelling rules (e.g., the plural of *vuz* is *vuzy*). There are some Russian words, however, which are today quite common in English (e.g., komsomol). They are not italicised in the text, and their plurals follow English spelling rules. The Library of Congress system of transliteration has been adopted. I have also followed the Soviet practice of transposing pre-1917 orthography into new.

1 Historical background

Up to the beginning of the twentieth century sociology was not taught in Russia as an independent discipline under that name but as an aspect of various areas of intellectual enquiry such as the 'philosophy of history', 'social foundations of economy', 'social psychology', and the like. By 1906–7, for example, Maxim Kovalevskii wrote: 'we have – in all – one chair [of sociology] in the whole Empire of 160 million inhabitants and that at a private university in the Psycho-Neurological Institute [in St Petersburg].' Kovalevskii, the first to hold the chair of sociology at the Psycho-Neurological Institute which specialised in psychiatry, neurology and experimental psychology, continued: 'I would be less surprised at the news that in Nanking or Peking a department of sociology was created than at hearing of the fact that Mr Kasso [Minister of Education] had started such a reform in Moscow or St Petersburg.'[1] By 1917, however, some universities were offering courses in sociology.

Although the formal science of sociology was hardly taught in Russian universities, the Russians were neither ignorant of nor unconcerned about social problems and ideas; quite the contrary. While it is beyond the scope of this study to discuss the work of the early Russian sociologists or to evaluate their contributions to sociology at large, it is clear that questions of the history of civilisation, the development of social ideas and ideas of progress, the nature of the state, the establishment of sociology as a distinct social science – as well as specific investigations into the family, the intellectuals, the role of women, etc. – were ardently debated in pre-October Russia.

Strong links existed between those concerned with these questions and European thinkers. In addition to the ties which the upper classes and intelligentsia had through European languages and cultures, many Russian professors emigrated to Europe in the early part of the

1

twentieth century. In 1901, a group of them in Paris (e.g., Kovalevskii, deRoberty, Kareev) set up a Russian section of the Higher School of Social Sciences attached to the Sorbonne; this later became the Higher Russian School of Social Sciences. The tradition of the Paris Higher School was continued when in 1905 a Higher Free School was opened in St Petersburg. It was this establishment which was the first to teach sociology as an obligatory subject.[2]

In general, Russian thought had experienced the same intellectual influences that had affected the rest of Europe, although through the process of adaption ideas were sometimes distorted. In sociology, in particular, there were extensive translations from the writings of German, French, English and American sociologists. Some Russian sociologists even argued that there were more sociology translations than original sociological literature.

The general impression which emerges from the various surveys of Russian social thought in this period is of the representation of a wide diversity of points of view, the satisfactory classification of which is a difficult if not impossible task. Principal among these various schools of thought were: the subjectivists, such as Lavrov, Mikhailovsky, and Iuzhakov, who by accepting positivist, empiricist philosophy rejected the biological-organic and mechanist schools; the mechanists, such as Voronov and Spektorsky, who interpreted social phenomena from the viewpoint of 'social mechanics' or 'social physics'; the behaviourists, such as Bekhterev and Pavlov, who began analysing physiological processes, proceeded to nervous processes and then applied their knowledge to social phenomena; and economic materialists, such as Plekhanov, Tugan-Baranovsky and Struve, who said that the basis of all social phenomena was economic.[3]

Articles on sociology and sociological problems were published in many weeklies and monthlies: 'rarely does an issue of one of our thick magazines fail to contain articles on some question of sociology.'[4] In 1913, Maxim Kovalevskii co-edited with E. V. deRoberty and P. A. Sorokin the first of a series of sociological yearbooks entitled *Novye idei v sotsiologii* (*New Ideas in Sociology*):[5] *New Ideas in Sociology* took the place of a sociology journal and helped to gain further recognition for sociology in the academic world. Under its stimulus, among other factors, the first Russian Sociological Society was established in 1916 in Petrograd (in honour of Kovalevskii).

The post-Revolutionary situation

The general situation in Russia after the Revolution in the 1920s and early 1930s was analogous to the slow process of re-furnishing a room. The old furniture was to be removed and replaced by the new, in a piecemeal fashion. For a while, the old and new co-existed. Gradually, however, the whole room took on a new character as the structure was re-designed.

The same process occurred in the field of sociology. The 'old philosophy' was gradually dislodged from its position in the journals and in the universities.[6] Private publications serving as the mouthpiece of 'bourgeois' views were totally eliminated by 1922. By 1924, the Department of Social Sciences at Moscow State University which included a chair in sociology was closed after its five-year existence. The chairs of sociology became chairs of the history of social thought; Marxist theory of society and social development became an obligatory subject.

The old idealist furnishings were to become materialist: the new structure was to be based on the *Weltanschauung* of Marxism. This transformation involved the struggle of proletarian ideology with idealism – philosophy, historiography, and sociology, of which the last was accused of disseminating the legend of the absence of sociology from Marxism. In the attack on bourgeois sociology, the concepts of *narod* (nation, nationality, folk), stratification, class, and progress were particular targets.[7] Marxist sociology was subsequently entrusted with applying the method of dialectical and historical materialism to social relations and with further developing historical materialism. At the same time, it was charged with popularising and propagandising the ideas of historical materialism and with teaching the masses about the construction of socialism.

The strongest opponents of these changes were to be found in Petrograd, the city which housed the first university to offer sociology and the first Sociology Society. Here, the discipline *qua* discipline had been most firmly entrenched prior to the Revolution. Immediately after the Revolution, Petrograd University opened a department of sociology and subsequently created a bio-sociological institute to study the relation between organic and social forces. The faculty of social sciences at the University offered courses in 1920–1 entitled the system of sociology, genetic sociology, history of sociological studies, history of socialism and criminology. In addition, there was established a society for studying the liberation and revolutionary movement of Russia. At the same time, the Kovalevskii Sociological Society was reactivated in 1920 – it had been interrupted by the death of its president, A. S. Lappo-Danilevskii, and the Revolution – and, according to a retrospective report by V. I. Klushin, its anti-Marxist direction was widely publicised by Pitirim Sorokin.[8]

Sorokin himself held a professorship at the Psycho-Neurological Institute and Petrograd University by the end of 1918. Writing from the perspective of 1925, Sorokin describes his life as a sociologist at Petrograd:[9]

My classes in sociology at the University became the largest and most closely attended in the whole institute, not because I was such a talented lecturer, but because sociology had now become such a vitally important subject. Not only the students, but the university clerks and the public attended my lectures. If my scientific data had favoured the Government, I should not have been sorry, because it would have made my lot much happier, but I had to present facts as they were. Being a sociologist under such conditions was a damnable business, but I had to be honest. I can hardly describe the difficulties under which I continued my work, which I knew might any day cause my arrest.

Sorokin was forbidden to teach in the autumn of 1921 but he continued his research at the Research Institute of the Brain (where he 'would not be harmful to students') and at the History and Sociology Institute of the University. In September of 1922 he, along with other bourgeois thinkers, was banished from the Soviet Union. Sorokin's Petrograd colleague, K. M. Takhtarev, wrote in October 1923 that 'at the present time, chairs of general sociology at the University do not exist. Sociology has been replaced by the history of the development of social (*obshchestvennye*) forms. . . .'[10] By mid-1923, the department of general sociology at the university had ceased to exist, although courses listed as 'historical materialism (sociology)' continued until the mid-1930s. In place of the department of general sociology there was organised a department of the development of social forms.

Qualifications to this gloomy picture of the state of sociology in Petrograd in the 1920s are offered in a contemporary analysis by the Leningrad sociologist, V. I. Klushin. He states that one of the major difficulties faced by those who sought to transform the system was the fact that the 'so-called official sociology in the university department was represented by professors who either did not hide their animosity towards Marxism or, having declared themselves to be Marxists, were no such thing and were not able to become Marxists.'[11] The non-Marxists were divided into two schools: 1. the positivists (e.g., Sorokin and Takhtarev) who, in spite of major differences, were united in their general approach to sociology as an empirical science and as an intimate of natural science, especially biology; and 2. the 'last of the Mohicans' (as Klushin calls them), a group of speculative philosophers of history of a non-Marxist kind (e.g., S. Frank and N. Karsavin). Disputes about the subject and content of sociology within and between these two non-Marxist schools – and between them and the Marxists – were the order of the day.[12]

The Marxists in Petrograd, the majority of whom were young,

spent much time in the early years after the Revolution popularising the ideas of the founders of Marxism-Leninism. Since there were only a few Marxists among university staff, they concentrated on political economy, history, and the materialist understanding of history, defending these from the attacks of the bourgeois ideologists. By the middle of the 1920s, the Scientific Society of Marxists (*Nauchnoe Obshchestvo Marksistov:* NOM), which had been formed in the Worker's Faculty (*rabfak*) at the end of 1919, had become the recognised centre of Marxist philosophical and sociological thought in Petrograd. NOM's journal, *Zapiski nauchnogo obshchestva Marksistov* (*Transactions of the Scientific Society of Marxists*), further helped to spread the ideas of the society.

The displacement of idealism by materialism was also accomplished by the creation of scientific institutes (mostly in Moscow) where both teaching and research in the social sciences took place. In 1918, the Socialist Academy was established as the centre for Marxist research. In its socio-historical section, the general introductory courses included genetical sociology and 'general sociology (historical materialism)'; in the political-juridical section, there were courses on the sociology of crime. The Marx-Engels Institute, whose philosophy library was arranged for historical materialism *and* sociology, was formed in 1920. A year later, the Institute of Red Professors was set up for the express purpose of training professors for higher education posts (a branch was opened in Leningrad at a later stage). The preparation of Marxist-educated university teachers was also undertaken by the Sverdlov Communist University, the Russian Association of Scientific Research Institutes of the Social Sciences (RANION), and others.

The impact of the new regime was felt not only in institutions but also in publications. In 1922, the first Soviet philosophical and socio-economic monthly journal, *Pod znamenem marksizma* (*Under the Banner of Marxism*) was published and was soon followed by other journals which treated theoretical problems of society and general questions of social philosophy. The contributors to most of these journals and the teachers at the universities were primarily specialists in dialectical materialism and the history of philosophy with the result that these fields were more fully represented in the published works than were the problems of (Marxist) sociology. Another reason for this was that the anti-Marxist literature was more philosophical than sociological in character and thus the criticism by the Marxists fell within the limits of the former.

During these years, several important questions on Marxist sociology were raised. These dealt mainly with the relation of method and theory in historical materialism, the relation of general and particular laws, productive forces and productive relations and the theory of the class struggle. Different interpretations of historical materialism were expressed. One treatment of historical materialism derived from mechanism whose theoretical sources were 'the subjective-idealist views of Bogdanov, the positivism of bourgeois philosophy, and the mechanistic tendencies in the natural sciences'.[13] Nikolai Bukharin appeared as the principal representative of this field in the realm of sociology; he presented an integral mechanistic conception of sociology, closely connected with the views of Bogdanov on the questions of methodology, as well as on such problems of historical materialism as the origin of class, the state and ideology. Up to the beginning of the 1930s, Bukharin's book, *Teoriia istoricheskogo materializma – populiarnyi Uchebnik Marksistskoi Sotsiologii* (*Theory of Historical Materialism: a Popular Textbook of Marxist Sociology*) was the centre of verbal and written discussions on historical materialism and Marxist sociology since in it he advanced the view that historical materialism *is* Marxist sociology. It was during the period of these discussions and criticisms (e.g., Bukharin's concepts were 'unhistoric', 'abstract', 'scholastic' and/or 'revisionist') that Soviet philosopher-Marxists were developing the content and structure of historical materialism as an academic discipline.[14]

A. M. Deborin and his students were critics of, and eventually successors to, the mechanists in the 1920s. Questions of historical materialism seemed to be of little importance and were even ignored in the Deborinite criticism because the Deborinites concentrated on the problems of dialectical, rather than historical, materialism. *Istoriia filosofii VI* (*History of Philosophy VI*) notes that:[15]

> Deborin himself and his group underrated historical materialism and declined in point of fact to work out actual problems of social development; they were not in a position to challenge the mechanistic sociological conceptions of Bukharin and others because they neither had a correct standpoint nor did they undertake thorough and concrete scientific research on the problems of social development.

Deborin and his students viewed historical materialism not as sociology but only as a social *methodology*, as a totality of abstract, logical categories with which the Marxist only 'approaches' the study of the laws of different social formations, that is, historical materialism provides the 'domain assumptions' of social analysis for the Marxist.[16] Sociology, according to these views, is the task then not for philosophers but for specialists. Consequently, social theory was taken out of the boundaries of philosophy.[17]

There were thus two views about historical materialism by the end of the 1920s and the beginning of the 1930s: Bukharin's, identifying the materialist understanding of history with sociology in general (i.e., historical materialism is Marxist sociology), and Deborin's, identifying historical materialism only with social methodology. At the All-Union conference of historian-Marxists in February 1929 (that is, just prior to the April 1929, Sixteenth Party Congress from which the Deborinites emerged victorious), the discussion about the Marxist understanding of sociology showed quite definitely that Marxist sociology had not yet been officially defined: questions as to whether it was a theory, a methodology, or both – and its consequent relation to historical materialism – clearly reflected both mechanistic and Deborinite tendencies.[18]

In the early 1930s debates continued over the question of the relation of historical materialism and Marxist sociology. These were largely a continuation of earlier arguments but refinements did occur. Some theoreticians underlined the mainly philosophical aspect of historical materialism, others saw sociology as historical materialism, while a third group considered historical materialism to be both an inseparable part of Marxist philosophy and a theory of social development.[19] In general, in comparison with the 1920s, little progress was made with regard to the development of the theory of historical materialism. Some theoretical analysis did approach less general questions about the transition to and construction of a socialist society. Advances were made in four areas in particular: works connected with theoretical questions of socialist construction were published; Leninism was established as making its own contribution to the analysis of problems of Marxist sociology; important questions were raised on culture and cultural revolution; and a number of texts and collections on historical materialism appeared, dealing with the role of ideas and the development of society, the role of the mass and related questions.[20] At the same time, with reference to the institutional context, some advance occurred through the development of the sociological groups within the Institute of Red Professors in Moscow, its branch in Leningrad, and in the philosophy branch of the Communist Academy.

Before turning to sociology in the period of *partiinost'* (party mindedness, commitment to the party line), we must examine the state of empirical research since the Bolshevik victory.[21] As early as 1918, Lenin, in defining the programme of the Socialist Academy of the Social Sciences, formulated the task of developing social research. At his suggestion, a broad programme of social research was initiated. The areas under study were: 1. labour, especially the conditions and organisation of labour and the influence of socio-psychological, educational and general cultural factors on labour production; 2. the economic mode of life and the income(s) of different categories of the population (e.g., the peasants); 3. class

7

relations and questions of the theory of classes; 4. culture; 5. religion; 6. socio-economic and socio-demographic data collecting and processing; and 7. methods and techniques of social research. It has been suggested that the research was not so much sociological as socio-economic and social in character. Assessment of this position depends upon a particular theoretical stance but certainly the research did have an applied character and relied to a significant degree on having statistical data and on using simple questionnaire methods and interviews. Of all the men mentioned in connection with research on new social processes, most often cited are S. Strumilin in connection with his research on the time budgets of workers, peasants and employees (*sluzhashchie*), L. Kritsman on the (class differentiation of) peasants and the economy of the village, and S. Vol'fson on marriage and the family.

In reviewing this early period, V. Kantorovich states that sociologists 'were able to rely on data, objective in their origin, considering that statistics were widely accessible and researchers did not have to provide themselves with visas and passes to statistical materials'.[22] However, Klushin is much more critical of the researches carried out in this period: 'There was not time for concrete research, which demanded a high degree of processing and comprehension of general methodological principles and methods', because in view of their inadequate theoretical training, the few Marxists in the field of sociology devoted themselves to considering abstruse problems of the materialist understanding of history.[23]

The 1930s saw an intensification of the influence of power-political as opposed to political social influence. Just as the mechanists had been eclipsed by the Deborinites in 1929, so the Deborinites were eclipsed by the Bolshevisers in 1930–1. Philosophy and sociology were to serve the party: the disciplines were to be politicised, Bolshevised and ultimately, Stalinised.[24]

> There is not and cannot be a philosophy [sociology] that wants to be considered Marxist-Leninist philosophy [sociology] while denying the necessity of ideational-political and theoretical leadership on the part of the Communist Party and its leading staff.

From the mid-1930s to the mid-1950s, sociology as an independent academic discipline virtually disappeared in the Soviet Union. Sociology was to have no distinct place in the Marxist system since it was considered a 'bourgeois' and, consequently, non-Marxist subject. Marxism-Leninism-Stalinism took its place.

The number of courses of philosophy and sociology in *vuzy* (higher educational establishments) diminished. The teaching of Marxist philosophy was entrusted to the newly created departments of

Marxism-Leninism. The departments of dialectical and historical materialism remained only in the universities and institutes where philosophy, history and literature faculties existed. Many sociological terms and concepts worked out by Marx, Engels and Lenin, were no longer used: 'the very word "sociology" in this period was found to be prohibited'.[25] Only that social terminology and those social concepts to be found in the works of Stalin were recognised. The basis of sociological and philosophical commentaries became the chapter entitled 'Dialectical and Historical Materialism' in *History of the CPSU(B): Short Course*, 1938. 'When only one man was recognised as having the right to scientific creativity, all that was left to the others was to comment, popularise and – admire.'[26] To the commentaries on Stalin's pronouncements may be added those on other Marxist-Leninist classics. There was very formal discussion of such subjects as class structure, marriage and the family, religion and atheism, ethics and morals, art and aesthetics, and basis and super-structure. In addition, there were general discussions of the laws of social development and the transition from socialism to communism. The net result was that theory and practice were split. There was a prevalence of 'scholasticism' (that phenomenon which describes detachment from life), the 'deducing' of life from theory, and the 'fitting' of new facts and phenomena to schemes and constructs already known.

Such sociological research as was carried out during this period occurred under the rubric of other disciplines. Ethnographers and anthropologists, for example, investigated religious behaviour and family patterns of various national and minority groups in the out-lying Soviet Republics; some did research on the kolkhozes (collective farms). Although it was mainly of a descriptive nature, this collection of data was a source of information about the impact of socialism and industrialisation. It is of course possible (though not probable) that work in sociology, as in some branches of psychology, was being done even though it was not published.[27]

Very few sociological articles appeared in journals which had once carried such articles. While Chagin suggests that gradually in the period 1939–40 some were published in *Pod znamenem marksizma* in which an attempt was made to go beyond the canons of Stalin's work, the journal itself was discontinued in 1944.[28] Until 1947, when the publication of *Voprosy filosofii* (*Problems of Philosophy*) began, there was no philosophical journal in the country. However, *Bol'shevik*, the organ of the CPSU, somewhat bridged the gap. It was there, in fact, that the second stream of writing during Stalin's rule – namely, criticism of bourgeois sociology – roughly began in earnest in the middle of the 1940s. Articles on this subject were published first in *Bol'shevik* and then in *Voprosy filosofii*.

9

Why was criticism of bourgeois sociology necessary? G. Aleksandrov, writing in *Bol'shevik* in 1945, suggested the answer:[29]

Soviet philosophers are obliged to continue the work on the substantial criticism of contemporary reactionary bourgeois philosophical and sociological theories. Our scientific and teaching staffs during the last years have had little information about the state of philosophical and sociological thought abroad. However, the struggle against the ideology of bourgeois reaction as regards the most real political questions is impossible without the exposure of contemporary reactionary bourgeois philosophical and sociological theories.

Although these articles were less subtle and more polemical than those of the late 1950s and 1960s, the targets for reproach were basically the same.[30] On the whole, bourgeois sociology was continuously represented as an abstract metaphysical approach to the study of society, whereas its counterpart, historical materialism (Marxist sociology), was presented as the only scientific approach. It was Marxism, Lenin had said, which had first raised sociology to the level of a science. And the theory of historical materialism was – and is – the Marxist science of society.

With the exceptions just noted, therefore, the period up to the mid-1950s represents the nadir of Soviet sociology. Only with the Twentieth Party Congress in 1956 did it experience any kind of renaissance. As Chagin says:[31]

The Twentieth Party Congress initiated the gradual elimination of dogmatism and subjectivism in the sphere of Marxist theory and the liquidation of the consequences of the cult of personality in the sphere of Marxist sociology. This was the turning point. The 1950s – these are the years when sociology rehabilitated many lost positions, renouncing dogmatic ideas of the period of the cult of Stalin's personality and tried to become an authentic research science, relying on the practice of communist construction and the theoretical legacy of Marxism-Leninism. This was a complicated and contradictory process. The canons and dogma did not disappear at once from the content of historical materialism. The ranks of sociologists were not re-built at once. Many still clung to the old. But the creative spirit of research continuously pierced through the dogmatic conglomerations. Soviet sociology, like all philosophy, in the 1950s defended its right to become a creative science.

What caused this to happen in the 1950s? As every Soviet account reiterates, 'After the decisions of the Twentieth Party Congress (and the subsequent four Congresses), the party defined the role and tasks of the social sciences, pointed out the main directions of research work, and directed the concrete study of the processes of communist construction.' In *Pravda* and *Kommunist*, the party orientation to the solution of theoretical problems appeared and the basic lines of the further development of philosophy and sociology were laid.

The party and 'practice' finally produced the demand for a search for solutions to many questions raised during the Stalin era, and the first steps in the rebirth of sociology were taken.* But while the party had at last opened the door for the development of sociology, it was not until the Twenty-Third Party Congress in March–April 1966 that sociology was recognised officially as a discrete discipline with distinct functions. In the preceding decade, there had been fought out a theoretical battle which also represented at the level of social forces a struggle for the legitimation of sociology. It is to this theoretical debate that we now turn.

*In addition to these internal factors, a major stimulus to the revival of sociology in the Soviet Union came from contact with the more highly developed sociology of Eastern Europe and in particular with Polish sociology.

2 Soviet and bourgeois sociology

The 1956 Twentieth Party Congress of the CPSU called for liberalisation in general and an end to the separation of theory and practice in particular. At that time, the discussion about sociology's renewed right to exist took the form of a debate on the classification and definition of the term sociology. Central to this discussion were questions about the tasks, the subject and the very legitimacy of concrete social (in particular, sociological) research:[1]

> The development of society has [had] confronted us with a host of new questions concerning the economy, the social structure, the state, the family. Whereas these questions used to be raised only in very general terms, now [after the Twentieth Party Congress] we are concerned with their practical – that is, their supremely concrete – content; the daily activity of the masses in various spheres of public life raises scores of concrete 'how's' and 'why's' and demands concrete, scientific answers to these questions.

In fact, empirical research on the 'how's' and 'why's' began while the philosophers were still defining and classifying sociology. While the terms of the philosophical discussion were the familiar ones of the relationship between sociology and historical materialism, the purpose of the debate was clearly to find ideological and philosophical justification for the discipline.

Within what terms was sociology established as an independent discipline? On one side of the crucial discussions were those who, following the discussions of the 1920s and 1930s, claimed that historical materialism is sociology. Historical materialism, it was argued, studies the general and particular laws of social development; sociology studies the general and particular laws of social development. The two are therefore identical. Because historical materialism already exists, there is no need for sociology as an independent science.[2] The central points of this position were as follows:

Sociology is a philosophical discipline.

According to its content, it coincides with historical materialism.

The subject of sociology is both the general laws of development of human history and the specific laws of the functioning and development of socio-economic formations.

Sociology, that is, historical materialism, studies social life at different levels.

Sociology, that is, historical materialism, is also defined as an experimental, empirical science.

The term 'sociological research' is avoided and in its place is 'social research' which all social sciences perform.[3]

On the other side were those who maintained that historical materialism is not simply equivalent to sociology. Here it was argued that it is the theoretical side of sociology alone which coincides with historical materialism. (The argument implicitly conflated general theoretical and methodological questions.) The empirical or applied side of social enquiry therefore becomes an independent science, sociology. Understood in these terms, sociology is synonymous with 'concrete sociological research', based on empirical investigations.[4]

In addition to these two principal positions, there were a variety of alternatives advanced on different bases. One of these differentiated between historical materialism and sociology according to the laws which each studies. Historical materialism studies the general laws of development of society as a whole, historically defined. These general laws are manifest at all stages of societal development and in all spheres of life. Sociology, on the other hand, should study the laws pertaining both to specific formation,[5] i.e., specific stages of social development, and to specific spheres of life, i.e., economics, politics, etc.[6] This proposition was somewhat altered subsequently by those who argued that historical materialism studies the laws of nature, society and thought, whereas sociology specialises in the study of society alone.[7]

A further position was that which saw sociology as a science studying laws which proceed from the more general to the particular. Within this hierarchy, three major distinctions are made. The first distinction refers to the general laws existing during the entire course of human history. This coincides with historical materialism, with 'all-sociological' (*obshchesotsiologicheskaia*) theory. The second distinction pertains to those laws which are present in different economic formations (e.g., capitalism, socialism, communism).[8] The third distinction refers to those laws, discoverable through concrete sociological research, which pertain to only one social formation.[9]

Distinct from but related to these alternative positions about the relationship between historical materialism and sociology were a series of views about the relationship between sociology and the social sciences. One of these claimed that sociology is social science in its most general form. Sociology is fuller and wider than other social sciences because it uses the results obtained from all social research and it also studies society directly. Thus sociology examines the entire system of social relations.[10]

A different view asserted that sociology – an independent science – is just one of the many concrete social sciences which study the social structure. Sociology, as a social science (and not as part of philosophy), is similar to the other sciences which share with sociology the theory and method of historical materialism. Related to this view is the argument that sociological research is merely one form of social research: social research is wider than sociological research because it covers social relations in such diverse fields as economics, law and the state.[11] As against this, there is the view that each of the three branches of Marxism-Leninism – philosophy, political economy and scientific communism – conduct social research.[12] Sociological research can therefore be subsumed under any or all branches.

It should be understood that no real resolution was arrived at over these various positions which were taken up in the years following 1956. In whole or in part, many of the debates continue to the present. The point which is emphasised here is that the latent significance as opposed to the manifest content of these debates was in their establishing that there was a legitimate area of discussion about the exact status of sociology and its nature as a social science. This, of course, meant accepting the initial premise of sociology's existence at all. Through a combination of the various propositions described above, sociology has – for all practical purposes – won the battle for legitimation and recognition as an independent academic discipline within the Soviet Union. In so doing, it has demonstrated that a science in addition to historical materialism should be created.

While there is no consensus on the above classifications, most Soviet sociologists would agree that in the most general sense theirs is a science which studies the laws of the functioning and development of society, a science proceeding from Marx's basic laws, embracing the socio-historic process and concerning social phenomena and their interaction. This science investigates the laws and motive forces of the origin, development and replacement of socio-economic formations. At the same time, it is concerned with the totality and interaction of social phenomena within society: sociology studies the social structure of society as a complete, organised system of social relations, institutions and social groups, interrelated with each other. Because the individual is viewed as the product of society, being both nurtured and moulded by it, society is defined as the broadest system of mutually interacting persons.

The Soviet view of bourgeois sociology

In general, the Soviet conception of sociology is inversely related to its view on bourgeois sociology. Since the 1920s, any means of constructing (Marxist) sociology has simultaneously been a way of combating bourgeois ideology which, according to this view, tries to construct sociology by basically ignoring historical materialism. Marxist sociology has long been considered to be in a state of ideological war with bourgeois sociology. The battlefield itself is the arena for, as well as the means of, an intense ideological struggle. Marxist and bourgeois sociology are enemies because they have opposing social, political and theoretical bases; their understanding of history, either materialist or idealist, is incompatible; and the former carries out 'scientific' sociological research whereas the other is plagued by empiricism.[13]

The most obvious and basic Soviet criticism of bourgeois sociology is its class character. The interests of the bourgeoisie are the *de facto* bases of bourgeois sociological principles. The bourgeoisie, as the ruling class, needs sociology to help solve numerous problems: sociology comes to its aid, just as it, in turn, aids sociology by readily financing research. Thus bourgeois sociology, as the executor of the direct social orders of the ruling class, has 'aided' research such as Project Camelot. This naturally raised in the Soviets' mind the problem of the relationship between sociologist and client.[14]

Furthermore, bourgeois sociology acts as the disseminator of bourgeois ideology, as the 'handmaid of imperialism'.[15] It recommends ways of strengthening the capitalist system and of rationalising and stimulating the organisation and productivity of labour.[16]

> Modern bourgeois sociology is nothing more than a mechanical aggregate of different social myths and utopias which express the age-old dream of a class peace, social integration, solidarity, harmony, etc, while preserving private ownership of the goods and means of production and, consequently, the exploitation of man by man.

Bourgeois sociology also undertakes to cure the individual ills and eliminate the conflicts within capitalist society, but it completely ignores the general social process of which these ills are merely particular manifestations. The individual is taught to be a loyal member of bourgeois society and to blame not the society but himself for any and all difficulties.[17]

The second objection to bourgeois sociology, namely, its lack of

15

and use of theory, is somewhat paradoxical. On the one hand, bourgeois sociology is condemned for not having a general, all-embracing theory of social development and for denying the significance of such a theory. But on the other hand, it is accused of professing idealism and metaphysics, rather then materialism and dialectics. In a similar vein, bourgeois sociology is criticised for giving credence to such diverse theories and philosophies as positivism, neo-positivism, pragmatism, personalism, existentialism, neo-Malthusianism, neo-Thomism, neo-Kantianism, etc.[18]

Although bourgeois sociology is not guided by a single, all-embracing theory (such as historical materialism), it is recognised nonetheless that it contains more limited sociological theories. Of these, three usually appear as targets of criticism. The first is the 'stages of growth' theory, originally proposed by W. W. Rostow as an alternative to the Marxist study of socio-economic formations. It is not difficult to understand why this comes under attack, especially if it is recalled that Rostow sub-titled his theory 'A non-communist manifesto'. The second refers to the concept of 'a single industrial society' which is closely related to convergence theory. While it is accepted that the two super powers are indeed industrial countries, one is capitalist and the other socialist, and the theory negates the root differences between the two. Convergence is neither feasible nor desirable. The third theory is associated with Malinowski and Parsons, namely, the theory of structural-functionalism. While structural-functional analysis may expose several links in society, its limits are obvious to Soviet critics:[19]

> In the first place, this [its limits] is explained by the disregard for the socio-economic basis of the social structure which is principally distorted by the concept of structure and function of social formations. In the second place, [this is explained] by the disregard for the genetic approach to the analysis of social phenomena [and] by the anti-historicism peculiar to functionalism. Marxist sociology proceeds from the organic unity of the structural-functional and genetic approaches [or methods] in sociological research.

The problem with the structural-functional approach to social phenomena, according to the Soviet critics, is a methodological one: the methodology of Marxism is ignored by the structural functionalists. Since Marxist sociology considers both functioning and development, the method of functionalism cannot be applied because it only discusses the former. In contrast, 'Marxism . . . examines any social system as maintaining a certain stability, [while] simultaneously becoming, appearing, developing and transforming into another system.'[20]

However, in the recent past more Soviet sociologists are stressing that the structural-functional approach is an organic part of the Marxist method of sociological – or economic – analysis. Marx in *Capital* – and Engels in his works on the family – is cited as a classical form of 'systems (structural) and functional analysis of capitalist economy as a complex dynamic system'.[21] Furthermore, 'to speak of structural-functional analysis as wholly the creation of Western sociology [and to argue that] Marxist sociology must be "re-armed" using it, means above all to ignore the real experience of the development of Marxist theory which there is at the present time'.[22]

A third major Soviet criticism of bourgeois sociology involves the connection between bourgeois sociology and social psychology or the assimilation of the former by the latter. Accordingly, the objective logic of social development is overlooked and the real nature of capitalist society remains obscured behind a façade of psychic interaction between people – behind the web of individual human relations, acts and intentions.[23] Thus sociology is converted into a theory of behaviour in which no distinction is made between objective phenomena and their reflection in the minds of men. By equating the concept of 'social situation' with the concept of 'social-psychological', 'purely ideal' phenomena are analysed without regard for their dependence on and conditioning by material factors.[24] Thus the human psyche becomes the fundamental basis of society and the role of economics is ignored.

At the same time that bourgeois sociology is censured for gravitating towards social psychology, it is accused of marrying empiricism. Lacking a general theory and refusing to show general social patterns, bourgeois sociology then becomes equated with empirical research. The particular (i.e., the fact) is raised upon a pedestal and the general (i.e., the law of the historical process) is ignored.[25]

As a result, social life is compartmentalised. This partially happens because 'society' itself is thought of as a 'mechanistic aggregate of individuals', as an aggregate of isolated social beings.[26] Man, the individual, is discussed in the abstract, outside of classes, outside of social groups. What follows is the growth of separate sociological disciplines – for example, the sociology of religion or the sociology of the family – each concerned with carrying out petty studies. These researches, non-historical by nature and devoid of generalised theory, tackle specific, and not long range, problems, the 'solution' to which aims at adapting people to the existing system. Even the use of objective methods is nullified by a subjective interpretation of data. And even in the best cases of this 'factology', only the relations existing at the surface of social life are discovered.

The definition and criticism of bourgeois sociology in the 1966

c

Kratkii slovar' po filosofii (*Short Dictionary of Philosophy*) aptly sums up the Soviet view:[27]

In capitalist countries sociology is a branch of knowledge [which has] a developed network of institutions in which a large number of concrete researches is conducted. The majority of these researches bears a practical character and is subsidised by private firms and monopolies. Contemporary bourgeois sociology is separate from philosophy. It ceased being a general theory of social development, having been split into a multiplicity of separate 'sociologies' – labour, political life, education, family, leisure, sport, etc. Empiricism prevails. . . . Sociology, in point of fact, is converted into social psychology. . . . Thus, in spite of sociology's declaration of 'independence' from philosophy, bourgeois sociologists inevitably proceed from definite philosophical theories, as a rule idealistic and metaphysical. The inability of bourgeois sociology to give a general picture of the development of social life is explained by the fact that the bourgeoisie, as the class which has lost its *raison d'être*, is not interested in the knowledge of the general laws of history which predict its demise. The class function of bourgeois sociology consists in working out practical means for smoothing over social conflicts, in justifying and defending capitalism. [This is] accompanied by attacks on communism. . . . Fearing to recognize the progressive development of society, bourgeois sociology prefers the concept of 'social change(s)' to the concept of 'progress'. . . . Criticism of contemporary bourgeois sociology and its methodological bases is one of the important tasks of Marxist sociology.

In spite of this blanket criticism, it should be noted that, in more recent Soviet writings, Western sociologists are divided into those with whom the Soviets should co-operate and those with whom co-operation is impossible. In more strictly political terms, there are two poles of thinking, one represented by C. Wright Mills and his criticism of the Cuban invasion and of the American ruling elite, and the other represented by W. W. Rostow, as one of the authors of the single industrial society theory. Most recently, the young radical sociologists who criticise conservative trends in the development of bourgeois sociology are favourably seen to present a new approach to sociology, especially in their 'non-conformist' research.[28]

The views presented above, gleaned from the considerable number of articles, monographs and books devoted to bourgeois sociology, represent the most general and widely held Soviet views concerning the functions and limitations of bourgeois sociology. By no means all of these arguments are found in each Soviet treatise, nor are they all upheld by everyone writing in the field. In fact, the majority of articles deal with specific, rather than with general, areas of sociological interest. In many cases, a most detailed account of bourgeois theory and research is offered, explained and criticised. While the degree of sophistication regarding the presentation of the critiques varies considerably, the prevalent sentiment is that bourgeois sociology by its very nature is not and cannot ever be Marxist sociology. Therefore those characteristics for which bourgeois sociology is criticised are considered not to be inherent in Marxist sociology.

In reviewing Soviet criticism of bourgeois sociology, it would be foolish not to note that in the first place, bourgeois sociologists criticise their own work and in the second, their criticism often falls within the range of shortcomings and criticisms noted and put forward by the Soviets. For example, Project Camelot was censured equally by Soviet and Westerner alike.[29] Or, more broadly, the single industrial society theory has stimulated some strong debates both for and against. However, it is not my intention to examine how valid these criticisms are, but rather to look at the positive role that the critiques of bourgeois sociology perform in terms of the development of Soviet sociology.

The invectives against bourgeois sociology have helped to establish and stimulate the growth of sociology if for no other reason than that after discrediting bourgeois sociology in various ways, those who endorse Soviet sociology can portray their own as the more superior science. Within a similar frame of 'ideological' warfare, some Soviets might argue that they need their own sociology to counteract both the theory and research of bourgeois sociologists.

On a more positive front, the explication of bourgeois texts has made bourgeois theory and research available in Russian to a large number of people, many of whom would not have had access to the originals. In the best instances, the theory or research is presented in detail before it is criticised. Often the theories and researches are traced through a period of time, sometimes dating back to the nineteenth century. Extensive bibliographies may accompany the discussions. In this way the Soviet sociologist learns about and may consequently utilise what is happening outside the Soviet Union. In this sense his intellectual isolation (particularly prevalent during and immediately after the Stalinist era) is diminishing, his sociological horizons are broadened, and he may be able to avoid some of the problems, in theory and methodology, which his colleagues abroad have faced and overcome. The process of adopting and adapting some aspects of bourgeois sociology becomes more apparent in the next chapter.

But before turning to that issue, it must be made clear that the discussions in the Soviet Union were about the classification and the definition of *Marxist* sociology. According to Soviet sociologists, Marxist and Soviet sociology are synonymous because the Soviets are unanimously engaged in Marxist sociology whereas the vast majority of sociologists in capitalist societies are engaged in what the Soviets typify as bourgeois sociology. Thus the generic term 'sociology' encompasses two mutually exclusive brands of sociology.

3 The theory of research

The more closely one examines Soviet accounts on research methods and techniques, the more one becomes aware that Soviet sociologists are as anxious as others to find those methods and techniques which will best serve to analyse social phenomena. Such differences as do occur in their writings may be traced to the Soviets' original attempts to obtain initial recognition of the most elementary ways and means of gathering, processing and analysing information. The usual process has consisted in explaining and qualifying a specific method and then appealing for its acceptance by other Soviet sociologists. Once the method has been at least partially accepted as valid for Marxist research, the sociologists plead for and indicate ways for its improvement. Viewed as a whole, the process represents a strategy for institutionalising sociological research practices.

As part of this process, more and more has been written about the benefits of studying the techniques employed by non-Marxist sociologists and engaging in critical borrowing of such methods. Justification for the use of such methods by Soviet sociologists has to be sought and the fact that they are used by bourgeois sociologists rationalised. Thus there has been a change from perceiving methods as 'bourgeois' to seeing them as 'acceptable' in terms of their general validity and applicability. Like bourgeois sociologists, Soviet sociologists are now more able to weigh the pros and cons of already established methods and to develop others.

Earlier blanket criticism of various methods has subsided. In its place there were discussions about the significance of using such indices as the arithmetic mean, the degree of variation from the mean and the degree of error. Gradually a variety of methods – game theory, the theory of optimal programming, the theory of probability, correlation analysis – became part of the sociologist's normal equipment. By this stage, the most significant criticism was concerned with the mechanical application – potential or actual – of methods worked out in other disciplines, without due consideration of their validity for sociology.

No matter which methods are used, the Soviet researcher is seen as ideally performing certain functions. He is to examine the general theoretical problems of society and analyse social phenomena which appear as a result of new forms of productive, social and personal relations. His studies should facilitate the 'all-round' development of man's personality (e.g., the 'new man'), thus linking societal with individual development in the process of building communism. By studying social phenomena, the sociologists should be able to influence the development of society in the capacity of a social planner: he is to extract meaning and a programme of action from the 'facts' he uncovers. He is to share his data with state, party and public organisations which, in turn, aid him in research. By analysing the results, he is to provide planning agencies, enterprises and institutions – especially in the techno-economic realm – with invaluable information and 'feedback'. Pre-conceived stereotypes are to be destroyed by such research and negative phenomena (such as crime) are to be eliminated. Bearing in mind that the Soviets equate sociology with social research, the following remarks by V. A. Iadov, a leading sociologist, are a representative statement of the Soviet view of the functions of such social research:[1]

First, the *informational* function – sociology uncovers social problems, provides scientific description of them, and classifies and analyses them. Then, the *critical* function – it collates new facts with those previously known, evaluates possible variations in explaining them, offers explanatory hypotheses with respect to the given sphere of phenomena. . . . Next, the *theoretical* function – the scholar builds a non-contradictory, integral concept, a model of the sphere under study. Next, the function of *prognosis* – forecasting possible paths of development or changes in social processes and evaluating the reliability of the forecasts. And then the *'engineering'* or applied function – the sociologist proposes optimum paths for active intervention in social processes in a socially desirable direction. (Italics mine.)

Concrete social enquiry is still said to be based on historical materialism which, in effect, serves as the methodology for sociology. Historical materialism should act in the research process as method and principle for determining subject matter, formulating hypotheses, compiling a plan of investigation and explaining results. How does it help to interpret social reality?[2]

The Marxist [read: historical materialist] interpretation of a social situation, free of metaphysical and idealist one-sidedness, regards it [a social situation] as a link in the general historical process, as an interconnection of material and ideological relationships, in which the economy plays a decisive but not inexorable role, and in which the common will and the conscious activity of the socialist collective are capable of accelerating to a considerable degree the course of historical development, operating in accordance with its objective guidance.

Less concisely, Soviet sociologists are formally guided by the following principles of research. First of all, historical perspectives, that is, the interrelationship between the past, the present and the future must be emphasised. Social enquiry is to be grounded on history; sociological research cannot be 'photography',[3] because it encompasses the historical situation. Second, sociological research is to be based on a materialist, rather than an idealist, understanding of social phenomena; laws and interrelations are objective and determined by material circumstances. Finally, sociological research is to be intrinsically objective and scientific because historical materialism is said to be the first scientific system for understanding and then directing the development of society.

In his studies, therefore, the sociologist should show how the general theoretical patterns are manifested and should prove the reality of the theory. But he must also uncover new *zakonomernosti*.[4]

Marxism-Leninism never laid claims to predicting historical events in all their specific details. After all, every historical event contains an enormous number of crisscrossing interactions and factors that add up to the inimitable uniqueness of a particular historical phenomenon. This is why Marxism-Leninism assumes it is necessary to study the changing reality *anew*, starting from preceding generalisations and facts, in order to perceive the sources of the new, in order to use, for study, the general principles of Marxism as a methodological medium. . . .[5]

B. A. Grushin similarly emphasises the contributions to be made to general theory by research into an immanent reality: 'the concrete study of social reality, which always proves to be *new social reality*, perforce must enrich general theory, must as it is clear that existing theory must guide concrete research, determine its structure, methodology, etc.'[6]

Theory and methodology are therefore considered to be fundamentally united: to improve one means to correspondingly improve the other. Some Soviet sociologists, however, do recognise the existence of two problems not unlike those faced by their Western colleagues. The first involves the connection between meta-theory

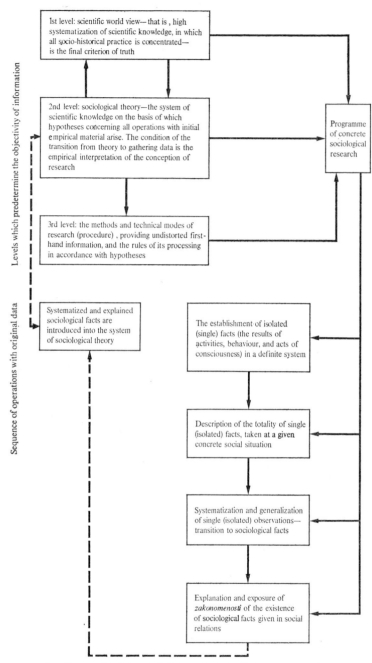

FIGURE 1   *General scheme of the sequence of operations of ascertaining objective sociological facts*

and research. Here the crucial question is: How can the original theoretical positions be embodied in the concrete research methods used for retrieving and analysing materials? The second problem is concerned with how one elevates research data to theoretical generalisations so that the research not only gives direct recommendations for practice, but also serves as the basis for the further development of theory.[7]

In attempting to deal with these problems, Iadov has inserted a transition stage between the theoretical and the empirical.[8] He suggests a three-tiered, interlocking system for ascertaining objective sociological facts and drawing up a programme of research. The highest level is the philosophical and scientific world view (the paradigm) – general notions about the processes of social and natural life (e.g., dialectical and historical materialism). The second level translates the concepts of the first into sociological language. This is the level of sociological theory and hypotheses, the level at which hypotheses related to concrete social situations are advanced; in other words, the level of 'middle range' theory. The third level involves the methods and techniques required for actual empirical research. (See Figure 1.)[9]

These three levels – roughly, *Weltanschauung*, sociological theory and research methods – are Iadov's basic methodological prerequisites for establishing a programme of research. Closely connected to this scheme is his view of the three levels of methodology.[10] Dialectical materialism occupies the first level, the level of universal scientific methodology; the dialectical approach is neither a supplement nor an addition to the methods and techniques of research, but rather acts as a directive for working out these research procedures. The second and third levels are, respectively, the general and the specific methodology of sociological research and are parallel to what Iadov terms all-sociological (*obshchesotsiologicheskaia*) theory and specific sociological theory. All-sociological methodology gives instructions related to the ways of working out special sociological theories which, in turn, contain particular methodological directions.

As is obvious, Iadov's two schema are very similar; the connection between theory and methodology is quite clear. He has further described and classified the methods and techniques to be used at the third stage. His scheme is a comprehensive picture of those areas of research methods which have been and are being discussed and used by other sociologists in the Soviet Union.[11] As such, these methods receive similar, if at times less sophisticated, treatment by Soviet sociologists as they would from other social scientists. (See Figure 2.)[12]

Iadov is certainly not the only sociologist concerned with these

Methods

Sphere of gathering first-hand information   Sphere of processing first-hand information

related to:

1. ascertaining single (isolated) facts	2. system of gathering first-hand information
observation	monographic enquiry
study of documents	complete enquiry
questionnaires	selective enquiry
	experimental observation (actual experiment)

description and classification

experimental analysis (actual and conceived experiments)

statistical analysis (survey of statistical laws)

systemic analysis

typologization

genetic or historical analysis

social modelling

Techniques

Sphere of gathering first-hand information   Sphere of processing first-hand information

related to:

1. ascertaining single (isolated) facts	2. system of gathering first-hand information
methods of qualitative control of first-hand information: adequacy validity stability	statistical equipment for selecting single (isolated) observations
	methods of qualitative and quantitative levelling out of characteristics
measurement of quantitative characteristics of first-hand facts ('scaling')	

logical means (for example, systemic analysis)

statistical methods (descriptive statistics, statistics of deduction and ascertainment of functional connections)

other mathematical means, not statistical (for example, linear progamming, use of the theory of graphs, mathematical modelling

techniques of processing sociological qualitatively-quantitatively compounded characteristics (indices)

FIGURE 2   *Methods and techniques*

26

problems. A. M. Rumiantsev and G. V. Osipov, for example, see four levels in the system of sociological knowledge, namely:[13]

1. general sociological theory – historical materialism, the most general laws of society;
2. theory of the social structure of society, which studies laws of interaction and functioning of different social systems within a given social structure;
3. theory of different social systems studying specific *zakonomernosti* (regularities, patterns) of functioning of different aspects and phenomena of social life (e.g., sociology of the family, of labour, etc.);
4. empirical level – research of social facts and their scientific systematisation.

This hierarchy represents an alternative formulation of the strategy of combining general theory with middle range theory and empirical research.

A general scheme to guide the sociologist in his research was constructed in 1967 by V. N. Shubkin who, like Iadov, is an eminent sociologist whose pronouncements carry considerable weight. The scheme was one of the first to indicate various stages of research, combining operational concepts and quantitative procedures.[14] (See Figure 3.)

More recently in his *Metodologiia i protsedura sotsiologicheskikh issledovanii* (*Methodology and Procedures of Sociological Research*), A. G. Zdravomyslov suggests five stages of research procedures: 1. working out the programme of research; 2. defining the objects and the unit of observation; 3. working out the means of gathering material; 4. gathering material; and 5. analysing material and its generalisations. Zdravomyslov sees no principal differences between Shubkin's scheme (which underlines and isolates quantitative aspects of procedures) and his own (which graphically depicts its logical junctions).[15]

In sum, the Soviet sociologist's original concern was to legitimate a body of tools to be used for sociological research within the framework of historical materialism. This process has gone on over time and to some extent accounts for the methodological weakness and lack of sophistication in much early Soviet research and some current investigations. It also explains the more recent and growing recognition by some Soviet theorists of problems concerning the relation between theory and methods, a relation which, in more official terms, is unquestioned and unquestionable because theory and method are united.

In general, their need to work out a theory of research has meant that the Soviets have not been great innovators with regard to specific

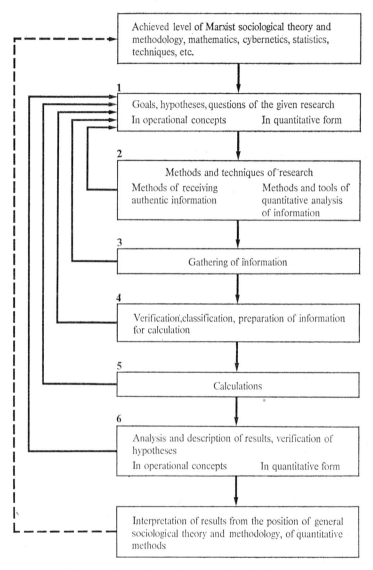

FIGURE 3 *Scheme of sociological research with the use of quantitative methods*

types of research. A major exception to this has been their 'perfecting' of time budget research which studies how people allocate their time. (This research is discussed in chapter 5.) The methods developed after much debate in the USSR have been utilised in cross-national studies sponsored by UNESCO's European Co-ordination Centre for Research and Documentation in Social Sciences.

4 The sociologists

The exact number of 'sociologists' in the Soviet Union is unknown. The term itself is still somewhat vague so that such a figure, if it were precisely calculable, might include the amateur as well as the more highly skilled and educated sociologist.* For the purposes of the following discussion, however, an individual is a sociologist if he defines himself as such. What is certain is that the number of people in this broad category is continually expanding.

The following profile of the sociologists is divided into three main sections. The first section discusses the training of the sociologists and their complaints about its inadequacy, a deficiency which may be traced to the discipline's origin in philosophy. This question of training is then continued in an examination of the activities of institutes carrying on professional training as well as research. The second section surveys the *Sovetskaia Sotsiologicheskaia Assotsiatsiia* (Soviet Sociological Association), the only body which represents the sociologists, and closely examines the participants it sent to the Sixth World Congress of Sociology. The final section looks at the role played by journals in informing their readers of current sociological research, in linking the Soviets with other socialist countries, and in reporting Soviet, socialist and international conferences and exchanges.

Training and research institutes

The sociologist's vocation is an unusual one. He must have a broad outlook and all round professional training. For this

*P. N. Fedoseev has stated that 'about 2000 workers in *vuzy*, scientific research institutes, party, komsomol, and trade union organisations are actively engaged in social research.' See his 'Marksistskaia sotsiologiia, ee zadachi i perspektivy', *Vestnik AN SSSR*, no. 7, 1966, p. 5.

reason we consider it advisable to open sociology divisions in the universities of Moscow, Leningrad, Novosibirsk, and Kiev, and to offer specialisation in this line of study for graduate students and upper-classmen in the humanities faculties.[1]

In March 1966, the noted Novosibirsk sociologist, V. N. Shubkin, published the above proposition in *Pravda*. A month later Academician A. Aleksandrov, writing in *Literaturnaia gazeta*, reiterated the call for improving the training of sociologists: training, he said, is 'conducted on an extremely limited scale, maybe at two or three universities, on the basis of the initiative of several enthusiasts in this field. . . . The impression is created that in the eyes of the USSR Ministry of Higher and Specialised Secondary Education this science does not exist at all'.[2] By the end of that same year, V. A. Iadov of Leningrad had joined the angry chorus:[3]

> The USSR Ministry of Higher and Specialised Secondary Education obviously thinks sociology should continue to develop 'on a volunteer basis'. Otherwise it is difficult to explain why for the third year now the Ministry is not reacting to persistent appeals to offer the appropriate specialities in at least three of the country's universities – Moscow, Leningrad, and Novosibirsk – where there are trained specialists.

The first 'sociologists' in the post-1956 era were trained as philosophers and became social scientists because they concentrated on social laws and theory. The majority of these men focused their attention primarily on ideological aspects, merely reiterating Marxist social theory on given topics; the minority became sociologists by performing actual empirical research. Data from the first All-Union Sociology Symposium held in February 1966 in Leningrad indicated that the composition of sociologists was changing. Sociologists at this conference received their education in the following fields:[4]

	per cent
Philosophy	25
History	27
Economics	10
Psychology	3
Other humanities	30·5
Technical specialists	4·5

It is quite apparent that none of the conference participants was educated as a sociologist *per se*, even though the majority were described as having been occupied with sociology for three to four years.

31

While there may be but little specific training in the discipline,* whatever training there is has come under scrutiny. For example, V. A. Iadov complained in 1966 that 'the level of training of many "professional" sociologists is, alas, very low at the moment. . . . We have neither teaching aids on the methodology and techniques of empirical research nor specialisation in sociological research in the humanities departments.'[5] Commentators at the Sukhumi Conference (April 1967) on 'Quantitative Methods in Social Research' pointed out that 'even if such a speciality were introduced in the next academic year (and the hopes of this are feeble), the first professionally trained sociologists would not appear for several years. There are extremely few people enrolled in graduate work in sociology.' Who, then, should train the sociologists? 'How could people

TABLE 1   *Dissertations, by year and subject*

	Total	Doctorate	Candidate
1964–5			
Historical materialism and scientific communism	98	16	82
History of philosophy (and bourgeois sociology)	65	16	49
Subtotal	163	32	131
Total (all theses)	340	54	286
1965–6			
Scientific communism	55	3	52
Historical materialism	30	5	25
Sociology	16	2	14
Subtotal	101	10	91
Total (all theses)	340	37	303
1966–7			
Scientific communism and sociology	75	9	66
Historical materialism	38	9	29
Subtotal	113	18	95
Total (all theses)	323	43	280

*For contrary evidence based on his first-hand knowledge of the situation in Moscow, see Wesley A. Fisher's letter to the editor in the November – December 1971 issue of *Problems of Communism*, p. 81.

[instructors in the social sciences at the institutes for raising qualifications] themselves unacquainted with sociology train sociologists? Or people who are familiar with it only theoretically?'[6] The general position presented by these views seems clear. The circle is complete: few places exist where those who want to become sociologists can be trained, while at the same time few institutions employ people capable of teaching the discipline.

There is, however, evidence contrary to this assertion. This evidence suggests that there is an apparently growing number of dissertations dealing with sociological topics. Since the beginning of 1966, data on philosophy dissertation topics and the institutions awarding philosophy dissertations have been published by the Supreme Attestation Commission's (VAK) appraisal commission (*ekspertnaia komissiia*). 'Sociology' receives different treatment in these accounts.[7]

In the six reports to date, sociology was only once – in 1965–6 – listed as an independent discipline: in 1964–5, it was listed as 'history of philosophy (including the history of bourgeois philosophy and sociology)'; in the years 1966–9 it was coupled with scientific communism; and in the last year, 1969–70, 'sociological research' (and not sociology *per se*) was attached to historical materialism. Consequently, it is impossible to get an exact figure for theses in sociology. (Table 1, however, gives some indication of the fluctuating number of dissertations. See Table 1.) The question of meeting this problem was first posed in the 1967–8 discussion when the introduction of Doctorate and Candidate degrees in Socio-political Sciences was suggested. Since then each report has re-emphasised this idea.*

To a greater or lesser extent, all of the reports discussed the themes of the dissertations in sociology. The earliest one only noted an uneven distribution of thesis topics and advocated stimulating research in the 'theoretical problems of sociology and methodological questions of concrete social sciences'. The next report again pointed to the insignificant number of theses written on the basis of concrete social research and, except for vaguely mentioning theses connected with the problems of working and free time, did not specify research topics. The 1966–7 account did elaborate the themes of the sociology dissertations including those on the (changing) content and character of labour and on social structure (especially on the *rapprochement* of the working class and intellectuals and on the evolution of different social groups). Two theses on time budget research – one by M. S. Aivazian and the other by V. A. Artemov

---

*The Doctor of Science degree (*doktorskaia stepen'*) is the highest academic degree, roughly equivalent to the D. Litt. or D. Sc.
The Candidate of Science degree (*kandidatskaia stepen'*) is a first post-graduate degree, roughly equivalent to an M.A. or M.Sc.

TABLE 2 *Locale of Universities and Academies of Sciences*

1964–5[a]	1965–6: Additions (compared with 1964–5)[a]	1966–7: Omissions (compared with 1965–6)[a]
Moscow (exception, see Table 3)	Perm	Perm
Leningrad	Irkutsk	Tashkent
Urals	Voronezh	Kirghiz SSR, Institute of Philosophy and Law
Novosibirsk	Khar'kov	
Bielorussian	L'vov	
Tomsk	Latvian	
Kazan'		
Gorkii		
Rostov		*Additions*
Krasnoiarsk Pedagogical Institute		(compared with 1965–6)
Kiev		Odessa
Tbilisi		Dagestan
Kazakh		Vil'nius
Tashkent		
Azerbaidzhan		
Erevan		
Tadzhik		
Saratov		
Kirghiz SSR, Institute of Philosophy and Law		

Academies of Sciences[b] *1965–6: Additions* (compared with 1964–5)	*1966–7*[c] (compared with 1965–6)
Ukrainian SSR	[d]
Kazakh SSR	
Uzbek SSR	
Bielorussian SSR	[d]
Kirghiz SSR	Missing *Addition* Azerbaidzhan

[a]Unless otherwise noted, all are state universities.
[b]The 1964–5 list did not list Academies of Sciences.
[c]Unless otherwise noted, the 1965–6 Academies of Sciences appeared on the 1966–7 list.
[d]These Academies of Sciences have two listings, the first as the Sector of Social Sciences and the second as the Institute of Philosophy.

(the latter's work is well known in this area) – received much praise. In the next academic year, two distinguished Soviet sociologists earned their doctorates, B. A. Grushin for 'Public opinion (methodology and methods of its research)' and V. A. Iadov for 'Methodological problems of concrete sociological research'. Out of the eleven who earned Candidate degrees, four studied problems of free time,* while the others concentrated on the problems of *byt* (daily life, customs), labour, socialist production team and spiritual interests of youth. The 1968–9 report did not specifically discuss the themes (or, more correctly, only discussed what was not examined). The final report, however, did. Doctorates were conferred on G. N. Volkov for 'Social problems of development of science and technology', D. M. Gvishiani for 'American theory of organisational management' and A. G. Zdravomyslov for 'Theoretical and methodological problems of research of social interests'. The candidates examined (principal) methodological problems of research of society and the individual, problems of the scientific-technical revolution and its influence on social life under capitalism and socialism, and contemporary bourgeois sociology.

As might be expected, the standard of dissertations varied a great deal, outstanding being the distinguished work of Iadov, Grushin and Zdravomyslov. The authors of the reports themselves criticised the general standards of the theses for a variety of reasons, namely, lack of originality, doubling of themes, lack of theoretical and/or practical significance, themes which are too comprehensive, and insufficient application of data obtained in concrete sociological research in the fields of scientific communism, historical materialism, scientific atheism, ethics and aesthetics. On the whole, however, the authors felt that the quality of the theses was improving.

Thus, philosophy students are writing theses in sociology and are, no doubt, getting some training in the discipline. This occurs in a few graduate or *ad hoc* seminars on theories and methods of sociology and through 'practical experience' either at universities or at research institutes. Where exactly are these people studying?

Once again, the Supreme Attestation Commission (VAK) provides an answer. While the 1964–5 information lists only the cities, the next two reports list the specific universities, institutes and academies of sciences where philosophy (and hence, sociology) students study; unfortunately, no indication was given as to the number of students per speciality per university or institute. Information is available regarding the names of the universities and academies of sciences by academic year and also regarding the omissions and additions per year. (See Table 2.) More specific information concerns the degree and training institutions in Moscow, the city where the majority of
*Artemov and Aivazian were listed here as well as in the previous year.

TABLE 3 *Degree and training institutions in Moscow*

1965–6	1966–7
Moscow State University, Philosophy Faculty	
Institute of Philosophy, USSR Academy of Sciences	
Academy of Social Sciences, attached to CC CPSU	
Moscow State Pedagogical Institute	
Moscow Institute of Economy	
Higher Party School attached to CC CPSU	Missing
State Institute of Theatrical Art	
Moscow *Oblast'* Pedagogical Institute	
Social Sciences Sector, USSR Academy of Sciences	Missing
Military-Political Academy	
	Additions
	Moscow Institute of Culture
	Moscow Institute of International Relations

philosophy training took place. (See Table 3.) (In 1964–5, Moscow was only listed as one of the cities and, consequently, there was no breakdown by institutions.) The last three VAK reports do not discuss individual institutions.

Tables 2 and 3 certainly do not list all of the institutions where training takes place, nor do they name all of the institutions which prepare sociologists for sociological research: scientific research institutes and *vuzy* (higher educational establishments) have sociological laboratories which do not offer degree and training programmes. The list of places for training and research is continually expanding, but, on the whole, it can be divided into three types: those institutes attached to the universities and *vuzy*, those associated with the USSR and republic academies of sciences, and those linked to other organisations, such as the party, komsomol, trade unions, enterprises and journals. Thus, in any given city (depending on its size), one might expect to find sociologists attached to one or more of these three types of institutes.

Before exploring some of the major centres of sociological research, let us enlarge the picture for Moscow. At Moscow State University, the Institute of Philosophy's Laboratory of Sociological Research has worked on problems connected with equalising the conditions of life between city and village, the influence of technological progress on workers (including socio-psychological research on the labour force), bourgeois sociology and problems of methodology. Other departments and laboratories within the University – such as the Department of Historical Materialism and the Laboratory for Labour Resources – also conduct sociological research.

The Academy of Sciences in Moscow comprehends a great number of Institutes, of which the following have units for sociological work: the Institute of State and Law (crime, delinquency and social management), Institute of Archaeology and Ethnography (culture and customs of peasants and the peoples of the USSR), Institute of Economics (social problems of technology and labour), and the Central Economic–Mathematics Institute (methodology of concrete social research and optimal economic planning). The Institute of Philosophy has a sector for studying new forms of labour and daily life which was transformed first into a Division of Concrete Social Research and then in 1968 into a full Institute of Concrete Social Research. The creation of this Institute within the Academy of Sciences, separated from the Institute of Philosophy, symbolised the legitimation of the discipline itself. At present, the Institute houses five sectors: a sector of methodology, methods and techniques; a sector of the problems of development of social relations of city and country; a sector of problems of development of labour collectives; a sector of sociology and socio-psychological problems of the individual; and finally, a sector of problems of public opinion and the effectiveness of ideological work. The Academy of Sciences' Social Sciences' section also set up, in February 1966, a learned council on the problems of concrete social research to 'co-ordinate concrete social research, including sociological research, which is being conducted in the country'[8] and 'to realise links with sociological centres of the Ministry of Higher and Secondary School Education and Ministry of Culture with different public organisations, enterprises, etc'.[9]

Moscow also houses: the Institute of the World Labour Movement's Social Research Division – 'the second national centre for the field [which] seeks to stress and develop comparative studies, of both communist and non-communist countries';[10] *Komsomol'skaia pravda*'s Public Opinion Institute (see chapter 6); the Central Statistical Administration of the RSFSR; and the Youth Problems Institute formed at the Komsomol Central Committee in 1964 to co-ordinate the work of fifty sociological groups and thirty-five youth centres in various towns and villages.[11] Not separately listed here are the numerous party, enterprise, trade union, etc., organisations which either conduct or commission research. (See below, pp. 39–41.)

Another leading centre of sociological research is Leningrad where, in 1958, a sociology seminar was set up within the framework of the

Soviet Sociological Association. In October of 1960, the first sociology laboratory, attached to the Philosophy Faculty of Leningrad State University, was established. In 1963, other social science laboratories – including the sociology laboratory – entered the Union of Integrated Social Research and in 1965, the Union became the basis of the Institute of Complex Social Research, the largest research institute in Leningrad. 'In the system of the University, the Institute acts as an inter-departmental scientific centre, as a singular base of all the humanities faculties.'[12] In a 1965 report on research in Leningrad, the Institute was said to have a staff of ninety, some of whom worked at the Sociological Research Laboratory.[13] On the whole, the Institute has three main research directions:

1. social planning for industrial enterprises,
2. working out optimal systems for administration and scientific organisation of labour, and
3. studying social problems of higher schools and the education of students.

Other institutes in Leningrad also have sociology laboratories. The Leningrad Mechanics Institute has a group of workers studying intra-class differences; the Electro-Technical Institute is working on mass communication and mechanisms of response to socially significant information; the sociologists at the Philosophy Department of the Leningrad branch of the USSR Academy of Sciences are studying the family, *byt*, and services, problems of city planning, change in the social structure, methodology of sociological research and problems of labour. Another centre for research is the Public Institute for Social Research which was established in 1963 without a paid staff. It concentrates on problems linked with the development of technology and on the results of atheistic education. In addition, the higher party school, the higher school of the trade union movement, and the komsomol city committee conduct research or have research done for them on a contractual basis, as do other interested organisations, such as the State Radio and Television Committee.

In Sverdlovsk, sociology is institutionalised in two places, at the University and at the Urals branch of the USSR Academy of Sciences.[14] At the former, a philosophy sector was opened in 1965 which was transformed in 1966 into a philosophy faculty, one of whose functions was to prepare workers for sociology laboratories and instructors of social science for *tekhnikumy** and secondary schools. Research under the auspices of the University has focused on three main areas: processes of raising the cultural-technical level of the working class (e.g., work by Iovchuk), problems of change in the

Tekhnikum – specialised secondary school/institute, with two- to four-year courses, including general education, usually from age fourteen.

social structure (e.g., Rutkevich), and the development of the spiritual life of working people (e.g., Kogan). The Urals branch of the USSR Academy of Sciences has two special sociological sectors, one devoted to the problems of management and the other to research on the cultural and intellectual life of society. While sociology is firmly ensconced in philosophy in Sverdlovsk, sociology in Novosibirsk seems to be rooted in economics and mathematics.[15] In fact it was a Novosibirsk *kollektiv* (team) at the Siberian branch of the USSR Academy of Sciences which originally began to study time budgets in the late 1950s, thus commencing empirical research after the 'thaw'. This branch embraces the Institute of Economics and Organisation of Industrial Enterprise, which studies labour resources, population movement, working and non-working time, the level of organisation of labour and production, etc., and the Laboratory of Economic and Mathematical Methods of Research, which studies the problems of youth, the choice of professions, job placement, labour turnover, and the methodology, methods and techniques of concrete sociological research. The Academy's Institute of History, Philology and Philosophy also studies sociological problems of youth, social mobility and cultural development of the peoples of Siberia and the Far East, and time budgets.[16]

A further guide to the present pattern of institutionalisation of Soviet sociology was offered in a review of philosophy and sociology in the Ukraine.[17] There, the centres of sociology are the Institutes of the Academy of Sciences of the Ukrainian SSR (especially the Institute of Philosophy), the university laboratories of concrete sociological research (in Kiev, Khar'kov, L'vov, and Dnepropetrovsk), sociological groups attached to *vuzy*, polytechnic and pedagogic institutes, party committees at *raion*, city, and *oblast'** level, komsomol organisations, and the editorial boards of newspapers. The basic themes of sociological research in the Ukraine have been: time budgets, change in social structure, attitudes of students to their elected specialities, the technical level of workers and their attitude toward labour, the role of public opinion in the management of industry and forms of religious belief. This has been the pattern in other established centres of sociology and there is little doubt that other areas in the country will set up sociological research along similar lines.

As this review of the centres for sociological work has shown, party, komsomol, trade union and other organisations are involved in training personnel and in conducting research. Courses in sociological methods for party officials, for example, have been (if not

Oblast' – region; an administrative sub-division of a Union Republic.
Raion – district; an administrative area within *oblast'*, *krai* or republic.

already introduced) strongly suggested: 'there is no provision what-soever for . . . the methodology of concrete sociological research in the curriculum [for the training of party officials]. But it is absolutely essential that a party official be conversant with these subjects.'[18] The Academy of Social Sciences, attached to the CPSU's Central Committee, now conducts yearly seminars for party officials and scientists. Some party committees have established departments of Marxist sociology at evening universities and at the Higher Party Schools.[19] Other organisations have set up similar facilities.

In terms of research, these organisations can, in the first place, rely on work conducted by the research institutes, the *vuzy* or other institutions. It has been argued that such research should enable party workers to analyse phenomena more scientifically, gather concrete information and utilise new methods for studying social problems. The sociologists, in turn, should benefit from collaboration with the party and other organisations because the latter should help in the development of a theory of socialist society, aid in gathering information and subsequently effect practical recommendations.[20]

In the second place, these organisations themselves carry out research of a social character by setting up research centres which unite teachers, scientific personnel, and workers from party and public organisations.* A good proportion of this research concentrates on the effectiveness of ideological-political work among different social groups (e.g., workers and technical intellectuals) on the effect of methods and organisation of a number of trends in propaganda and agitational work, on ways of forming public opinion and on a study of the party *aktiv* themselves.[21] Other party 'research' falls into the broad category of gathering information of a socio-economic and socio-political nature (e.g., the work situation, contexts of crime and drunkenness).†

The exact position is not clear, but it appears that social research involving the party and other organisations is frequently carried out on a co-operative basis. A picture of the type of inter-dependence involved is provided in a discussion of some research carried out in Estonia on the influence of art. Figure 4, showing the organisational structure at the questionnaire stage of research, indicates the division of labour involved.[22]

From Figure 4 it is impossible to say precisely where co-operation ends and supervision begins. It is clear, however, that many types of

---

*An example of this is the public institute of sociological research set up under the *gorkom* in Dnepropetrovsk.

†A.G. Zdravomyslov points out that this information is not concentrated and analysed as a whole, nor does it have a systematic character. He suggests creating indices of this information gathered by the party committees. See *Metodologiia i protsedura sotsiologicheskikh issledovanii*, Moscow, 1969, p. 57.

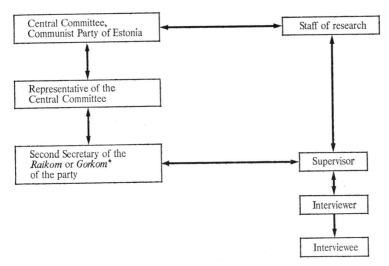

FIGURE 4   *Organisational structure*

Raikom – district committee of the party. *Gorkom* – urban committee, usually of the party.

social research in the USSR are carried out by a combination of party workers and social scientists, an unknown number of whom are themselves party members.

The Soviet Sociological Association – Sixth World Congress of Sociology

The Soviet Sociological Association was founded in 1958. According to its statutes, it is to follow two courses:
1. to participate in the activities of the International Sociological Association and disseminate Soviet sociologists' work abroad, and
2. to assist in the development of scientific research work inside the USSR. However, at the third general meeting of the Association, held in February 1966,[23] 125 participants weighed up the work of the Association and concluded that, on the whole, the Association had fulfilled the function of guaranteeing representation of Soviet sociologists abroad, but had focused little attention on internal problems.*

One of the major problems revolved around the question of collec-

*The first general meeting was in 1958 and the second in 1961. Since no further reference was made to a general meeting until 1966, it has been assumed that the latter is the date of the third meeting.

41

tive as opposed to individual membership. At the time of the Association's second general meeting in 1961, there were twenty-four collective members, chiefly Institutes of the Academies of Sciences. In February of 1966, there were fifty collective members, and by November of 1967, seventy-nine organisations and institutions had been accepted as collective members. However, at the 1966 Leningrad meeting the question arose as to the advisability of admitting individual members into the Association. It was argued that the inclusion of individual members, most of whom were working on sociological problems, would help to unite and co-ordinate their frequently isolated efforts. Along with the motion for individual membership came a suggestion that individual members be bound regularly to inform the presidium of the Association about their research; there was also a proposal to create an institute of 'probationary candidates', the fact of admission attesting to the qualifications of the individual researcher. The suggestion for individual membership was accepted: in November 1967, the Association was said to have 580 scholars as individual members and by September 1970, 1469 people were individual members and 273 institutions were collective members.

The February 1966 meeting also considered some motions for enlarging and improving the functions of the Association. Some members proposed that the Association conduct yearly seminars and symposia. Others suggested the creation of branch associations and research committees at the *oblast'* and/or republic level to discuss and carry out research, while others proposed the creation of a regular *apparat*,* attached to the presidium of the Association, to co-ordinate sociological research. Branch associations have since been set up in Moscow, Leningrad, Novosibirsk, Sverdlovsk, Kiev, Kharkov, Perm, Tallinn and other large centres; twenty-four permanent research committees have been established to co-ordinate the activity of sociologists.[24] In general, the training of sociologists and the publication of study aids and a journal devoted to sociology were included in the proposals which were aimed at further uniting sociologists and improving the quality of their work.

Before the Soviet Sociological Association was established, the Soviet Union was represented for the first time at the Third World Congress of Sociology of 1956 in Amsterdam. Subsequently, the Association sent delegates in increasing numbers to the Fourth Congress in Stresa in 1959, the Fifth Congress in Washington in 1962, the Sixth Congress in Evian (France) in 1966, and the Seventh Congress in Varna (Bulgaria) in 1970. Soviet sociologists are now taking an active part in these international meetings.

Apparat – system/machinery of administration; staff, personnel of the system/machinery of administration; the organisation.

Because many of the foremost sociologists attended, a close look at the Evian Congress's eighty-two Soviet delegates presents an excellent opportunity of supplementing this profile of Soviet sociologists.* The sample is biased in favour of the 'better' sociologists but, nevertheless, a picture of the composition of Soviet sociologists in general can be drawn.

The number eighty-two is derived from the Liste des Participants, Supplement II du Bulletin d'Information no. 3, in conjunction with a list prepared by V. S. Semenov in an article entitled 'VI vsemirnii sotsiologicheskii kongress'.[25] Those whose papers were read in their absence are not included in the discussion. Of the eighty-two participants, information was found on seventy. Therefore, the following discussion is based on seventy, rather than eighty-two, sociologists. The Evian delegates are also compared with those from the previous (Washington) Congress; all but four of the eighteen Soviet participants returned to the Evian Congress.[26]

The overwhelming majority of participants in 1962 and 1966 were from the Moscow area. But whereas in 1962 only two republics were represented (seventeen participants from the RSFSR and one from Latvia), the 1966 delegation represented seven republics. The regional breakdown is as follows:

RSFSR
Moscow	44
Leningrad	6
Novosibirsk	3
Sverdlovsk	3
Volgograd	1

Ukrainian SSR
Kiev	4

Georgian SSR
Tbilisi	2

Byelorussian SSR
Minsk	1

Uzbek SSR
Tashkent	1

Latvian SSR
Riga	1

Kazakh SSR
Alma-Ata	1
Unknown	3
Total	70

*This part of the study was completed before the Varna conference where 300 to 400 Soviets were present, a fact which would have greatly extended an already complex examination of the sociologists.

One can generalise from these data that sociology is indeed spreading throughout the country into the national republics.

The delegates' educational background is as follows:

Doctor of Science	35
comprising	
Doctor of Philosophy	28
Doctor of Historical Science	2
Doctor of Law	1
Doctor of Economic Science	3
Doctor of Juridical Science	1
Professor	2
(listed only as Professor, no academic degree listing available: this title does not include Doctors of Science who are also professors)	
Candidate of Science	16
comprising	
Candidate of Philosophy	12
Candidate of Economic Science	3
Candidate of History	1
Unknown	17
Total	70

Two of the delegates were full members of the USSR Academy of Sciences; three were corresponding members. All in all, then, in terms of academic honours and achievement, the delegates ranked very highly: over half of the participants had doctorates or were professors, almost one quarter had candidate degrees, while the rest remain unknown. If we leave aside the figures for the unknown, then the ratio of doctorates to candidates is almost two to one. This was not the case at the 1962 Congress where the number was more evenly divided; four of the eight candidates at that Congress had, by the time of the Evian Congress, earned their doctorates. One could generalise from this that more and more practising sociologists are obtaining higher degrees.

The institutional positions of the participants have been separated into three tables, the first listing affiliation to universities and institutes, the second to the Academies of Sciences, and the last, to other organisations, such as party, komsomol and journals. Individuals have been noted twice if their affiliation with more than one institution is known: a plus (+) appears for each of the two affiliations. The date of affiliation is taken to be correct as of 1966, that is, as close to the Evian Congress as possible, but I have also indicated when an individual changed his position. An asterisk (*) means that the

TABLE 4 *Institutional position of the participants*
I. *Universities and institutes*

Moscow		
Moscow State University	7	
Philosophy Institute	2	
Department of Historical Materialism	1*	
Department of Scientific Communism	1	+
Sociology Laboratory	1*	+
Humanities Faculty		
Department of Historical and Dialectical Materialism	2*	
Leningrad		
Leningrad State University	5	
Philosophy Faculty		
Department of Sociology and Philosophy	1	
History of Philosophy	1*	
Institute of Complex Social Research	3*	+
Sverdlovsk		
Urals State University		
Philosophy Faculty	2*	2+
Kiev		
Kiev Medical Institute		
Chair of Philosophy	1*	
Tbilisi		
Tbilisi State University	1	

participant is the head of his institute or organisation. (See Tables 4, 5 and 6.)

In addition to indicating where each participant works, these tables put in some perspective the distribution of participants per type of institution. Thus, the number of people from the three types of institution is:

Universities and institutes 16 of whom 5 are listed twice
Academies of Sciences 34 of whom 11 are listed twice
Other organisations 24 of whom 12 are listed twice
Unknown 10

Of the fourteen men listed twice, three were listed simultaneously under universities and Academies, eight under Academies and other organisations, and two under other organisations and universities; one was listed in two places on the table for other organisations. On the whole, the distribution emphasises the affiliation of a large number of sociologists with research institutions.

45

TABLE 5   *Institutional position of the participants*
         II. *Academies of Sciences*

Moscow, Academy of Sciences, USSR		
Institute of Philosophy	9*	3+
Theory of Culture Section	2*	
Sector of Historical Materialism	1*	
Sector of Contemporary Bourgeois Philosophy and		
Sociology of Countries of the West	1*	
History of World Philosophy Department	1*	+
Social Research Unit	1*	+
Sector of Psychology	1	+
Institute of History	1	
Institute of Economics	1	
Institute of State and Law	2	
Vice-President for Social Sciences, USSR		
Academy of Sciences (until Spring 1967)	1	+
Leningrad Branch, Academy of Sciences, USSR		
Department of Philosophy	1	+
Siberian Branch, Academy of Sciences, USSR		
Institute of Economics and Organisation of Industrial		
Enterprise	1	
Sociology Sector	1*	
Laboratory of Economic and Mathematical Methods		
Social Research Section	1*	
Urals Branch, Academy of Sciences, USSR		
Sociology sectors (2)	2* (each*) +	
Academy of Sciences, Bielorussian SSR		
Institute of Philosophy and Law	1*	
Academy of Sciences, Kazakhstan SSR		
Institute of Philosophy and Law	1*	
Academy of Sciences, Ukrainian SSR		
Institute of Philosophy	2	
Academy of Sciences, Georgian SSR		
Institute of Economics	1	
Academy of Sciences, Latvian SSR	1	
Academy of Sciences, Uzbekistan SSR	1	

It is also evident from the tables that almost one-half of the people affiliated with universities and institutes were heads of their respective departments; almost one-third of those with the Academies headed their departments, and three-eighths of those attached to the other organisations were heads of their institutions. Therefore, taken in conjunction with academic achievement, it would appear that the 1966 participants were considerably weighty men in their professions.

TABLE 6   *Institutional position of the participants*
           III. Organisations: party, komsomol, trade union and
           journals

Moscow		
Academy of Social Sciences (attached to the Central Committee, CPSU)		
Department of Philosophy (became head of Department of Dialectical and Historical Materialism, early 1967)	1*	
Department of History of Soviet Society	1*	
Sociological Research Group	1*	
Higher Party School (Central Committee, CPSU)	1	+
Department of Marxism-Leninism	1*	+
Institute of Marxism-Leninism (Central Committee, CPSU)		
Sector of Scientific Communism	1*	
Institute of the World Labour Movement (money from All-Union Central Council of Trade Union, yet formal tie to Economics Department, USSR Academy of Sciences)		
Social Research Division	1*	
A sector of the above	1	
Institute of International Relations (Ministry of Foreign Affairs)	1*	
Komsomol'skaia pravda's Public Opinion Institute	1	
Editorial Boards		
Voprosy filosofii	2	2+
Filosofskie nauki	5*	5+
Kommunist	1	
Voprosy psikhologii	1	+
Sovetskaia etnografiia	1	
Novosti	1*	
Soviet Sociological Association		
President	1*	+
Vice-President	1	+
Learned Secretary	1	
Institutional position unknown	10	

What, then, are their main areas of specialisation in regard to sociology?* As in the previous tables, some individuals are listed under two classifications on Table 7: no pattern, however, emerged from this cross-classification. (A plus (+) appears for each of the

*Each person was classified according to his publications, the conferences he attended in the Soviet Union, and the meetings he participated in at the Congress.

TABLE 7   *Areas of specialisation*

Philosophy, theory		
Marxist philosophy	15	3+
Modern moderates	2	
Nationality questions (including concepts of national sovereignty, patriotism, and race)	6	+
International relations (including military history, co-existence, conflicts)	3	
Socialist revolution	2	2+
Sociology, theory and research		
Social theorists	3	+
Theory and methods of bourgeois empirical research	3	+
Comparative socialist research	3	+
Methods and modelling	6	4+
Fields of concrete social research		
Labour	11	5+
Social structure	7	4+
Marriage and family	1	
Urban sociology	1	+
Criminology	1	
Law	1	
Religion, ethics, morals, and values	4	+
Art and mass communication	2	
Public opinion research	1	
Time budget research	1	
Peripheral fields		
Psychology and social psychology	2	
Ethnography	1	
Demography	2	
Listed only by groups participated in at Congress		
Mass communication and leisure	1	
Leninist national policy	1	
Sociology and other sciences	1	
Unknown	1	

two classifications.) What did emerge is further evidence of the declining role of the 'grand theorist' philosophers and the growing research orientation of the sociologists.

In Table 7, the men classified under 'Marxist philosophy' include those working in dialectical and historical materialism, scientific communism, political economy, history of philosophy and culture and history of the CPSU. Ten of these people head their departments. At least eight of them are definitely Communist Party members, and at least eleven of them are over forty-five. A very similar combination of age, party membership and directorship applies to the people listed under 'nationality questions', 'international relations' and 'socialist revolution'. Thus it appears that the men in the 'philosophy-theory' category are the old-time stalwarts.

Quite a different picture emerges for those actually engaged in sociological research. On the whole, these men are in the thirty-five to forty-five age bracket: although some in this group are older or younger, the most dynamic work seems to be coming from the middle group. Moreover, in comparison with the older group, these sociologists are scattered throughout the country: there is less concentration in the Moscow area. In terms of their education, these sociologists are equally divided between candidates and doctorates although several of the former have since earned their doctorates. Only about one-third of them are in charge of their respective departments, but their ages would certainly be the crucial factor here.

From this profile, it would appear that Soviet sociologists roughly fall into two, not quite mutually exclusive, groups. On the whole, those who are described as actually engaged in research are becoming the rule, rather than the exception.

Journals

Sociologists do not as yet have their own periodical. This has resulted in the appearance of articles on sociology in other journals, especially in those concerned with philosophy, but also in economic, historical, political, ethnographic, juridical and anthropological journals, as well as in the daily press.

Two journals have indicated that they are to be published on a regular basis. The first, *Sotsial'nye issledovaniia* (*Social Research*), has appeared six times: the first issue came out in 1965, then one in 1968, and four in 1970. It is presently sponsored by the Academy of Sciences' Institute of Concrete Social Research and the Soviet Sociological Association. It publishes articles on general problems of sociology as well as devoting issues to specific problems, such as the family and marriage or time budget research. The other journal, *Chelovek i obshchestvo* (*Man and Society*), was first published in 1966. Its subsequent issues appeared once each in 1967 and 1968, three times in 1969, twice in 1970, and twice in 1971. It is sponsored by Leningrad State University's Institute of Complex Social Research and as such reflects the Institute's interests in problems of a sociological, psychological, economic and juridical nature. For example, articles have appeared concerned with social planning and management, the individual and all aspects of labour and youth and socialisation.

49

As a rule, however, two regularly published philosophy journals, *Voprosy filosofii* and *Filosofskie nauki*, carried the majority of articles on sociology.* *Voprosy filosofii* has about twice as many articles in the field of sociology as does *Filosofskie nauki* and its articles cover a wider range of topics. Besides informing their readers on past, present and future research in the discipline, what other functions do these journals perform?

From the early 1960s, the journals began quite regularly to carry reviews, summaries and/or surveys of philosophy and sociology journals from the other socialist countries. *Voprosy filosofii* has tended to review a number of journals from these countries at one time, whereas *Filosofskie nauki* has tended to investigate articles from different magazines on a specific problem (such as dialectical materialism) or has chosen to concentrate on journals from one country: this division, however, is not hard and fast. Meetings of representatives from the editorial boards of the philosophy and sociology journals in the socialist countries have been reported since the first meeting in 1962. Books on philosophy and sociology from the socialist countries are reviewed. For example, in 1965 *Voprosy filosofii* reviewed Czech publications from 1960 to 1963 and, in 1966, Polish literature on sociology for 1960–4.[27]

The journals also report exchanges between and conferences of Soviet and other sociologists. In November of 1962, for example, an exchange between Leningrad State University and some Polish universities focused on the general questions of method and technique of sociological research and on the study of labour activity.[28] Conferences sponsored by one socialist country and attended by Soviet delegates also receive coverage. Typical of these was one called in November 1966 by the Sociology Institute of the Czech Academy of Sciences, the Social Institute of the Slovak Academy of Sciences, the sociology society and the Institute of Marxism–Leninism from *vuzy*.[29] The journals report inter-socialist conferences which, for example, have discussed the problems of the social structure of socialist society or the theoretical problems of labour turnover. Finally, they discuss international gatherings of which the most notable are the international sociological conferences.

The journals also aid Soviet sociologists by reporting the conferences held in the Soviet Union. The conferences themselves provide both individual and institutional contact for sociologists and they may also act as a collective platform for the discipline as a whole. While the journals undoubtedly do not cover all of the conferences, they do give a fairly good picture of the range and depth of the conference papers.

*The universities and Academies of Sciences also publish general journals on the social sciences which often contain articles on sociology.

These conferences do not include meetings or seminars which are regularly scheduled (biennially, annually, etc.). Such meetings, also reported in the journals, might, for example, discuss the work of the *vuzy*, the results and problems of co-ordinating and planning research, and the work of special seminars set up by various bodies and devoted to some problems of social science.

The journals themselves also hold meetings with their readers. The readers appear to voice their approval and/or disapproval of varying subjects, including the contents of the journal. For example, in 1965 at Cherepovets, the head of the Department of Marxism–Leninism at the Cherepovets Pedagogical Institute requested more articles on concrete sociological research (and 'not only on questions of methodology and methods'), asserting that only five such articles appeared in 1964.[30] An opposite view was expressed at a conference in Tbilisi where one man complained about the increase of non-philosophical themes in the journal, including concrete sociological research.[31] He was answered, however, by the corresponding secretary of the editorial board of *Voprosy filosofii*, I. V. Blauberg, who stated that since there are no specialised periodical publications on questions of concrete sociology, *Voprosy filosofii* must study these problems. In general, all of these conferences of readers mentioned the subject of sociology and usually requested more coverage in this field.

By far the greatest task of the journals, however, is to inform their readers about current research in the discipline. In describing research, they have also given valuable information as to who is doing what – and where. In the absence of a professional periodical, these journals have been the substitute, informing sociologists about their profession, the growth of the discipline and their colleagues' work. In so doing they have played a significant role in the process of institutionalising sociology in the Soviet Union.

5 Areas of research

Since the mid-1950s, the areas of Soviet sociological research have expanded in number and scope. Subjects once thought to belong only in the realm of bourgeois sociology are coming under scrutiny, while more and more advanced methods are being employed to study topics always considered acceptable.

This chapter singles out and surveys seven areas of contemporary Soviet sociological research, namely: 1. time budget research; 2. labour; 3. social structure and stratification; 4. marriage, the family, *byt* (daily life, customs), divorce and the woman's role; 5. urban development, city planning and urban-rural relations; 6. criminology and juvenile delinquency; and 7. religion. Of these, the first three are examined in greater depth. The fields have been chosen because they appear to be the areas of greatest activity, both from the theoretical and empirical points of view.* Beginning with a

---

*One detailed empirical case study on public opinion research is treated separately, in depth, in chapter 6. While not discussed below, a further area of increasing interest for Soviet sociologists is that of youth and their problems. The youth are frequently studied as separate components of the class structure. They are therefore subdivided into working class youth, collective farm youth, young intellectuals, students, etc. The topics of research undertaken by sociologists include the attitudes of working class youth towards labour, the cultural level of young workers and stimuli for getting an education or further education, life plans of youth, professional choice and motivation of rural youth, and problems of student life. Apart from this concern with the social location of youth and its consequences, the specialised sociologies often discuss their specific topic with reference to youth (e.g., sociology of leisure and the problem of the use of leisure by the young). See, for example, B. G. Anan'ev and D. A. Kerimov (eds) *Chelovek i obshchestvo: Sotsial'nye problemy molodezhi*, Vol. 6, Leningrad, 1969; V. I. Dobrynina (ed.) *Molodezh' i trud*, Moscow, 1970; S. N. Ikonnikova and V. T. Lisovskii, *Molodezh' o sebe, o svoikh sverstnikakh*, Leningrad, 1969; L. N. Kogan (ed.) *Molodezh', ee interesy, stremleniia, idealy*, Moscow, 1969.

very brief chronological review of past work, the following accounts generalise about a field or highlight specific research findings.

A number of general points must be made about sociological research in the Soviet Union. In the first place, the sociologists are aware of the fact that theirs is a society sharply demarcated by urban-rural differences. While not always spelled out, the underlying processes, and effects, of industrialisation and urbanisation provide a broad background to specific research areas and problems. Second, references to 'survivals of the past', as *the* most prominent cause of certain types of social behaviour, occur more often in the more theoretical discussions as opposed to actual research; that is, the gulf between official theory and actual research is conspicuous. Third, much of the research deals, to a greater or lesser extent, with the creation of a new socialist form of social institution, for example, the city or the family. In this connection, for example, questions are raised regarding a 'Soviet' as distinct from a 'universal' city or family. Fourth, many research reports discuss what the various sub-divisions of sociology should study (e.g., the sociology of religion). The research itself attempts to define specific fields of inquiry. At the same time a closer interaction between the various sociological sub-divisions is noticeable. For example, researches on urban planning and on the family, although carried out by different individuals, are beginning to contribute to a better understanding of both. In many instances research published in one area tells a great deal about another; using the same example, research on the family may describe work in urban affairs and vice-versa.

On the whole, the utilisation of statistics is a problem shared by all of the researchers. Many are rather critical of the careless use and misuse of 'home-made' statistics. For example, researchers are admonished for presenting a table without stating the base number for their figures, for drawing 'statistical' conclusions from unrelated 'facts', or for assuming that correlation means causation. Equally crucial is the situation which refers to inaccurate statistics.* Here is one case reported by P. Fedoseev in a discussion of time budget research:[1]

What results had this research yielded? When scientific methods were used to determine losses of working time in production, it turned out that these were substantially greater than was apparent from the data of ordinary statistics. Ordinary statistics stated that losses of working time came to about one-tenth of one per cent for the country. But the results of the research showed that the figure was actually much higher – about ten to fifteen per cent for the annual total of working time. This means

*This applies to national statistics as well as to the 'home-made' variety.

that the question of making effective use of working time in production is far more complex than could be assumed from the statistical data.

The practice of withholding statistical material is also widely condemned by sociologists. As B. Grushin stated at a round-table discussion in 1966: 'The statisticians do not give us many data, being obviously captive to outdated considerations.' The other participants unanimously 'expressed the wish that the statistical administrations ... would be wise and sensible in separating those data that are indeed state secrets from those that are senselessly buried in the depths of statistical institutions because of someone's absurd over-caution or failure to understand true state interests'.[2] The absence of statistics in vital areas (for example, in crime), as well as the over-all lack of data on the socio-demographic structure of the country, has considerably hampered the work of the serious sociologist.

An enumeration of other suggestions for specifically improving research in their respective areas is a feature common to many researchers' reports. In writing up his research, the author usually described the project, reported the results and then concluded by expressing the need for the following: 1. improvement and expansion of demographic data available to the sociologist; 2. similar improvement of research methods and techniques, especially in regard to mathematical and statistical methods; 3. better training of sociologists; 4. more co-operation between sociologists as well as co-operation with other social scientists; 5. the publication of a sociology periodical; and 6. the translation and printing of sociological works published abroad, by both socialist and bourgeois sociologists.

Although not explicitly stated, the research described below is indicative of the growing diversification of views on any particular topic. Nonetheless, the unifying thread running through the research is the attempt (and the word attempt must be underlined) to answer or solve particular problems. For example, much labour research is concerned with the real problem of labour turnover and migration. In this and other fields, the desire to deal with particular problems produces an awareness of the lack of adequate social and sociological information and acts as a stimulus for the collection of basic data. Whether the information gathered is actually applied is a moot question.

Time budget research

One of the first areas of empirical research to surface after 1956 was time budget research, that is, research primarily concerned with how people spend their non-working time. A sequel to earlier Soviet research initiated in the 1920s by Academician S. Strumilin and others, this research was originally designed to show the important changes in the lives of the workers in the first years of Soviet power. The second stage of research was the result of the transition to the seven-hour work day at the end of the 1920s and the beginning of the 1930s. The third wave of research began in the late 1950s and early 1960s, coinciding with the 'building of communism' and the shortening of the work day. Since that time, a considerable number of studies have been conducted in the USSR.[3]

A strong impetus to time budget research throughout the Soviet Union was given in 1958 when the Siberian Research Institute of Labour and Wages and the Siberian Branch of the USSR Academy of Sciences launched a two year programme on how workers in Siberia and the Urals spent their non-working time. The fifteen investigations of the more than 25,000 time budgets of workers, engineering and technical personnel (ITRs) and white-collar workers in a number of industrial enterprises were collected and presented in one volume.[4] The editors stated in the introduction that the fundamental task of their investigation of time budgets was to work out recommendations for methodological practices in the study of non-working time; they warned that it is necessary to regard the collection only as a preparatory stage to the publication of further work on the problem of non-working time.

Surveys were conducted in order to determine the workers' use of time over a twenty-four hour period. Interviewing was conducted at the enterprise during non-working time – before the beginning and/or after the end of work, or during the lunch break – or at home. The general information included the following: sex, age, education, residence, location of work, type of worker, wage category, fulfilment of norms, length of service, marital status, number of children, living conditions, and what appliances (and similar things) the family owned. The informant himself kept a diary of his time use for the twenty-four hours: his non-working time was divided into four categories* and was examined on a workday, a day off, and a holiday. (See Appendix IA and IB for Prudenskii's questionnaires.)

The commentary on the data usually explained some peculiarities of the region or the enterprise under investigation, presented the tables with explanatory notes and discussed with criticisms and suggestions (which sometimes were direct party programme quota-

*Prudenskii's schema was as follows:
I. Working time
II. Non-working time
    A. Time expenditures connected with the stay at production
    B. Housework and care of self
    C. Sleeping and eating
    D. Free time

tions) the particular misuse or waste of time. Mention was usually made of the changes in the structure of non-working time: the changes were measured in terms of the findings of S. G. Strumilin's earlier research in the 1920s.* No statement was made as to how respondents were chosen. Although these respondents could not remain anonymous, the authors pointed to the need for conducting the sample on a strictly voluntary basis.

By the end of 1960, the Institute of Economics and Organisation of Industrial Production of the Siberian Branch of the Academy of Sciences held the first conference on 'The free time of working people under the conditions of the reduction of the work day'. The conference, which grew out of the necessity to exchange experience and work out methods for this type of research, was divided into two topics: 1. the rational use of non-working (including free) time, and the improvement of cultural and *byt* amenities; and 2. the methods of studying non-working time of the workers. The participants noted that time budget research conducted by scientific institutions or trade unions must be co-ordinated with party and state statistical organs. They recommended polling either by a registrar or by self-registration as *the* method for observation. The poll could either be conducted on the basis of enterprise or territorial classifications. The period of observation could vary: the most complete study would cover a week's time, but if this was impossible, then a three-day survey (including a weekday, a day preceding a day off and a day off) would be acceptable. A time budget for a weekday and a day off was also possible. The two seasons suggested were winter and summer.

The recommendations from this conference and the proposals and methods from the Siberian study have been the bases for further time budget research. On the whole, relatively few changes have been introduced in the procedure, but researchers have continued to question certain aspects of this form of research. For example, should the period of observation be daily or weekly? Should a control group be used? What is the definition of 'satisfactory' representativeness? Should the data take into account national and ethnographic peculiarities?[5]

The classification of time use has been an area of debate between

---

*Most of the studies do compare their data with the earlier findings of Strumilin, but they often fail to mention that the 1924 Strumilin study interviewed 625 people of whom 9 per cent came from Moscow, 6 per cent from Leningrad and the remaining 85 per cent from the provinces; they were people who lived near the factories and the large towns, and hence may be characterised as urban. The tendency to compare present studies with those in the past seems, however, to be diminishing. In its place is cross-national or cross-socialist comparative research. See S. G. Strumilin, *Problemy Ekonomiki Truda*, Moscow, 1957, 733 pp. and *Rabochii Den' i Kommunizm*, Moscow, 1959, 64 pp.

time budget researchers. Each researcher has found his own way of classifying time while at the same time attacking the other systems.[6] As a result, no one opinion on the classification question exists. However, more standardisation is quite possible on account of the link-up of the Siberian department with the multi-national research on time use, conducted under the auspices of the European Co-ordination Centre for Research and Documentation in Social Sciences.[7]

In general, the basic unit of the time budget studies is the type of work: each study is billed as the non-working time of workers, engineering and technical personnel (ITRs), office workers or kolkhozniks:* of the research carried out in the years 1958–66, 88 per cent was devoted to the time budgets of workers, ITRs and office workers.[8] The difficulty with these classifications, however, is that either they are not held constant or they are not precise enough. The problem is particularly acute with the classification of the ITRs, that is, the engineering and technical personnel 'with a higher or secondary education engaged in technical management or industry or transport'.[9] This category, like the others, encompasses a wide range of working people; at times, it also includes the term *sluzhashchii* (white collar or office worker). Many studies combine the two groups so that the distinction is blurred or overlooked.†

Time budget researchers usually describe and chart the variables which influence the amount and use of non-working time. While different researchers concentrate on different variables and omit others, the list of variables may include: conditions of employment and character and content of labour; calendar day; season of the year; type of occupation; age and sex; marital status and composition of the family; size and character of dwelling and presence of public amenities; presence of household equipment and cultural articles; income; educational level and commitment to studies; term of work in one's speciality and one's qualifications; brigades of labour; party membership; length of working day. Two types of charts usually appear in the research write-ups. The first involves the composition of the sample. For example, age variables are charted against sex or educational level against age. The second type, which

*The 1965 Pskov study, which was linked to and regulated by the UNESCO multi-national time budget research, is based on the adult population of urban and industrial areas. The basic unit of this study, then, is the urban industrial centre.

†One study, the Baikova study, sometimes calls the group 'engineering and technical *workers*', while at other times 'engineering and technical *intelligentsia*'. This may perhaps be explained by Baikova's insistence on developing the ITRs as leaders and organisers of production, as a technical vanguard. See V. G. Baikova, A. S. Duchal, and A. A. Zemtsov, *Svobodnoe vremia i vsestoronnee razvitie lichnosti*, Moscow, 1965, p. 271. (Italics mine.)

is by far the more common, compares the given variable (e.g., sex, age or occupation) with different types of time expenditures (e.g., time on housework or leisure time). In most instances two variables are correlated. (The 1965 Pskov study does co-ordinate more factors.) In other cases, some data said to be collected are not tabulated or discussed.

As regards the sample itself, in most cases we do not know how the sample is chosen nor how representative it is of the population. We might assume that the sample is representative of a certain factory and of its workers, but surely this is not so in all cases.* Thus the time budget studies are reports of specific workers in specific types of factories. Moreover, regional characteristics are but briefly indicated in the studies. But even if they were more fully explained, the combination of worker classification and regional classification would still limit the possibility of generalising about the entire Soviet Union. Perhaps this concern is unwarranted since the main divisions of time expenditures (e.g., working time, time on housework and free time) are relatively constant, and the use of time follows certain broad trends. Variations do occur, but many of them may be explained by an examination of working and/or regional conditions.

What then is the significance of time budget research? Many researchers state that it should discover the uses of non-working time and have the important function of establishing the dependence of the development of different processes (e.g., the all-round development of the personality) on the presence of non-working time. The presence and use of non-working time are considered to be positively or negatively connected with the development of the mental and physical capabilities of the individual. Non-working time is also considered to be important as a period in which the individual 'reproduces' energy which is then utilised during working time. Thus society, as well as the individual, profits from non-working time. At the same time, non-working time is viewed as one of the indices of the level of development of the individual, of a definite social group and of society as a whole. Time budget research, therefore, is to define the reserves of growth of non-working time and subsequently improve the structure of non-working time. This, in turn, seeks to answer the question: Does the individual have sufficient non-working time to satisfy his intellectual and physical needs? By studying different groups of the population, time budget research indicates the importance of variations in standards of living, the state of *byt* and cultural

*For example, the Leningrad sample had (proportionally) too many well-educated workers. See E. V. Beliaev *et al.*, 'Izuchenie biudzheta vremeni trudiashchikhsia kak odin iz metodov konkretno-sotsiologicheskogo issledovaniia', *Vestnik LGU*, no. 23, 1961, pp. 96-110.

services and national ethnographic differences (e.g., differences in tenor of life, level of culture, leisure pursuits).[10] Most time budget research is also concerned with ways of 'rationalising' the use of non-working time. Rational use of time applies to time spent on 'necessities', such as sleep, as well as to free time. Time use is considered 'rational' if it positively affects the intellectual and physical development of the individual and 'irrational' if it has a negative affect.* For example, time spent on housework and on work connected with production (e.g., travel to work) is considered irrational. Thus it is important and essential first to shorten time on these activities and then to ensure that this time is spent more rationally.

The results from the research are intended to be used for planning a more rational use of non-working time by developing communal and service facilities and cultural amenities and utilising labour resources more profitably. Blaming shortcomings in planning for the present situation, each of the researchers offers suggestions for improving living conditions and increasing the material and cultural level of the workers. Several of the researchers' suggestions have been applied. For example, some transport systems have been altered on account of the research. However, at the second conference on time budget research, the researchers themselves concluded that the success rate of introducing research results into practice has been quite low.[11]

Time budget research has another function which is becoming increasingly evident. Criticism of existing conditions forms a good part of the reports. The complaints are mostly concerned with the absence or inadequacy of facilities and services – with objective, rather than subjective, factors. Most of the criticism falls within accepted limits. It also parallels many of the regime's complaints, but often the researchers can back up their observations with more specific 'facts' than the regime spokesmen.

Labour

Sociologists have been accused of trespassing on the territory of the economists, but with the increasingly successful application of the sociologists' findings, the criticism is subsiding.[12] Be that as it may, it would appear that the economists are primarily interested in the

---

*At the second conference on time budget research held in June 1969, it was noted that while rational use of time was the aim, no criteria of 'rational use' were listed nor was there any discussion of a 'sociological theory' of free time. See E. V. Klopov, 'Biudzhet vremeni i sotsial'noe planirovanie', *Vop Fil*, no. 9, 1969, p. 152, and V. A. Artemov and B. P. Kutyrev, 'Biudzhet vremeni i sotsial'no-ekonomicheskoe planirovanie', *Fil Nauki*, no. 6, 1969, p. 186.

economy at large – in production, distribution and the management of resources – whereas the sociologists concentrate on the individual in his relation to labour and production, and on labour in relation to society. The industrial sociologist specifically studies the organisation of labour, labour relations, labour turnover, occupational structure, job qualifications (education and training), technological (and also societal) progress, automation and leisure.[13] But all Soviet sociologists are involved, albeit indirectly, with 'labour'. After all, in fundamental Marxist terms, 'the mental, physical and moral development of the working man is conditioned by the content and character of labour, by the rhythm and conditions of labour, and finally, by the socio-psychological life of the productive collective'.[14]

Sotsiologiia v SSSR has stated that the basic task of sociological research on labour consists in establishing what influence the present production activities of different people have on the formation of socialist and communist relations (e.g., the new society) and on the development of the individual (e.g., the 'new man'). The functional requirements of the developing society, however, may diverge from the individual's requirements. It is at this point or, ideally, before this point that the sociologist must offer suggestions and/or warnings so that the objective requirements of society are fulfilled. His task involves manipulating two sets of factors. The first set, which refers to such things as the organisation and conditions of labour, must be immediately altered: in other words, these factors, on account of their very nature, can (and must) be made to coincide at once with societal requirements. The second set of factors, which includes, for example, the presence of unqualified types of labour and the low cultural and technical level of the individual, must also be modified; this process, however, is much slower than the first because it involves gradual change.

Thus the sociologist is to balance individual and societal requirements, with the latter taking precedence. Keeping this in mind, sociologists have done a considerable amount of research into the relationship between the individual and labour and production. Part of this research concerns labour efficiency, that is, how workers utilise their working time. Such research – basically time budget and labour efficiency research – takes into account the differences between various grades of workers and managers. Related research has been carried out in connection with the ways and means of increasing production. This research examines workers' incentives – both material and moral – and workers' satisfaction or dissatisfaction with their jobs. Questions as to how best to utilise human resources and the causes of labour turnover – both within one sector of the economy and between different sectors of the economy – are also closely related to the basic problem of work satisfaction.

Another topic of research is the worker's relations with other workers. The working patterns of various groups are examined in an attempt to find out why some work groups function better together than others. Factory conditions and the impact of technology and automation have also been studied for their effect on the work group, the individual and labour production.

A further area of research relates to the education of workers. Education in this case refers primarily to raising labour skills and to additional training in one's own profession or re-training in another. But it does also encompass education in cultural and intellectual spheres. What one does during non-working time is seen as being closely related to labour performance: the more fully-rounded individual is the better worker. Taking non-working time into account, other sociologists have studied the role of labour in the development of the individual and the methods of moulding the new personality.

Intensive work on many of the problems listed above has been carried out in various parts of the country. The following account discusses some of the most important studies in labour sociology: these either initiated further research in some specific area, indicated changes in attitudes toward a specific research problem, or made suggestions for improving or coming to terms with a particular problem.

The Laboratory for Economic and Mathematical Research at Novosibirsk State University is among the leading research centres for labour sociology. Under the direction of V. N. Shubkin, the Laboratory has concentrated on the related problems of education and occupation and on social mobility.[15] Accordingly, a major project sought to answer questions on the following:[16]

the social prestige and attractiveness of different occupations and types of work; the objective and subjective factors influencing the education, occupation inclinations, choice of occupation, job placement . . . of various groups of young people; social, occupational and geographical mobility in choosing an occupation; the effectiveness of the system of production training in schools and some ways for improving the planning and preparation of qualified cadres; and improving the system of vocational guidance and counselling.

The research, mainly by individual questionnaires, included a follow-up survey two years after the first (1962) trial survey of 300 secondary school graduates and an intermediate study of 9,000 secondary school children.

Concentrating on all aspects of job placement, the researchers discovered two gaps in vocational training and actual work. First,

61

vocational training in secondary schools did not correlate with job placement: only 11 per cent of those interviewed entered the trade for which they were trained. Thus vocational training was relatively ineffective. Second, the individual's plans for higher education diverged from his actual placement both in industry and in education: while 80 per cent of the respondents wanted to continue their studies, only 44 per cent were actually able to do so. Demographic, social and material conditions were shown to affect the possibilities for further education. Like the Rutkevich research on the hereditary nature of the intelligentsia, the Shubkin team found that social origin affects educational opportunities and influences the individual's evaluation of future jobs. According to the data, social differences manifested themselves in inequality of opportunities for continuing education among young people from urban professional families and the working class on the one hand, and rural youth on the other. The same occupations were found to have different degrees of 'prestige' among urban and rural young people and among children of workers' families and children of the intelligentsia. The latter point was discovered in the course of research on occupational preferences, done along sex–age and urban–rural lines.

The Novosibirsk study was one of the first to discuss these problems. In 1965, surveys employing techniques identical to those of the Novosibirsk study were conducted in Leningrad (by the Sociology Laboratory of Leningrad State University under the guidance of V. A. Iadov and V. Vodzinskaia), in the Buriat ASSR (by the Buriat Interdisciplinary Research Institute of the Siberian Branch of the USSR Academy of Sciences under D. Lubsanov), and in Poland (Institute of Philosophy and Sociology of the Polish Academy of Sciences and the Higher School of Economics under Professors A. Sarapata and A. Rajkewicz).

Workers' attitudes towards labour have been the object of several studies by Soviet sociologists. The most advanced and comprehensive of these was conducted by the staff of the Sociological Research Laboratory of Leningrad State University (begun in 1964).[17] At twenty-five Leningrad enterprises, 2,665 workers under thirty years of age were selected 'by random, regional cross-section, according to the nature of their work'. In addition to gathering the usual objective data (e.g., on sex, age, occupation), the researchers attempted to characterise the worker's performance in his job by determining his degree or level of conscientiousness, discipline and initiative. They also studied subjective factors, namely, work satisfaction, satisfaction with wages and organisation of labour, interest in work and motives for choosing the occupation.

The workers were ranked into six groups according to the degree of technical skill required by their occupation. 'Satisfaction with occupation' was found to vary from a negative attitude among heavy unskilled manual labour to a highly positive attitude among the most highly skilled group, panel operator setters. The factors in the work situation giving rise to satisfaction or dissatisfaction in work were ranked (index) as follows:[18]

Content of work (does it require ingenuity or not)	0·72
Pay	0·61
The possibility of improving skill	0·58
Variety in work	0·48
Organisation of labour	0·38
Management's concern for workers	0·35
Physical effort	0·32

The authors of the study placed strong emphasis on the fact that the content of work emerged as the most significant factor determining job satisfaction. They argued that the content of work was the crucial determinant of whether or not material rewards furthered or hindered the formation of positive or negative attitudes towards work. In the case of workers engaged in occupations with a low (non-creative) content of labour, high wages acted as a form of compensation for work and furthered the establishment of attitudes which regarded work as a means of satisfying needs lying outside the work activity itself.

On the one hand, therefore, findings of the study in so far as they emphasised technology as a determinant of attitudes towards work were in agreement with a similar 'technological' perspective in Western industrial sociology.[19] On the other hand, the emphasis on material rewards as a compensating factor for intrinsically unsatisfying work gives support to a quite contrary position.[20] In this connection, it should be noted that Iadov and his colleagues have been criticised for underestimating the significance of material incentives as determinants of job satisfaction.[21]

It was an important contribution of the Leningrad study to recognise the need when carrying out research into job satisfaction to take into account occupational differences and the diversified attitudes of various groups. Problems of planning and management were seen to be soluble without identifying differentiated groups of people in terms of similarity of occupation, qualifications, needs and work motivation.

Sociological research on labour turnover has, it is argued by Soviet sociologists, disproved the opinion widely held by economists that labour turnover is a purely economic phenomenon and that the means of controlling it should derive from improvement in economic circumstances, motivating a more efficient use and redistribution of manpower. This, for example, is the position of E. Antosenkov (head of a team of economists and sociologists affiliated with the Institute of Economic and Industrial Engineering of the Siberian Branch of the USSR Academy of Sciences and the Laboratory for Economic–Mathematical research of Novosibirsk University).[22] He and his team carried out studies in the years 1964–9 in Western and Eastern Siberia and showed that labour turnover is the result of the inter-action of economic, social, socio-psychological, demographic and other factors.

Before the early 1960s, according to Antosenkov, the tendency was to subject all aspects of economic and cultural life to planning by directives. A corollary of this was the concept that labour turnover was a process not inherent in socialist economy. The reasoning was as follows:[23]

As the national economy plans reflect (or should reflect) all kinds of labour mobility necessary from the point of view of national economy, any other labour force movement is inconsistent with the national economy interests. Hence, the above mentioned concept of the labour turnover followed [that] which was not represented (and could not even be so) in any plans. This situation was most clearly reflected in the 'Short economic dictionary (1958)', where an attempt was made to analyse the economic nature of this process. Two points were emphasised by the authors of the 'Dictionary' in the first place: the uncontrollable character of the labour turnover and its incompatibility with a planned system of socialist economy. They believed that labour turnover under socialism was not a consequence and a *sine qua non* of the existence and development of the socialist mode of production and of the social labour organisation inherent to it. Hence they concluded that such a phenomenon could not be tolerated in socialist economy and should be fully eradicated by all possible means.

With the help of sociological research into the effect on turnover of such factors as the level of organisation and working conditions, the ways of recruiting and assigning personnel to jobs, the labour force shortage, especially in skilled trades, and living standards (among them housing and wages), the concept of labour turnover has been altered. Antosenkov suggests that labour turnover can now be defined as a result of the fact that the goals of certain working people, certain enterprises and the national economy as a whole do not co-incide, e.g., interests have not been satisfied.

Closely related to the above questions is research into the influence of population movement on the manpower problem. Studies by V. Perevedentsev, also from Novosibirsk, have demonstrated regularities of population movement and also the fallacy of the idea that only planned migration exists or even predominates in the USSR.[24] (In particular, population movements were shown to be associated with the instability of the labour force.) Among the variety of reasons advanced for movement by migrants, economic factors were predominant. These included unsatisfactory wage levels and the actual character of work and living conditions. Further it became apparent that migration for supposedly different reasons (e.g., personal motives, such as moving to relatives) was actually strongly influenced by economic considerations. A major consideration emerging from the work of Perevedentsev and his colleagues, much of whose work was concerned with migration on a regional basis, was the fact that population movement, and hence labour turnover, when viewed societally emerged as being very closely related to differences in living conditions and educational opportunities between the urban and rural population. Among the agricultural population in Siberia, for example, the move to the cities was shown to occur principally among the youngest and more highly skilled sections of the labour force. Other studies have stressed that urban residents are better off than their rural counterparts on the same social level and that this has to be considered as one of the main reasons for the rural population deficit.[25]

As has been emphasised previously, a major source of Soviet sociological studies is the confrontation with practical problems. Evidence of this in the field of labour sociology is the concern with the influence of alterations in the length of the working week. It was found, for example, that approval of a reduction in the length of the working week – from six to five days – was positively correlated with residence in large, as opposed to small, cities. The basis for the greater approval in larger cities emerged as resting upon greater opportunities for utilisation of the time made available in the form of leisure pursuits.[26]

A further example of the practical results of labour research is to be found in evidence available about the social consequences of the impact of research centres such as that at Novosibirsk. This evidence largely relates to the presence and role of sociologists in Soviet factories. A report from the first Secretary of the Altai *kraikom*, for example, specifically links the application of sociological surveys by the Novosibirsk department with the subsequent employment of sociologists in factories and to the establishment of a bureau of sociological research. As a result, it is claimed that labour turnover has been reduced.[27]

Social structure and stratification

Since the beginning of the 1960s, previous theoretical work in the

65

field of social structure and stratification has been revitalised by concrete sociological research which has, in its turn, produced modifications in the general concept of social structure. Sociological work in this field started from the general position that while the path towards social unity and a classless society was originally paved by the liquidation of an exploiting class, classes still do exist, namely, the two non-antagonistic classes of workers and peasants. There is, in addition, one stratum, the intelligentsia. However, with the advent of more concrete sociological investigations, utilising sociological and psychological variables, increasing stress is placed on examining intra-class, rather than inter-class, differences. In fact, it is in the area of intra-class study that the most advanced research is taking place.

The first All-Union Conference on the 'Changes of the social structure of Soviet society' represented a turning point in research in this area.[28] Held in Minsk in January 1966, the conference was sponsored by the Social Sciences Branch of the USSR Academy of Sciences, the Institute of Philosophy and Law of the Bielorussian SSR Academy of Sciences and *Znanie*. More than three hundred scholars took part.

The opening paper at the conference was delivered by V. S. Semenov (Institute of Philosophy, USSR Academy of Sciences). His talk essentially said that the division of the population into working class, collective farm peasantry, and intelligentsia and employees was correct, but far too general. Within Soviet society there exist 'many social developments, degrees, and variants'.[29] He then outlined four basic trends of social class development on which writers on social structure have concentrated, namely:[30]

1. class differences between the working class and the kolkhoz peasantry, based on two forms of socialist *property*;
2. social differences between physical (workers and peasants) and mental (intelligentsia) *labour*;
3. socio-economic and cultural-*byt* differences between urban (urban workers and urban intelligentsia) and rural (peasants and agricultural workers and rural intelligentsia) *regions*;
4. social *differences within* the working class, kolkhoz peasantry, intelligentsia and employees. (Italics mine.)

The other conference participants filled in Semenov's four-fold scheme. Some, like Professor G. E. Glezerman, adhered to the position which stresses property relations as paramount. Others expanded the second proposition on labour: V. C. Podmarkov, for example, discussed occupational structure after stating that the most general principle of the professional structure was the division between mental and physical labour. The third argument was propounded by

G. P. Davidiuk in his discussion of kolkhoz peasantry and the problem of shifts in population. And finally, many participants recounted their studies on the internal structure (hence, the intra-class differences) of the workers, the peasants and the intelligentsia. In addition, new definitions of 'class' were proposed by some who said the term was no longer valid for socialist society. Iu. I. Shiriaev of Kiev said that the Leninist definition of class consists of two parts: a general definition, which is related to all classes (both the exploiting and working classes), and a particular definition, which is only related to the exploiting classes. Shiriaev complained that the general definition is upheld today even though the social composition of classes under socialism is principally different from that under capitalism. Furthermore, he said that the particular definition is not applicable to socialist society since there are no exploiting classes. All in all, the term 'class' does not allow for the changes which have occurred in socialist society. Another participant, N. A. Aitov, agreed that 'class' demands another definition. Since at present there is only one kind of relationship to the means of production, there are no classes; but since there are differences according to forms of property, there are classes. Therefore 'class' refers to class and non-class phenomena simultaneously. Hence, a redefinition is in order.

While a new definition was not accepted, it is clear that the participants went a long way from merely mouthing former concepts of class. Not only were inter- and intra-class differences elaborated in the discussions, but conclusions from concrete sociological research were cited as evidence. Therefore, it seems that modifications of the concept of class (both as property-based and antagonistic) were proposed.

Three participants at the Minsk conference are particularly noted for their work in the field of social structure. They are M. N. Rutkevich, Iu. V. Arutunian and O. I. Shkaratan. All concur in the primary role of intra-class differences. Each specialises in one social group. Before reviewing their work individually, let us examine their more general comments on the study of social structure.[31]

There is agreement that a major task confronting Soviet students of social stratification is the development of a new theory which would make possible the analysis of a novel system of social relations. Progress towards the development of this theory has been hindered by the neglect of intra- as opposed to inter-class relations. Such intra-class relations are, it is agreed, determined by the over-all structure of class inter-relations, but nevertheless have an independent significance with respect to the pace and direction of social change.

With regard to the question of relations between classes, the writers whose work is about to be examined in some detail have made a number of discrete but complementary points. Arutunian, for example, has emphasised the deficiencies of available data with respect to class composition. In particular he has argued that the inclusion of the two anachronistic categories in the census returns (namely, private peasants and handicraftsmen not in producers' co-operatives and capitalists, landlords, merchants and kulaks) is a significant obstacle to progress in the analysis of class relations and their evolution. Paralleling this type of empirical criticism, Rutkevich has pointed out the theoretical difficulties which arise from the fact that sociological literature, while emphasising the novelty of class relations in the Soviet Union, at the same time underestimates the essential novelty of the social process and therefore of the groups involved in the stratification system. This position would appear to amount to an argument for the lack of any possibility of comparison between the social situation of the working class prior to 1917 and the social situation of the group referred to by the same concept subsequently. Such a position is not incompatible with that advanced by Shkaratan. With regard to the question of the influence of pre-Revolutionary social conditions, Shkaratan questions the plausibility of treating class relations within the Soviet Union as being essentially homogeneous in character given the very wide variation in economic and socio-political circumstances of different regions at the time of the Revolution. Shkaratan's emphasis upon the need for a longitudinal historical dimension in the analysis of stratification is both novel and important. Of similar significance is the argument that he has advanced for the impossibility of discussing changes in both class and professional profiles independently of a study of urbanisation.

Professor Rutkevich of Sverdlovsk is specifically engaged in identifying the intelligentsia.[32] He divides mental workers into two groups – the employees or non-specialists (*sluzhashchii*) and the specialists. The former are defined as less qualified non-manual workers whose work does not require higher education; the latter are those people who have received a secondary special or higher education and who are, by profession, engaged in mental labour. In other words, not all mental workers are included in his definition of intelligentsia. Much of Rutkevich's work is concerned with implementing this, as against the more official, definition.

Another phase of his research includes an examination of the sources of recruitment of the intelligentsia. Although he did conclude that the main replacement of the intelligentsia came from the workers, the peasants and the non-specialist employees, he also indicated that the opportunities for further (i.e., high school) education – and thus entrance into the intelligentsia – were greater for urban families of 'comfortable circumstances' and of greater education themselves. On the basis of discovering the hereditary nature of the replenishment of the intelligentsia, Rutkevich has suggested that the social composition of the students should conform more closely with the social composition of the population.

Extensive work on the social structure of the rural population has been done by Iu. V. Arutunian of Moscow State University.[33] In his research on this subject, he maintains that the nature and quality of labour determines the nature of the social group within the class.* 'Differences in the quality of labour are linked with the social division of labour. Labour that is socially dissimilar in quality falls into two basic categories, physical and mental.' These categories, each of which appears in the state and collective sectors, are further sub-divided into skilled and unskilled labour. Once he had determined these divisions, Arutunian showed that variations between sectors (state and collective) and between classes (workers and collective farmers) were much less substantial than they were within them: the greatest differences were between people of skilled and unskilled labour.

Arutunian has three basic criticisms of the current analysis of the social structure. First of all, he says the problems of the rural regions are reduced to problems of the peasantry and therefore the state sector is eliminated. Second:[34]

in considering the differences between the working class and the peasantry on the basis of the country as a whole, without regard for the kind of workers – urban or rural – the investigators are dealing with, . . . it remains unclear to what degree the differences between workers and collective farmers are caused by different relations to property, and to what degree they are caused by the specific nature of city and countryside, of industry and agriculture.

Arutunian sees the undervaluation of intra-class differences as the third and chief shortcoming of this research: 'it is inadequate for an analysis of social relations in a socialist society to base the division of society solely on the relationship of social groups to the ownership of the means of production.'

The study of intra-class structure is also stressed by O. I. Shkaratan of Leningrad.[35] In his research on the working class, defined by him as workers in the sphere of physical and mental labour, engaged in material production and employed in enterprises and institutions which are publicly owned, he sees differences in the 'complexity of labour' as the dominant factor in social differences. He sought to establish an index of 'complexity of labour' which would permit a

---

*At Minsk, according to Arutunian, the speakers were virtually unanimous in choosing quality and character of labour as the criterion for the intra-class structure of the peasantry.

measure not of the quality of labour itself, but of the differences between groups of people in different jobs. 'The fact that members of one and the same class belong to groups of workers with different skills, holding unequal positions in the system of social production, is decisive today in determining the social importance of the individual.'[36] Therefore, 'intra-class divisions into groups according to their socially heterogeneous labour determines the social cast of the individual and influences the possibility of advancement of those who come from these groups.'

Elsewhere Shkaratan set out to test and document the following theses:[37]

1. the development of a classless society will be accompanied by profound structural changes in the class units themselves, which will lose their class character and take on characteristics consonant with the character of the new society;
2. the boundaries of the working class will expand to include those doing non-physical labour, including the technical intelligentsia;
3. during the transitional period from capitalism to socialism, and during subsequent development, the working class (while unified by a common relationship to the means of production, by a leading role in the societal organisation of labour, and by common sources of the basic means of existence) is still internally differentiated in many ways;
4. intra-class structure is derivative not only from the type of over-all social structure in the society, but also from the stage of development of social relationships;
5. the social structure of both society as a whole and its components is stable within stages, given the same social order; this is connected with the level of development of social and economic relationships.

In general, therefore, sociologists in the field of social stratification have shifted their emphasis from a study of inter-class differences to one of intra-class differences. As a consequence, they stress that, in order to achieve a homogeneous society, differences between as well as within classes must be removed.

However, there is no real consensus on how to differentiate or delineate classes, let alone differentiate within a class. For example, some define the intelligentsia as all who are employed in mental labour; others define them as a stratum between two classes, the workers and collective farm workers; others say there are two classes and each has its own intelligentsia. Nor is there agreement on differentiation within a class, be it in terms of qualifications (educational and cultural), character of labour (mental or physical), wages or place of work. However, once these intra-class differences were recognised as analysable, other dimensions, such as nationality differences, family and living conditions and cultural variations, have begun to be considered.

Thus the sociologists have begun to paint a picture of a differentiated and stratified society in which different classes and different groups within the classes have varied attributes, interests, life styles. The painting has been hampered, however, by brushes clogged with past theories and by a lack of new styles of composition.

Marriage, the family, *byt,* divorce and the woman's role

The study of the development of marriage, the family and *byt* under socialism – that is, as social and interpersonal institutions which fulfil biological, economic and emotional functions – is increasingly becoming an area of concern for Soviet sociologists. Supplementing the more general discussion of a socialist form of marriage and family, sociologists are concentrating on the family because of the large increase in divorces, the falling birth rate and the large number of juvenile crimes.

A. G. Kharchev from Leningrad was the sociologist who broke the silence of the Stalinist era with his work on the family.[38] He seems at present to be the most prolific writer in the field and his book, *Brak i sem'ia v SSSR (Marriage and the Family in the USSR)*, represents the 'first contemporary attempt at a sociological study of this extensive problem (more accurately, not problem but rather sphere of social life)'. So wrote I. S. Kon in his review of Kharchev's 1964 book.[39] The volume looks at marriage and the family as objects of sociological research, at the social nature of these institutions and finally at the changes in, development of and differences between the family under capitalism, socialism and communism. In addition to his own research, Kharchev made extensive use of literature from other fields (e.g., ethnography, economics, jurisprudence).[40] He also relied on Western literature; in fact, according to reviewer Kon, 'it [the book] . . . is free of that vulgar-nihilistic attitude to non-Marxist sociology which still sometimes rears its head in certain works and causes obvious damage to Soviet science'.[41] Another critic maintains that the 'sexual-psychological' aspect is a weak part of his research and that he has not offered enough recommendations from that research.[42] However, Kharchev was praised for his substantial contribution to sociology.

Kharchev's research is based on his 1962 survey of 500 couples who were getting married at the Leningrad City Registration Bureau (ZAGS) and also on an analysis of the data of these bureaux for the Uzbek SSR, the city of Kiev, the town of Tiumen' and the Mga *raion* of Leningrad *oblast'*. The aims of the investigation were;[43]

71

1. To discover what those who intend to marry consider to be vital for a stable and happy family life, and how the choice of a future husband or wife is motivated;
2. To find out the differences in the ages at marriage and the main trends of these differences;
3. To establish the proportion, and importance, of marriages which involve the overcoming of certain prejudices and hence require a stronger subjective justification and greater personal responsibility for the decision. These include all marriages between people of different nationalities and, especially, of different cultural, religious or ethnic groups;
4. To obtain data on premarital acquaintance, including its duration.

With these aims in mind, he gathered data on the social composition of the couples (age, family background), how long the couples knew each other, where they met and why they married. On the whole, Kharchev's research begins to give some answers to these relatively unstudied questions.

An over-all survey of other areas of concentration of family sociology is simplified by the fact that in January 1967, the first All-Union symposium of sociologists working on the problems of marriage, the family and *byt* was held in Vil'nius.[44] Kharchev, who chaired the hundred-man symposium, opened the proceedings with a description of research in Leningrad where, he informed the symposium, researchers were concerned with three phases of research. The first focused on different aspects of marriage and family relations, the formation of the family, and the liquidation of conflict within the family so that the family might successfully carry out its role in educating the 'new man'. The second phase linked family research with urban and architectural problems (e.g., a study of the present and future composition of the family so as to ensure that housing meets the needs of the population). And the third direction of research concerned the leisure of youth or, more specifically, the problem of leisure in relation to personality development, unregulated leisure and informal youth groups.

Many other topics, such as rural families, student marriages and the role of the family in socialisation, were discussed at the symposium. The approach of bourgeois (in this case, American) and Polish sociologists to the subject was also examined. Problems of methodology and methods of research in this field were reviewed by participants from all over the Soviet Union. Particular emphasis was laid on the role of statistical (e.g., tables of marriage and divorce rates) and ethnographical (e.g., family histories) methods.

Divorce as a subject of social research – that is, the causes of divorce, including both subjective and objective factors – was also examined at the Vil'nius conference. Why study divorce? According to a *Nedelia* commentary on the conference: 'Everyone has long known the aphorism that all happy families are alike, but each unhappy one is unhappy in its own particular way. But it has also been established that the path to family disintegration has its own laws and causes. It is essential to study them.'[45]

In documenting the causes of divorce, the researchers stated that divorce itself was not indicative of the decay of the institution of marriage: 'The individual is not running away from family life in general, and destruction does not at all threaten the family nucleus in our society.'[46] The best proof of this, they said, is the large number of repeated or second marriages. Noting that research findings are relatively constant throughout the country, the researchers stated that intellectual and moral differences were the main causes of the disruption of a marriage. Drunkenness, the pet source of many social evils, and a 'lightminded approach to marriage', a trait often manifest in the young, were also cited as causes of divorce. Directly related to the latter is the feeling among some sociologists that physical maturity has proceeded more rapidly than emotional or economic maturity. Some suggested programmes for sex education and special pedagogical or family consultation services to help remedy this situation. Others suggested that the state make financial provisions to cover the expense of setting up a home. This last proposal was echoed a few years later (1970) in some Bielorussian research on the family: long-term, interest-free credit from the state to help newly-weds set up home was recommended.[47] At the symposium, proposals to enlist sociologists in the courts to work on cases involving 'violations' of family life and juvenile delinquency were put forward. Also voiced was the hope of studying separately urban and rural families as well as families from various sized cities (e.g., large, average and small).

The role of the woman – as wife, mother and worker in production – was another major topic at the Vil'nius conference. The basic contradiction between the professional and family roles for women was discussed. Z. A. Iankova, for example, told of research she had conducted with the Section of Sociological Research of the Institute of Philosophy (USSR Academy of Sciences) in 1965–7 and the Institute of Concrete Social Research of the USSR Academy of Sciences in 1969 in Moscow, Penze and Leningrad on the structure of the domestic role of women and its influence on the process of overcoming residues of inequality between the sexes. She concluded that the structure of the domestic role depends in many instances on: the content and character of labour in social production and therefore is connected with the woman's professional preparation and orientation; the structure of the family (e.g., is it nuclear or extended?); and the models of domestic roles (e.g., does dusting have any prestige?).[48]

As indicated in Iankova's study, sociologists are concerned about the woman's role as housewife. The excessive burden of housework and the resulting 'retardation' due to the consequent absence of free time are causes of concern. Time budget research has shown that women do more than their fair share of housework. 'The patriarchal tradition of "household bondage" lives – and flourishes! The age-old division of labour that takes over on the thresholds of our homes is dying hard.'[49] Mixed with criticism of household duties and the consequent loss of free time is a plea for time and labour-saving services.

Sociologists are also examining the woman's role in production. In 1966, A. I. Pimenova discussed those factors which define and limit a woman's participation in socially productive work and sought to discover those conditions which would extend her participation.[50] Factors such as income and education were found to have a direct bearing on women's professional activities. Economic as well as 'moral' stimuli were cited as motives prompting women to work: economic stimuli included the desire to receive additional means for the maintenance of the family, while the moral reasons included contact with people and the desire to be of some use to society. The research yielded three practical suggestions:

1. to take additional measures to raise the professional qualifications of women, especially among the middle aged and the housewives, and increase average earnings;
2. to establish places to take care of the children of working mothers; and
3. to organise special commissions on the problems of women's labour.

In general, research in this field invariably produces suggestions for solving or alleviating some of the problems which initiated the research: not surprisingly, most of the plans are linked with state aid or intervention, as in the case of living accommodation or services. The research also inadvertently indicates contradictions between theory and reality. In theory, the socialist family, a new type of institution, is a happy one, but at the same time divorce must be explained; similarly, women are theoretically supposed to be equal to men, but in reality women are doubly burdened with career and family and home obligations.

Urban development, city planning and urban–rural relations

The over-all task of the sociologist studying the social problems of the city and the village is to examine the interdependence between the new forms of social relations in labour and every day life (i.e., the communist forms of social relations) and the existing or planned forms of urban and rural life.[51] The sociologist is to investigate the *zakonomernosti* of the development of different forms of urban and rural life, the paths and means for most quickly eliminating the differences between urban and rural areas, and the ways of creating relatively similar conditions in these regions. Currently, he is concentrating on urban planning.

The main debate on urban development is centred around the problem of the size of the city. Adherents of the officially sanctioned group are in favour of the theory of 'optimal cities'. According to this theory, a city should be limited to that size at which life in the city is at the optimum: criteria for determining this optimum range from health and public safety factors to retail facilities and educational opportunities. Consequently, regulating the growth of large cities, intensifying industrial development in medium-size cities and invigorating smaller ones have all been encouraged. Adherents of this school of thought stress that regulation of the growth of large cities is not an end in itself: 'without such regulation it is impossible to site production forces in the country rationally and economically, and it is impossible to strengthen the industrial role of medium-size and small cities.'[52] In other words, city growth should be planned – and not planned in isolation from long-term schema for development of entire economic regions.

The other group maintains that large cities will not and should not perish as has been both assumed and suggested. On the contrary, new cities, as well as existing cities, will and should grow even larger. Adherents of this plan maintain that a 'new, higher, social-spatial form, based on an unconstrained layout of extensive areas, on specialisation and on the spatial separation of functional zones, contrasts with the old urban form and constitutes a means for overcoming and resolving its [the old urban forms'] contradictions'.[53] According to these people, the concept of extensive zones of intensive development has two advantages over the opposing notion of optimal size cities: first, it envisages a territorial linkage between industry and agriculture, thereby providing the necessary condition for the elimination of the difference between town and country, and second, it resolves the problem of the rational utilisation of inter-city space. Other critics of the 'theory of the optimal city' stress that the criteria of optimality or effective growth are absent: they maintain that there is no evidence to prove that city growth has to be restricted or that smaller cities are more functional than larger cities (e.g., optimal size cities display no special advantages over other cities). V. Perevedentsev pointed out that 'the productivity of labour in large cities is many times higher

75

than that in the small ones, and in the super large cities it is many times higher than in the large cities.'[54] If the productivity of social labour is generally considered to be the chief criterion for effectiveness in distributing productive forces, the author suggests that the case for large cities is obvious.

While this debate continues, most sociologists concur that present knowledge about the economic, social, demographic, public health and other aspects of the growth of cities is inadequate. One has gone so far as to say that 'our present knowledge in the area of the sociology of the city is such that it does not qualify for attention in a serious discussion'.[55] L. N. Kogan and V. I. Loktev have also complained of the lack of research on the influence of social factors on the construction of urban plans. They suggested that a city 'portrait', consisting of the state of social resources, contacts between inhabitants, type and structure of neighbourhood units and the possibilities for cultural development, become a subject of sociological research.[56]

Plans for social development of a different order have also been made by sociologists. N. Aitov, for example, has discussed plans which were drawn up at the request of the city party committees and the executive committees of their Soviets in two cities in Bashkiria, namely, Neftekamsk and Sterlitamak.[57] His study uncovered, for example, an adequate number of cinemas in these cities but an inadequate number of children's institutions. Lack of co-ordination between the local authorities, departmental agencies and the various ministries was blamed. Aitov then suggested that a city social development plan include a demographic forecast and on this basis provide for growth of the city economy and long-range development of all service, cultural, educational, athletic and sports facilities. Aitov advocated that the city Soviets themselves should develop this social plan for a five- to ten-year period. This somewhat veiled request for more city autonomy seems to parallel similar requests by other sociologists.[58]

It would thus appear from this brief look at urban sociology that one of the main problems considered is how to balance planning and non-planning in the urban context. Planned intervention in the formation of an urban environment has not been entirely successful: the failure of the *mikroraiony* (neighbourhood units) to develop tightly knit communities within the larger city environment is a case in point.[59]

Criminology and juvenile delinquency

The revival of criminology began in 1957 when the first articles advocating a renewal of the study of the causes and prevention of crime appeared.[60] While these articles expanded and eventually

developed into monographs, surveys and texts, research was trans-
ferred from governmental institutions to the universities where, in
1964, courses in the study of crime were introduced into all legal
institutes and law faculties; by 1965–6, certain institutes of pedagogy
and psychology had initiated similar courses. Concurrently, the case
was argued for studying crime not only as a juridical but also as a
social and/or sociological phenomenon. Within the latter context,
how is crime defined for research? Why does crime exist? And what
indeed are its causes?

'The *backwardness of social consciousness* relative to the objective
conditions of life in socialist society contains the possibility of the
violation of the principles of socialism, and it is the violation of these
principles that leads to the existence of crime.'[61] Socialist society *per
se* lacks inherent social causes of crime, but 'there are objective causes
which, although they do not derive from the nature of socialist
society, *still do objectively exist.*'[62] Socialist society has two kinds of
crimes: 1. crimes caused by the existence of capitalist countries; and
2. crimes derived from vestiges of capitalism in men's minds and
behaviour. Although these two interact, the first are insignificant in
number, while the second indicate the 'lag in social consciousness
behind social existence'.

Since subjective and objective factors cause crime, both must be
studied. Different theorists have stressed one or the other of these
factors, the more official line being that the objective factors are the
most prominent. But opinion seems to be turning to the view
expressed in 1965 by S. S. Ostroumov and V. E. Chugunov: 'a
number of objective conditions influence the manifestation of anti-
social views and habits. . . . Yet it is not the conditions of material
life which drive [people] to crime. Everything rests on the level of the
consciousness and culture of these individuals.'[63] Like the theorists,
the majority of the researchers focus on the objective aspects of crime,
while the minority concentrate on subjective factors such as the
psychology, temperament and character of the offender. Increasing
emphasis, however, is being placed on the latter.

This is easily illustrated by research on juvenile delinquency. The
purely juridical approach to the problem of crime in the past was one
which consisted of merely listing those objective factors which
correlated with crime, in this case, with juvenile delinquency.[64] For
example, a direct relation was discovered between criminality and a
low education, poor upbringing, drunkenness, etc.[65] However, the
present trend is towards an approach which combines an analysis of
objective and subjective factors. Thus, in a paper entitled, 'Typical
mistakes in the family upbringing of adolescent lawbreakers'
delivered at the Vil'nius conference on the family, Z. Baeriunas discussed the 'mistakes' as follows: 'In some families, more significance

is attached to social factors, while in others, to psychological [factors].' Parents' employment (or unemployment), an incomplete family and low material security were cited as 'social factors'. 'Psychological factors' included: 1. pedagogical neglect of the child from a very early age and then a hasty attempt to re-educate him; 2. strict authority over the child from infancy, but the inability to sustain this influence in adolescence; and 3. independence from an early age which the child did not know how to handle.[66]

Others looking at the motives of crime are debating the relative importance of the social and the biological in the criminal act. In 1969, for example, B. D. Ovchinnikov discussed both sides of the question and concluded by pleading for an investigation of both aspects.[67]

In general, the discussions admit that Soviet society, for a variety of reasons, has crime and it must be studied. Motives for crime are more or less connected with the 'moral formation' of the individual and with the concrete living situation, with the subjective and the objective. On the whole, the individual, and not society, is at fault. On the other hand, society is expected to solve the problem of crime.

What, then, are the measures suggested for the prevention and cure of crime in general and juvenile delinquency in particular? Almost all commentators would agree that, in the first instance, an analysis of crime requires research to help discover, understand and subsequently eliminate those causes of anti-social behaviour which society can influence. Such research should include the reasons for the fluctuations in the incidence and nature of crime and in the personal characteristics of the law breakers.[68] The desirability of predicting overall indices of the state of criminal activity throughout the country and then of drafting measures to eliminate those negative influences which stem from unfavourable conditions are readily achnowledged.[69] For example, to combat drunkenness and its effects, economic measures (raising the price of vodka), educational measures (publicity) and administrative measures (forbidding the sale of liquor) have been advocated.[70] Plans against 'boredom' include building sports facilities and other amenities for helping to broaden leisure pursuits as opposed to anti-social acts.[71] Greatly favoured are measures to help in the 'moral formation' of the individual, that is, before he or she performs an anti-social act. In addition, it is argued that crime prevention research should examine and determine the effectiveness of the methods of 'curing' this social ill (e.g., the forms of punishment) and should include a programme for re-educating the people connected with offenders (e.g., the family members as well as the offenders themselves). It should also list specialists, such as psychologists and sociologists, in the agencies engaged in crime prevention or in institutions for corrective labour as is done in

Poland.[72] Finally, statistics on crime should be made available.

Religion

Like so many other fields, the sociology of religion and atheism lay rather dormant during the cult of personality. This dormancy was most noticeable because in the preceding years empirical investigations into religious sectarianism, investigations of a local, regional, historical and ethnographic nature, were of special importance.[73] Research all but ceased at such institutes as the Academy of Sciences, the Communist Academy and the Union of Militant Atheists. But in the past several years research on religion has been resumed, mainly by scholars at institutes of philosophy, history and ethnography attached to the USSR Academy of Sciences, the academic institutes of the Ukraine, Bielorussian, Kazakhstan, Moscow, Leningrad and Kiev universities, and others. The Institute of Scientific Atheism of the Academy of Social Sciences, along with its institutional network in the republics and *oblasti*, is also taking part in this type of research.

According to the Soviets, the sociologist of religion should be concerned with the following.[74] First, he seeks to explain the extent of the practice of religion by different social groups in Soviet society and in different regions of the country. Once the believer is identified, the researcher should define the degree and character of religious observance among different groups of believers (e.g., different sects) and consider the motives for performing religious rites, the psychology of the believer and the causes of the vitality of religious survivals.[75] He should analyse the relationship between consciousness and behaviour – namely, the correlation as between the consciousness of religious and non-religious elements, the transformation of religious ideas under the influence of socialism and the relationship of the intellectual, emotional and spiritual in the believer.

Another aspect of the sociology of religion involves education in atheism. Sociologists are supposed to continue the struggle with religious ideology – and its defendants; they are to help prepare cadres of Marxists familiar with problems of religion and atheism. Various research teams do in fact include party workers and propagandists of atheism. Hence the sociology of religion might best be retitled, problems of scientific atheism and eradication of religion.

Questions on anti-religious training, the history of religion and atheism, sociological research, and philosophical criticism of religion came under detailed scrutiny in a review of the past fifty years of research.[76] In addition to stressing that one of the decisive conditions for the success of anti-religious training is a *sociological* analysis of the causes of the existence of religion in socialist society, the authors of the article stated that a new philosophical criticism of religion is feasible at the junction of the (Marxist) study of religion, on the one hand, and sociology, ethics, aesthetics, demography, ethnography, archaeology, anthropology, social psychology and other sciences, on the other. In other words, a more concrete analysis of the *social* nature and roots of religion can and should be attempted by applying both philosophy and sociology. Instead of merely emphasising the ideological side of religion, the philosophical, historical and sociological aspects are now being studied jointly: this fact does not preclude independent research on the essence and value of man, ethical and cultural ideas, and modernist tendencies in religion – all of which are still fields of concern for the philosophers. Religious beliefs and the moral doctrines of religion, including the class character of religious beliefs and morals, the incompatibility of religion with communist morals and the teachings of the Bible, the Koran and other books of this nature, are being examined and criticised. But the *sociology* of religion is emphasised more and more.

A study done in 1963 by the Institute of Sociological Research in Leningrad is a good example of sociological research in this area.[77] The aim of the research was to discover the causes of the vitality of the baptism ceremony and the motives for baptism. A positive correlation was found between baptism and less skilled workers and between the influence of religious ritual and the believers' level of education. Particular emphasis was placed on the influence of 'survivals of the past' and on the role that relatives play in preserving religious ritual. In some cases, the performance of religious ceremonies was associated with nationality. The main conclusion drawn from the data was that the 'reason for baptising children in the majority of cases is not the religious beliefs on the part of the parents, but their indifference, their conciliatory attitude towards religion combined with the influence of incidental factors.' To remedy this situation the author suggested the development of new rituals based on folk traditions and customs, permeated with elements of the new socialist culture.

Another study of religious observance was undertaken by the members of the Department of History and Theory of Atheism at Moscow State University.[78] The research was carried out during a number of years: the department periodically sent expeditions to different regions of the country (e.g., to Orenburg *oblast'* in 1962, to Krasnoiarsk *krai* in 1963, to Leninsk *raion* of Moscow in 1966). In order to direct atheist upbringing, said the researchers, we must know the social, professional, age and sex composition of the believers, their specific and unique religious conceptions and sentiments and the fluctuation(s) in their beliefs in response to contemporary conditions. On this basis, the researchers proceeded. Like the previously cited research, these researchers found that a large part of the believers had low occupational qualifications and a low level of education; a large part of the believers were women and were elderly (in the fifty-six to sixty-five age bracket or over sixty-five). These findings coincide with similar studies of various sects throughout the country.[79]

These researchers from Moscow State University concluded by noting that concrete research in the sphere of religion is still not organised throughout the country, that the degree and character of religious observance in all social groups are not studied and that comparative data about the dynamics of such observance in different regions of the country are not sought. They suggested organising instruction in atheism among different groups of the population (including the various groups of believers) and advocated the improvement and co-ordination of concrete sociological research on religion.

The application of some research on the effectiveness of atheist upbringing was reported in *Pravda* by N. Andrianov, Rector of the Pskov City Party Committee's Public Institute for Social Research.[80] Having investigated the believers and finding that they were predominantly old, with neither a higher education nor specialised occupational skills, the researchers suggested that the present system of atheist education be reconstructed, improved and diversified. Hence the sociological research led to changes. Propagandists became more informed about the basic trends in the re-orientation of the church's ideological positions. According to Andrianov, their training began to focus not only on a historical criticism of religion, but also on questions of deepening the social bonds, linking the individual with society, developing new forms of human spiritual and cultural life, etc.

In sum, the sociology of religion aims to unearth and explain various aspects of religious observance and stress the weakening of religion, and suggests ways either to eradicate religious beliefs or provide some form of substitute. A by-product of the research is the collection of material of an ethnographic nature on various religious groups situated throughout the country.

81

6 Public opinion research

Public opinion research in the Soviet Union has undergone many changes in the past few years in both theory and methodology. The expansion and improvement of this form of research reflect the increasingly pragmatic trend in sociology, the growing belief among decision-makers in the functional value of such research, and the greater acceptance of sociological research by the country at large. A survey of public opinion research affords an excellent opportunity of chronologically tracing changes in the field of social research in general.

According to Soviet theory, a public opinion poll in and of itself constitutes a means of activating opinion by focusing attention on important social problems. The educational importance of polling is further advanced by publishing the most characteristic answers to the questionnaires in the periodical press, thus exposing the collective opinion, evoking 'nation-wide' discussion and giving the Soviet people the further possibility of replying through the newspaper. In answering questions, it is argued, the people speak about themselves and describe their needs and desires. Thus envisioned, public opinion polling is a learning and educating process for the party, the researchers and the public.

The theory underlying the alleged function of Soviet public opinion research has undergone substantial changes. In the past, a distinction was made between socialist and bourgeois public opinion. Bourgeois public opinion research was characterised by the fact that it: 1. seeks to explain how effective bourgeois propaganda is; 2. interferes in the actual formation of opinions; and 3. maintains the illusion of the democratic character of the administration and management of capitalism.[1] The essential difference between this bourgeois public opinion and socialist public opinion was that in the latter only one opinion existed. More recently, however, it has been admitted that public opinion in socialist societies is not unanimous on all subjects. 'It is foolish when some critics arrogate to themselves the exclusive right to speak in the name of the people. . . . The people are not a faceless mass with identical tastes.'[2] Or more strongly stated in a Soviet review of a book entitled *Obshchestvennoe mnenie sovetskogo obshchestva* (*Public Opinion in Soviet Society*):[3]

> The political and ideological unity of our people does by no means signify a full unity of opinions of all of the Soviet people on the questions of social life – moral, legal, aesthetic, etc. We have arguments about taste, norms of behaviour, morality, art, literature, etc. As a result of such discussions there is a serious polarisation of opinions in the course of which there arise significantly diverging and even mutually exclusive opinions.

The gradual recognition of these 'significantly diverging and mutually exclusive opinions' has demonstrably altered the scope and value of this type of research.

The announcement on 19 May 1960 by *Komsomol'skaia pravda* of the opening of its Public Opinion Institute – the first of its kind in the Soviet Union — marks the turning point in the study of public opinion. Soviet development in the field of public opinion research closely followed, albeit at a lag of several years, the Polish example. In both countries the communications media initiated the surveys — in the Soviet Union, the komsomol newspaper, and in Poland, radio and television. In the early attempts of both countries, the sampling and representativeness of the surveys were poor; the answers to the questionnaires merely suggested the existence of certain phenomena but permitted no evaluation of their scope and generality. But as Polish sociologists suggest, these scientifically questionable efforts on the part of the press broke the ice for more strictly controlled surveys by making the idea palatable to the public. In fact, according to some Soviets today, the popularisation of the public opinion poll was too successful: questionnaires as such have been used indiscriminately by many unqualified people. In many such cases, the questionnaire is hastily and poorly constructed, and the generalisations or conclusions drawn from it therefore appear unfounded. Such flimsy research impedes the work of the more competent and serious professional sociologists by sullying their research. But even with this 'notorious questionnaire mania', public opinion polling has become an accepted method of research. *Komsomol'skaia pravda's* Public Opinion Institute initiated this by institutionalising public opinion research.

From May 1960 until the end of 1967 the Institute conducted two polls separately and fourteen polls through the newspaper: several of the latter were also conducted simultaneously by interview. No new polls have appeared since the end of 1967. The number of respondents per poll has varied from a few thousand to 46,000. The duration of the polls' press coverage has lasted from one month to three years, and since some of the results from the polls are as yet unreported the time span must certainly increase.

The usual procedure has been to print a questionnaire, with closed- and open-ended questions, in *Komsomol'skaia pravda* and ask the reader to reply; in some cases, however, people are interviewed directly. After an indefinite time, some 'typical' replies are printed and further requests for the newspaper readers to participate are made. Subsequent presentation of the poll may either involve quotations from the respondents' replies, interspersed with or without much editorial comment, or lectures from 'responsible' individuals on the subject, or a polemic on one isolated area of the poll. The final coverage is usually written by a staff member of the Institute who summarises and tabulates, sometimes with charts and graphs, the results of the poll, and offers comment and criticism on the topic.

The topics of the polls range from 'How has your standard of living changed?' and 'How can you best spend your holidays?' to 'In the name of what are you studying?' Some of these subjects, such as 'What is your opinion of the young family?', emphasise 'accepted' attitudes towards the subject and their findings reveal the extent to which the assumptions of a formal morality still dominate Soviet thinking on such matters. A more sophisticated variety was the poll entitled 'How do you rate our service industries?', a poll which permitted government and party representatives to present changes to be introduced since the fall of Khrushchev. Other polls took the form of consumer research, eliciting the demands and complaints of the consuming public and, at the same time, offering gifts to those readers who supplied the most valuable suggestions. Another poll was a type of audience research by which the newspaper attempted to ascertain the character, preferences and reading habits of its readers. And the 'free time' poll corresponded to an intensive study of the same subject by other social researchers.

Since the beginning of the Institute's endeavours, many changes – in method, presentation and results – have occurred. Developments occurring within and between the various polls are now examined and evaluated, chronologically by topic.*

A poll on averting war was the first carried out by the Public Opinion Institute. Ten localities along the thirtieth meridian, which runs through four Union Republics, were chosen on the basis of the social and occupational diversity of the respondents. Of the 1,000 people

*The *Komsomol'skaia pravda* public opinion polls are listed in chronological order, by topic, in the Bibliography. The questionnaires themselves are in Appendix II.

chosen at random, the sex ratio was sixty–forty in favour of men. About 50 per cent of the respondents were workers, 12 per cent collective farmers, 12 per cent office employees, 10 per cent students, 10 per cent servicemen, and 5 per cent pensioners and housewives. Thus the proportions in the sample for the sex and occupation categories did not follow those of the population as a whole. The same applies to the last two of the four age groups, namely, the sample's thirty-three to forty-five bracket and the over forty-five group did not correspond with the proportion of the Soviet population as a whole, whereas the fourteen to twenty-five and the twenty-six to thirty-two categories did.

'*Komsomol'skaia pravda* sees in the result of the poll a complete vindication and support of the Soviet government's foreign policy. Judging by the replies that are printed, this is not an unfair interpretation since many of them are written in the familiar formulae used by Soviet propaganda.'[4] But not all. The range of differences was interesting. Some respondents replied that war will be averted because 'war is not a means of settling international disputes – the history of the last two world wars proves this'. A collective farmer in the same region suggested that 'the people do not want war, and since the people do not want it, they will have their way'. A student at the S. M. Kirov Pedagogical Institute at Vitebsk pointed to the tragedies of Hiroshima and the German concentration camps as 'facts which live in people's minds; therefore people will not permit a war'. The majority, in affirming that mankind will succeed in averting war, gave as their reasons either the downfall or the 'senility' of capitalism, Soviet rocketry, her technological and scientific strength, or the staunch policy of the CPSU and the government.

Five months later (in October 1960) the second poll – 'How has your standard of living changed?' – was conducted. The questionnaire was distributed by railroad conductors to the occupants of a single carriage on each of sixty-five trains leaving Moscow on one day, a total of 1600 people in all. As Soviet critics have pointed out, the poll poorly represented the kolkhoz workers while it overrepresented those people travelling 'under orders' or on holiday. Once again, the proportion of men to women (three to two) and the occupational categories did not coincide with the population as a whole. Moreover, the poll did not include a question on the respondent's level of education, an important factor in improving one's standard of living.

The poll showed that while the standard of living did not change for 20 per cent of the respondents, it did increase for 73 per cent; this rise occurred for all strata throughout the country. The replies from the 7 per cent of the sample whose standard of living had declined were discussed in connection with suggestions for improving

85

the standard of living. The Soviet pollsters concluded that the Soviet people link the standard of living with the policies of the CPSU and wholeheartedly support these policies. They also noted that, with the exception of fifty-nine people, every respondent made suggestions as to how standards might be raised. This was interpreted to mean that the broadest strata of the public are objectively interested in nation-wide social development.*

The third poll, begun in January 1961 and tabulated by July, was on a subject of great contemporary interest – Soviet youth. At the end of twenty days the Institute had received 19,000 responses, 1,500 of which were disqualified for sundry reasons. The respondents were the youth aged fifteen to thirty who read *Komsomol'skaia pravda*. *Komsomol'skaia pravda*'s circulation was 3,400,000 in 1960. Therefore half of 1 per cent of its readers answered the poll, and of these, only 11 per cent (1,933 out of 17,446) were from the countryside. The overwhelming majority of answers came from city 'activists'. Like the first two polls, this poll proved that the overwhelming majority of the Soviet youth enthusiastically supported the regime. But the open-ended questions allowed for valuable (self-) criticism. In fact, the editors themselves said that the 'young generation cannot be accused of lacking self-criticism; they speak out boldly about their short-comings'.

The request to name the strong traits of the Soviet youth yielded predictable responses: love of homeland, patriotism, resoluteness, heroism and collectivism made up the list. The answers to the question 'Are there any negative characteristics common among young people?' were more varied. The number one target was drunkenness. The second was the *stiliagi* (the teddy boys) – their worship of foreign fashions, music and dancing. Then came the complaints about time-wasters, the passive people, the parasites and those totally occupied with sex. A twenty-nine-year-old chauffeur considered the desire to 'stand out', to 'make a better appearance than others', a negative trait. A negative characteristic was one which distinguished the individual's behaviour and beliefs from the norms set by the group or the society as a whole.

There was one notable exception to the favourable appraisal of the young generation. A nineteen-year-old working girl from Moscow wrote the following:

The fact is that life is not very interesting. And this is not only my opinion but the opinion of the people I go around with. . . . One feels a lack of discipline and culture in the behaviour of

*The day after the results of the poll were published, *Komsomol'skaia pravda* printed comments by various state ministers praising the findings and dis-cussing the suggestions.

young people. . . . Money is everything. Luxury and well-being, love and happiness. You condemn those who do not work, who do nothing. Why, they are only to be envied, because they are enjoying life. We only live once!

Her letter sparked off many denunciations from other youth, but some agreement with her views was carefully interspersed with the criticism.

The fourth poll, conducted through the newspaper in the middle of August 1961, was entitled, 'What do you think about the scouts of the future?' The questionnaire attempted to elicit answers on readers' attitudes toward work-production teams, such as the brigades of labour, the competition for labour and the acquisition of honorary titles. The respondents were asked to indicate the shortcomings in the competition for communist labour and any necessary changes in the system of receiving honorary titles. In addition to stating occupation, age, education and residence, the respondent was also asked, 'Are you taking part in the movement for communist labour? If not, why not?' Then if he wished, the respondent could indicate his name. The questionnaire was first published on 16 August. Additional replies were requested on 23 August and 30 August, when responses from brigade leaders and other foremost communist workers were published.

The Public Opinion Institute also directly interviewed some members of collectives of communist labour. The Institute retained six of the seven questions from the questionnaire originally published in the newspaper and added four others to it. The additions focused on the distinguishing features and benefits of a collective of communist labour but provided no room for negative replies.

One year later, the results were tabulated and printed in the newspaper. Curiously enough, the number of participants from the two parts of the poll was not specified. Instead, the entire group – 1,662 in all – was divided according to the participant's relation to the movement: about one-half of the participants were not taking part in the movement, a little more than one-quarter were working for honorary titles, and a little less than one-quarter were members of a collective of communist labour. All of the replies to the questions were tallied according to these three groups. The authors concluded that although the principles of communist labour are clear, the best experience has not yet become the norm for everybody. In order to attain this end, they suggest a further study of the weak and strong aspects of the movement.

The fifth poll – 'What do you think of the young family?' – was published on 10 December 1961; readers were requested to reply by 31 December. The first replies were published on 17 December and a second batch on 6 January 1962. In both cases, no editorial comment appeared. Such comment was only published when the results of the questionnaire were tabulated in July 1964 – three years after the first questionnaire on this topic appeared. Earlier, in February 1964, *Moscow News* published an English version of the results. Here, emphasis was placed on 'building' a Soviet marriage and a Soviet family. Failures did occur, but 'money worshipping, petty selfishness, disloyalty and jealousy' were to blame. But by the end of the article the basic reason for success or failure in married life had become the presence or absence of love with true ideals, moral integrity and moral respect.

The *Komsomol'skaia pravda* presentation interspersed quotations from the respondents' replies with much editorial comment. This report was based on replies from 12,104 participants, whereas *Moscow News* cited 14,000. Moreover, the author of the *Komsomol'-skaia pravda* article concentrated on the question, 'In your opinion, how prepared are the young people who are entering marriage to create a family?', whereas the other report surveyed the entire twelve-question questionnaire. On the basis of the data, the *Komsomol'skaia pravda* author concluded that opinion on this question is basically negative. 'Public opinion considers that the youngsters are far from always prepared to create a family, first and foremost, morally. Almost one-half of those who answered negatively spoke of this.' Thus the two presentations differed in their emphasis, although both may be said to be connected with the moral code set forth in the 1961 Party Programme.

Between the poll about the young family and the lengthy sixth poll on the study of free time, *Komsomol'skaia pravda* printed questions it had asked 1000 students at Moscow State University in the spring of 1962. Neither a discussion of the sampling method nor the results of the poll were published: instead, ten replies appeared without any comment. The most interesting question was the first: 'Which of the motives below induced you to devote yourselves to your chosen speciality?'

1. tradition of your family
2. romanticism of the profession
3. the relative ease of the job
4. the desire to gain popularity and glory
5. sense of mission
6. high pay for the given profession
7. striving to move in cultured circles
8. impossibility to study your choice
9. not thought of it
10. if possible, what other kind of motive?

The ten respondents concurred on the force of tradition and romanticism, while they also favoured the sense of calling or mission. Commenting on this question in his book *Sila obshchesvennogo mneniia* (*The Force of Public Opinion*), B. A. Erunov, obviously with more access to material than the readers of the newspaper, stated that almost no one had included as a motive the relative ease of a job, high pay or the impossibility of studying a chosen vocation.[5] On the contrary, he wrote, everyone discussed romanticism and love of profession. The only conclusion to be drawn from the ten replies printed in the newspaper is that everyone is deeply dedicated to his profession-to-be, to knowledge and to learning; the only thing that can hinder one's goal is war, illness or an unhappy marriage.

Soviet youth were thus given another plus rating. The next task of the researchers was to see how the youth were spending their free time. Inaugurated on 4 January 1963, the free time poll was to appear sporadically on the pages of the newspaper until February 1966. It is a model of Soviet public opinion polling and, at the same time, the boundary between the early and later forms of polling.

The questionnaire's six questions covered the following points: How much time, on the average, do you spend each day on the following (work, housework, physical needs, going to and from work, etc.)? What do you do with the remaining time? What do you do on your day off? What would you like to do with your free time? What prevents you from spending your free time as you would wish? What are the most important ways you see for making better use of leisure time? Thus, half of the questionnaire was designed to elicit specific answers; the other half permitted the respondent to express his opinion on how to improve the given situation. This division seems doubly beneficial for the researchers who could thus amass such data on actual time use and then could suggest, on the basis of the respondents' replies, ways of remedying a poor situation or controlling an already valuable one.

The presentation of the replies at first followed the format of previous polls. A week after the poll's first appearance, the questionnaire was re-published along with four responses from Moscovites and people from Moscow province. The same procedure was used the following week. Then, after a week's time, five replies were printed in response to a letter (printed in *Komsomol'skaia pravda* on 11 January) from a girl who said she had no goal in life; she could find no interesting way to use her time and she had to 'compel' herself to study. She 'simply lives'. She was advised to develop a speciality, go to school and love her work.

The next discussion of the free time poll appeared in mid-February. This time the readers were subjected to a discussion of 'collectivism' and public spiritedness (*obshchestvennost'*), including civic acts. In

March, a member of the research team discussed young people's hopes and plans for using leisure. T. Gromova was specifically concerned with criticising the practice of aimlessly wasting free time and she ended with 'to spend time waiting is to waste life'. Several months later the questionnaire was discussed by a teacher who reviewed answers received from other teachers. She came to the conclusion that teachers do not have sufficient free time, a fact which she found especially appalling since a teacher must develop his personality not only for himself but for the *kollektiv*. In the June write-up, a Moscow architect linked the use of free time with the housing problem and suggested a new 'complex' which would unite housing with social and productive activities. A similar discussion took place in August when the first secretary of the Orskii city committee spoke about youth dormitories.

The November commentary shifted from an instructive and authoritative tone to one of ridicule. People who did not indicate their addresses on the questionnaire forms were compared with Goncharov's nineteenth-century character, Oblomov. With tongue in cheek, the author painted a picture of the modern Oblomovs. For example, asked 'What do you do on your day off?' they replied, 'The devil knows what!' 'What do you like to do with your free time?' elicited 'Lie on the divan', 'Sometimes read – but not more than a book a month', or 'Nothing!' 'If you wish, indicate your name.' . . . 'What for?' The main difference between the original Oblomov and the present day Oblomov was that the former would not have had enough energy to fill out the questionnaire or spend four kopeks for postage. Continuing with jabs at parasites and praise for komsomol workers, the author ended the article by hoping 'first and foremost to infuriate Il'ia Il'ich [Oblomov] and force him to pick up the gauntlet thrown in his face. Of course', he cautioned, 'this act requires definite moral strength. But – we shall hope'.

By the end of December 1963, the Institute had received 12,000 replies to the published questionnaire. A separate questionnaire 'by a specially worked out model' was then used when people at forty points throughout the country were interviewed; these points were supposed to represent the main geographic regions of the country. The results obtained from one point, Ust-Kamenogorsk (situated in the heart of the Altai mining region), were then printed.* The authors of the article turned to the theme of social or civic work, specifically complaining that not only was there a lack of civic work in Ust-Kamenogorsk, but also that the use of the term 'civic work' was often inconsistent. Here is one of the first acknowledgments of the crucial

---

*From the figures supplied, it is impossible to determine the exact composition of the 103 respondents: about one-quarter were students, two-fifths workers, and perhaps the remainder were intelligentsia and white collar workers.

role that semantics play in obtaining data. Also discussed were the cultural attractions and detractions of the city.

Two further communications with *Komsomol'skaia pravda's* readers appeared exactly a year after the first publication of the questionnaire, that is, in January 1964. Imitating the youth poll of 1961, the editors of the newspaper turned to the people who are 'prominent [among] and popular' with the youth to explain their views on problems of interest to the youth. A separate questionnaire asked these older representatives to describe how they spend their leisure time and how they integrate it into their busy lives. The replies, printed on two days, gave advice to the *Komsomol'skaia pravda* readers from Heroes of Socialist Labour, a CPSU member since 1896, a composer, the USSR Minister of Defence, a people's artist and an academician.

A year and a half later, in June 1965, 450 ninth-grade and 550 eleventh-grade pupils – a difference not mentioned again in the results – filled out the free-time questionnaire in Smolensk. Combining the replies for a school day and a Sunday, the pollsters concluded that most free time was spent on passive activities such as reading and watching television. Those activities which required 'active intellectual output and bore the beginnings of creativity' ranged from tenth to twentieth place. However, the replies to 'How would you like to spend your free time?' reversed this order. Obstacles to spending free time as one wishes, listed by the 700 pupils who were not completely satisfied with the way they spent their spare time, were, in order of frequency: the amount of school work, personal laziness, unfavourable home conditions, parental interference and limited material means. Only the last reason – limited material means – was mentioned again in the final tabulation of the entire poll. Complaints were also voiced about the high price of tickets, the lack of sports facilities, and the 'lack of a place to meet without adult chaperonage, a place to converse and make declarations of love, and a place to dance.'

Six months later, in February 1966, the conclusions from the two-part free-time poll were given a three-day spread in the newspaper. Some 2,730 people participated in research conducted in thirty cities which, according to the researchers, sufficiently represented the main geographic areas of the Soviet Union with the exception of the Baltic and the Trans-Caucasian regions. These cities were then classified according to the size of their populations; the proportion of people in each of the four designated population groups (up to 10,000; 10,000 to 100,000; 100,000 to 500,000; more than 500,000) was then compared with the proportion of people in comparable cities throughout the USSR, according to the 1959 census. This comparison forced the researchers to conclude that the poll was weighted on the side of the larger cities. Here, for the first time, the collected characteristics of the sample population were revealed and discussed in terms of the over-all population, a fact which should subsequently allow independent researchers to evaluate and validate the data. In the poll, the proportion of people in the seven listed occupation groups compared favourably with the proportion of the Soviet population: the group of pensioners and housewives (who received 3 to 5 per cent more representation in the poll) was the exception. The sex ratio of the participants very closely resembled the ratio in the Soviet population at large. As for age, there was a 'dislocation' in favour of the young adults. Least analogous to the population at large were the proportions of the different levels of education of the sample population: the questionnaire's respondents had more education.

Some 10,392 people participated in the newspaper variety of the poll. They mailed their responses to the questions, indicating at the same time – as did the participants of other polls – their sex, age, occupation, education, family status, living conditions (e.g., separate flat, communal flat, hall of residence), and city of domicile. As could be expected from a self-selecting sample population it deviated from the proportions of the entire Soviet population. The respondents were more educated (37 per cent of the sample had a secondary education and 14·3 per cent higher education) and younger (82 per cent were sixteen to twenty-nine years old) than the population of the Soviet Union; 61·1 per cent were male. Residence differences, so carefully distinguished in the other half of the poll and so significant in the discussion of free-time use, were not described.

For the first time, the *Komsomol'skaia pravda* researchers discussed the representativeness of a poll in comparison with the total Soviet population. On this basis, they cautioned the readers to bear in mind that the poll is weighted in certain directions. Second, in regard to the newspaper poll, the pollsters did not claim that the replies represented the entire Soviet youth. On the contrary, they stressed that the participants were active, young and educated. This is a strong indication of the composition of former poll participants.

The significance of the free-time poll lay not only in its greater size in comparison with its predecessors, but also in the fact that subsequent discussion revealed greater sensitivity to the methodological problems involved. For the first time, the pollsters included a chart which outlined the respondents' proposals for ways of improving leisure. Increasing free time, expanding the facilities for leisure, increasing the income of the population, improving organisational work, improving housing and amenities, and cultivating and improving the quality of free time were the six alternatives, listed here in descending order of general popularity.

The poll uncovered two basic problems – one, of increasing the amount of free time, and the other, of developing its structure (make-up). The former, it was argued, should be tackled by decreasing non-working, rather than working, time (e.g., time spent on housework and travel to work) and the latter by studying and then remedying the inequality in the distribution and utilisation of leisure time. The poll found that inequality in the distribution of leisure exists because different social groups use their time differently and because various ways exist for enjoying leisure. Hence, leisure time is structured unequally, according to the following factors: 1. 'biological factors', e.g., students spend less time with children; the young, more time on tourism; 2. the process of 'abolishing problems', e.g., workers study more than the intelligentsia because they need to raise their educational level; 3. 'neutral factors', e.g., men attend sports events more frequently than women; 4. 'clearly developed social character', e.g., the intelligentsia and students have a more developed or 'progressive' structure of free time than housewives or pensioners. Left unmentioned was a correlation between the uses of free time and the participants' desires for using their free time.

The question of subjective and objective factors also entered this discussion. Subjective factors, based on the 'low culture' of free-time use, played a secondary role. Objective factors, which included (in order of importance) the shortage of free time, the insufficient development of the material and technical base of leisure, the shortage of personal means, and the deficiency in the organisation of leisure, were first in importance.

The conclusions from the poll are in no way startling. The pollsters were quick to point out that their basic findings coincided with those reached by G. A. Prudenskii and his *kollektiv* at the Siberian branch of the Academy of Sciences in 1958–60. However, they emphasised the fact that the size of the urban population is a main factor in time use, disuse or misuse.

A year after the results of the poll appeared in *Komsomol'skaia pravda*, B. A. Grushin published a lengthy book in which he described and analysed the poll and simultaneously examined the problem of free time.[6] He was primarily concerned with trying to determine the size, structure and content of free time. His over-all conclusion was that the way to increase free time is not to decrease working time but rather to change the structure of non-working time. Moreover, objective, not subjective, factors were the main cause of the insufficient development of free-time elements. Of special interest here is Grushin's reference to income: groups possessing large material means have the possibility of increasing their free time as a result of decreasing time spent on labour connected with their occupation, transport and, especially, daily needs. He therefore concluded that a further increase in the working man's income will enable more extensive development of all elements of free time. Grushin also refused the misconception that everyone takes equal advantage of facilities provided by the state: the fact that the Soviet Union has so many thousands of theatres does not mean that all Soviets take equal or similar advantage of them.

Furthermore, Grushin's discussion of the content of free time is unique because he examines the issue of quality as well as quantity. The quantitative factor encompasses: 1. the subject of the action (doing *what*); 2. the character of the action (*how*, in what form); 3. the number of activities (*how many* different ones); and 4. the proportional time spent on each action (*how important* is each activity to the individual). The qualitative aspect includes: the difference between an active and passive activity; the attitude of the individual toward a given type of activity; the relations between different types of activities; and the presence of contradictions between different types of activities and between different population groups. The study of both the quantitative and the qualitative sides of the free time problem should add a further dimension to this form of research.

Of much less consequence is the seventh questionnaire, entitled 'To Mars, with what?' Given twenty-five days to complete the questionnaire, the reader was asked which fifteen items – the best representatives of twentieth-century civilisation – should be included in a rocket to be sent to Mars. The newspaper published several replies in March, April and June 1963; the last consisted of answers received from foreign countries. Then, in October, the results were tabulated over a four-day period.

Some 6,425 people contributed to the *Komsomol'skaia pravda* search for the best expressions of (Soviet) achievements in the arts and sciences. They identified the most important document of the century (the CPSU Programme), the great man of the epoch (Lenin by 98·2 per cent) and the person whose exploit has glorified the twentieth century (Iuri Gagarin). Answers to other parts of the poll, concerning *the* technological invention, work of literature, score of music and reproduction of a painting or sculpture, were more varied. Those that fell outside the generally accepted responses were used to illustrate a point. For example, the question about which musical score to send to Mars elicited thirty-three responses in favour of jazz. Commenting on this, the editors single out this 'insignificant in size, but extremely eloquent, figure of 0·5%'.

We do not in the least have a malicious feeling of 'victory' over jazz, which has become all but the symbol of moral decay in the eyes of some of our bigoted culture-bearers. No! We are glad of something else, and we have our own interpretation of this figure. It is simply pleasant to be made aware that our youth, while by no means adverse to jazz or to light music in general, do not make a shibboleth of the saxophone.

The next two polls, which appeared in the middle of 1964, introduced material incentives. The first was carried out jointly with the All-Union Scientific Research Institute of Technical Aesthetics. In the introduction to the poll, the Institute said that the time had passed when a consumer bought everything that a store offered for sale and traced the problem to a question of taste. To test this view, the poll was conducted. To ensure a large response, the editors of the Public Opinion Institute promised three prizes – two transistor receivers and one receiver – and several 'stimulatory bonuses' for the most valuable suggestion on the construction and improvement of television, radios and record-players. One-third of the questions were designed to elicit the readers' preference in style(s). Another third queried the need for remote control and automatic record-changers. The last part of the questionnaire requested the participant to name the brand of equipment he had and then to discuss the pros and cons of the said instrument. Suggestions for changes were welcomed. Some 14,000 people, mainly with engineering backgrounds (if we can judge from the composition of the winners), participated in the month-long contest. The three winners' answers were published in *Komsomol'skaia pravda*, along with the minutes and official statements of the judges; those who received 'stimulatory bonuses' were named and their occupation and place of residence noted.

This poll, the first of its kind in *Komsomol'skaia pravda*, was basically a form of consumer research. Using the *Komsomol'skaia pravda* readers as the chosen population, the researchers were able to elicit the demands and complaints of the consuming public. The poll was set up in such a way that mere praise of the existing services was of no benefit to the participant. Since deficiencies were already stated as the cause of the diminution of sales, prizes were given for concrete suggestions and not for praise. It may be presumed that the pollsters did obtain thoughtful and useful suggestions from the consuming public.

The second contest, entitled 'An Innovation demands a Name', began with the publication of the results of the first contest. Lasting for about a month, this poll requested the participants to name seven types of communications equipment, e.g., television and radiograms. Ten prizes for the best names were offered by the Administration of the Radio-Electronic Industry of the *Sovnarkhoz* (Regional Economic Council) of the USSR. A year later the results were announced. 46,000 people participated! This is by far the greatest response to any poll conducted by the Public Opinion Institute. Unlike the previous contest, the only 'information' obtained was a suggestion for a name. The names, however, were to be recommended to the specific industries involved. These contests seem to demonstrate at least one advantage of offering a material incentive, namely, the probability of obtaining a large number of replies. They certainly indicate the willingness of the public to offer suggestions in the field of consumer goods.

At the beginning of August 1964, the paper printed some replies to a questionnaire which the Institute had conducted among nine- and ten-year-old schoolchildren. The purpose of this poll, conducted in well-known Komsomolsk-na-Amur and little-known Komsomolsk in the Ivanovskaia *oblast'*, was to determine the meaning of fifty words relating to phenomena of the past. The researchers stated that they had a control group as well as a group of older children. They were also concerned with distinguishing replies from city and country children: 500 from the city and 500 from the rural regions were interviewed. The poll was intended to show the withering away of 'survivals of the past', bad habits and Old Testament ideas. Words describing religion, the kulaks and the class struggle had lost their original meaning. 'The Virgin', for example, was defined as 'a woman who works in a vegetable garden'.* 'But', added one commentator, 'ask them what *blat* [string-pulling, "fixing"] and *nakhlebnik* [parasite] mean. It would be better if they were less informed on these questions'. Another pollster stated that although the children did not have first-hand experience with the words in the questionnaire, their understanding 'reflects the subjective perception of the adults in their family'. 'Bureaucrat', for example, was defined as 'Father wanted to go on holiday but they did not allow him to do so.' On 'bribe', 'this is when money is given on the sly so that no one sees'. Over half of the participants knew what a 'speculator' was.

Like the earlier poll taken at Moscow State University, the pollsters failed to indicate the composition of the sample or to tally the results: the control group and the rural-urban differences were not discussed. While it is obvious that the schoolchildren were unable to correctly identify the meaning of such terms as 'dowerless girl' or 'house spirit', their knowledge of present-day evils (e.g., bureaucracy) or 'survivals of the past' (e.g., private property) seems to indicate the presence of the same in the society.

The tenth poll conducted by the Institute began in November 1964 and has not been given final coverage in the press. The topic was designed to increase the researchers' knowledge about the present conditions of, complaints about, and suggestions for the service

---

*The children were obviously confusing *Bogoroditsa* (the Virgin) with *ogorodnitsa* (market-gardener).

industries; thus, 'How do you rate the service industries?' Included in service industries were trade, communal eating, transport, medical facilities, combines (*kombinaty*) of everyday services, cultural institutions, sports centres and communications enterprises. These industries, in turn, were to be rated according to the following conditions: unnecessary expenditures of time, inconvenient hours of service, unsatisfactory organisation of supplies, poor fulfilment of orders and low standards of personnel. When judging the quality of the services, the respondents were asked to state the basic reasons for the shortcomings and to propose improvements. Positive comments were also solicited.

The first few press reports concentrated on one aspect or another of the poll. On 7 January 1965, a L'vov-and-Moscow based reporter discussed the problems associated with commercial advertising. The function of advertising, he asserted, was to inform consumers, describe the qualities and properties of the goods, and educate people's tastes. He complained that there is an advertising paradox, namely, that while windows and neon are abundant, they are almost completely useless and unused.

The next month's report revolved around the relations between consumers and salespeople. It was compiled from the responses of those readers who replied 'Poorly!' to the question, 'How do you rate the service industries?' The author condemned the rudeness of the salespeople, some of whom do not even bother to respond to enquiries, and the inexperience of the salespeople, most of whom appear to be young. She also stated that stores close too early and do not open promptly at nine o'clock; moreover, the consumer is often not sure that the salesgirl will eventually come and open the shop. Finally, the author arrived at the heart of the matter: buyers are many and goods are few.

A week later some letters from specialists in various service departments were introduced by the editors as follows:

> Judging by the answers of the service workers, they are united in their sincere interest in their work, in their warm striving to satisfy (as much as possible) the enquiries of the people, and in their feeling of resentment towards and annoyance with the shortage of equipment and materials for work, and with the stagnation, inefficiency and carelessness in the organization of their labour.

Two letter writers from the Central Mechanical Computing Station (run by the Central Statistical Board) suggested the use of a state network of electronic computer centres to solve the ever-growing problem of serving the nation. They proposed using computers to determine sales and demands and to allocate and distribute goods.

97

H

The subject for March included the reasons why enterprises do not work to their full capacity (e.g., there is only one shift or the hours of opening are unsuitable). This topic was followed by a discussion of the relation of profit and pricing. Then complaints about repairs and orders which are not filled on time were aired. Answers to these and other complaints were supplied by the author, a former *Gosplan* (State Planning Commission) expert; the system of payment and incorrect organisation of production were blamed.

In April, 346 visitors to Detskii Mir (a Moscow department store for children) were interviewed. The majority of them complained about the impossibility of procuring children's goods. Why can't children's articles be bought? 'Deficit' was the cry. 'But look at the shelves. There is a surplus of impractical stock.' Another answer was offered: children's goods are not produced because they are un-profitable. A third reply referred to the disdain for studying consumer demands. 'Specialists . . . do not know how to and do not want to distinguish consumer demands. . . . Today nowhere and no one studies (with the exception of the firm of Detskii Mir) the demand for children's goods. No one knows the existing demand.' The plea for consumer research was most explicit.

The fact that the poll data could be utilised with the explicit intention of bringing about policy changes was made clear eight months later when *Komsomol'skaia pravda* discontinued its previous practice of asking relatively unknown authors to discuss specific service problems. Instead, three ministers of trade were interviewed. The interviewers, furnished with the answers from the 6127 respon-dents, seemed to assume that the respondents' answers to the ques-tionnaire were the correct ones. For example, 'One-quarter of the respondents said this. . . . How can *you* explain this?' 'Well, *you* said this – they say that. How can *you* justify the difference?'

The first to be interviewed was A. I. Struev, Minister of Trade. During the interview he admitted that the demand for goods is greater than the supply; his solution for studying consumer demand was the establishment of branches of the already existing All-Union Scientific Research Institute. Then he partially attributed dissatis-faction with the way in which goods were distributed throughout the country to lack of stores. He further agreed with the poll participants that store hours were not convenient for factory workers. Finally, he concurred with the participants that salespeople are neither profes-sionally trained nor given enough authority: he would also consider changing the system of payment to salespeople.

N. N. Tarasov, the Minister of Light Industry, was the second to be interviewed. Agreeing with the poll participants that there is both an insufficient quantity of and poor quality of goods, Tarasov noted future plans to remedy the situation, plans which included the creation of a ministerial sub-branch of the Ministry of Light and Foodstuffs Industries. Responding to a question on the study of current and prospective consumer demand, he cited the ties between industrial and trade enterprises (e.g., the Bol'shevik experiment). He was enthusiastic about the practice of sending the tag from purchased articles back to the factory which has produced them so that the factory would know which items were most popular. He further suggested raising the material incentive of workers so that, for example, samples demonstrated in the House of Models and at exhibitions could appear more quickly as consumer goods on the shelves.

The last to be interviewed was the RSFSR Minister of Automobile Transport and Highways, S. P. Artem'ev. Unlike the previous interviewees, he seemed hesitant to recognise the problems which the respondents raised about the general malfunctioning of the transportation system. A particularly large number of critical letters on this topic came from people in the countryside, but city inhabitants also supplied complaints.

These three ministers were thus presenting some solutions to the problems which beset the service industries. As government or party representatives, they also indicated to *Komsomol'skaia pravda* readers the changes to be introduced since the fall of Khrushchev. Since the press presentation has not been completed, no further comment is possible.

Such is also the case with the next (and last) three polls which first appeared in April, June and October, respectively, of 1966. Coinciding with and conducted at the Fifteenth Congress of the Komsomol, the first of these, 'Komsomol members about the Komsomol', focused on problems connected with the life and activity of the komsomol. The three-fold questionnaire explored the main tasks of the komsomol, the relations between the komsomol member and his local organisation, and the most pressing questions in the life of the komsomol organisation. At this first stage of research, 3,000 city and country komsomol members, aged fourteen to twenty-eight, were queried; attention was given to their demographic, social, professional, educational and komsomol characteristics. The researchers stated that at a second stage of interviewing non-komsomol members of the corresponding age group would be questioned. In the meantime, the newspaper readers were asked to fill in a shortened version of the questionnaire.

So far, this poll has received only two notices in the newspaper. The extremely short May 1966 articles, which concentrated on question four from the original poll (i.e., 'How has the komsomol helped in the fulfilment of life plans?'), aired the views of five respondents. The September 1966 article centred on the principle of

99

'free and open discussion' (*glasnost'*) or, in this case, on the absence of an 'upward' and 'downward' flow of information between the rank-and-file and the local komsomol leadership. This striking situation, however, seemed to be of little concern to the komsomol committee workers who, according to the author of the article, did not as yet see this as a problem.

The twelfth questionnaire, begun in June 1966, continues the more and more pragmatic pattern of the Institute's research. This particular research, as has increasingly been the case with much other sociological work, was performed by the Institute in conjunction with other research bodies. And here again, different state agencies have the opportunity of ascertaining opinions, suggestions and criticisms, and then applying their knowledge to the problem at hand, namely, 'How do you best spend your holidays?' and 'How do you wish to spend your holidays?' In fact, the poll seems to be an outgrowth of the polls on free time and the service industries. This link should further enable the researchers to evaluate the results and the accuracy of these previous polls and, at the same time, continue to amass data – some overlapping and some completely new – on the structure and organisation of the annual holiday.

Although there was no indication at the time of its introduction that the poll would consist of more than one questionnaire, the two parts of the poll – the first concentrating on the present and the second on the future – were published within a month of each other. Three of the twelve questions of the first questionnaire considered the pros and cons of the organisation of the annual holiday. Then came questions on the most valuable type of holiday, the location and timing of such a holiday, the problems involved in co-ordinating parents' and children's holidays, and ways of furthering mass tourism. Another question, most unusual in approach, asked the participants to indicate which categories of people – distinguished by age, occupation, social position, etc. – have the best organised leisure and which have the worst; manifestations of these differences were requested. Finally, a question which duplicates one from the free time poll asked for proposals for improving leisure. Two of the six suggested replies from the free time poll were omitted, but they were either previously covered or irrelevant here. The remaining four suggested answers were listed as follows: expand the material base of leisure, increase the income of the population, raise the 'culture' of leisure, and increase the length of the holiday.

A week after the printing of the first part of the poll, the questionnaire was reprinted with several questions omitted. Once again, the editors stressed that the information obtained from the questionnaires would help the Soviet, trade union and komsomol organisations and the organs of public health to find an optimal solution to many holiday problems. At the same time, they emphasised that the questionnaire should also turn the reader's attention to his own attitudes toward leisure, e.g., 'Is it always sufficiently creative?' Then several replies were published. Within a week four more replies appeared on the pages of *Komsomol'skaia pravda*; after another two weeks, several letters were printed.

With the announcement at the end of July that the Institute had received 600 replies, the second part of the questionnaire appeared. Two of the poll's ten questions were related to the material base of leisure. Two others focused on the development of tourism, another on the relation between mass tourism and transportation facilities, and another two on the effect of different sources of information on the choice of location for and type of holiday. Another question sought to discover the reader's preference first for a holiday with or without a free travel warrant,* and then a holiday in one or in several places. Additional questions tried to discern the purpose of a holiday and then to discover ways of achieving it (e.g., by material means or whatever). The last query sought to answer the question, 'Holiday with whom? – Family? Friends? Colleagues? Professional colleagues? Unknown company? Alone?'

Two months later, the question of winter as opposed to summer holidays was discussed. The number of advocates of a summer holiday was considerable; their battle cry was 'sea, sun, cheap fruit and cucumbers'. At the same time, the defenders of winter holidays lauded winter sports and stressed the possibilities of taking advantage of big city attractions. (Theatres, for example, are closed in the summer.) Explaining that many of the respondents were in favour of a change, the author of the article complained that winter holidays were poorly organised and under-publicised; winter facilities, moreover, were clearly inadequate. And, as in the case of many of the other polls, the author directed the attention of organisers and planners to further developing and exploring the possibilities of winter holidays.

Within five days, the head of a department in the Central Scientific Research Institute of Experimental Planning stated that no sphere is as weakly studied or as poorly planned as leisure. Candidate of Architecture N. Shelomov sees leisure as a rich source of income and, in this connection, suggested the creation of an independent section of the economy devoted to leisure, a section which would completely centralise the 'industry of leisure'. He subsequently touched on the problems of protecting natural areas such as the Caucasus and the Baltic regions and developing additional areas.

The last write-up to date reverted to the favourite Institute

*A free travel warrant (*putevka*) is authorisation for officially sponsored (recreational) travel, accommodation or remedial treatment.

practice of relying on known and popular people of the older generation to explain their views on the given topic. Offered here are eight letters on leisure, leisure and work, and leisure and youth. Unlike the Shelomov report, this November 1966 article did not concentrate on the existing deficiencies in the organisation of leisure, but instead turned to the absence of a 'culture' of leisure and to the problem of the people's 'inability' to rest. The youth, in particular, had these problems. Hence, the lessons from their elders.

The very last *Komsomol'skaia pravda* poll marked the beginning of an approximately two-year study on 'The reader about himself and about the newspaper'. The Institute was to study the newspaper's audience in the hopes of determining readers' thoughts about and proposals for the newspaper. The first part of the research attempted to discover subscription practices, content preferences,* satisfaction and dissatisfaction with this newspaper in comparison with others, and length of time spent reading. No further mention of the poll has appeared since the printing of the questionnaire form, but judging from this form, it would seem that *Komsomol'skaia pravda* should be able to ascertain the composition of its audience. Such knowledge is indispensable for future polling.

It will already have become clear from the preceding survey that public opinion polls are on the whole characterised by an increasing concern with methodological questions, such as the representativeness of the sample in relation to the population at large. Indeed, one significant contribution of public opinion research was its stimulation of debate about survey methods. Almost from the outset, the *Komsomol'skaia pravda* polls came under direct attack. Thus, in June 1961, after the results of the first three polls had been published, a conference was held to consider public opinion polling.[7] At this conference, the main concerns were open and closed questions, sampling methods and the role of statistics. A debate developed between B. Grushin of the Public Opinion Institute, who defended the open question, and F. D. Livshits, Candidate of Economic Science, who spoke in favour of the closed question. Stressing the importance of the choice of the subjects to be investigated, Livshits condemned the second poll on the standard of living because, he stated, the Central Statistical Administration already conducts research on this very question. The other participants did not criticise the topics of the investigations but they did attack the general sampling procedures. A. G. Volkov of the Scientific Research Institute of Labour said that the respondents were not selected at random. V. D. Mirkin from the RSFSR Central

---

*Out of the forty-nine headings for the different types of articles, the Institute's articles came in sixteenth place.

Statistical Administration added that all population groups were not represented. All the conference participants stressed the need to use statistics and statistical methods in doing public opinion research. By June of 1963 comment on the third poll was available.[8] Candidate M. Kh. Igitkhanian said that although the organisers of the youth poll had not been able to 'typify' the composition of the sample population in advance, the poll was nonetheless representative and characteristic of Soviet youth.[9] This, however, was as far as his praise went. He said that Soviet researchers did not know how to conduct public opinion polls; they were ignorant of general statistical principles, concrete methods of typology and tests for the reliability of the polls' results. He then stated that polls conducted through the newspapers ascertained the opinion of isolated individuals rather than collective opinion. Finally, he warned that neither a detailed elaboration of the methods of opinion polling nor an improvement in the techniques of analysis could by themselves ensure accuracy: the results of a poll could reflect true public opinion only if, along with provisions for representation in sampling and objectivity in analysis, the very subject of the poll was of interest to the respondents.

In 1965, a major contribution to the debate over public opinion research was made by B. A. Grushin in an article which examined and weighed the past efforts and outlined future possibilities of this type of research.[10] The material from the first seven polls formed the basis of his discussion. Grushin stated that most often a public opinion poll proceeds from a study of a part to a generalisation about the whole. In other words, the researcher receives a picture of a particular phenomenon and then 'enlarges' it to generalise about the whole. Therefore, 'if we want to form an opinion about a social object on the whole, it is necessary that the sample – in whatever form and to whatever degree – reflects all of the existing features of the structure of the studied object.' He argued that the sample must be large enough so that one may generalise about society in general and separate social groups in particular; furthermore, it must be objectively proportional to different groups in the social structure. Another factor which plays a very important part in the definition of these groups is those objective and subjective 'possibilities' which the researcher has at his disposal. As far as the Public Opinion Institute was concerned, noted Grushin, it 'continually had to take into consideration the absence of the necessary number of workers who would be fully qualified to study programming, conduct questionnaires and analyse the received material'.[11]

Grushin then turned to the problem of sampling, namely, selective sampling as opposed to random sampling or a combination of the two. The pros and cons of these methods were discussed. The treatment and recognition of the 'errors' of spontaneous research (i.e., the method most frequently used at the beginning of the Institute's work) received special note. Such errors referred to the (possible) distortion due to readers' self-selection. For example, the kolkhozniks, the less educated, the women and the more passive youth were minimally represented in the *Komsomol'skaia pravda* questionnaires. Or more positively, the most conscious, active and literate part of the population, the 'foremost' youth, responded to the newspaper questionnaires. One of Grushin's several suggestions for remedying this situation – and here he echoes Igitkhanian's remarks – is to construct a questionnaire on topics which directly involve the respondent.

Grushin sees the problem of representation (and hence, of participation) of certain groups as follows:[12]

> The essence of the problem is that people do not want to express their opinion. Thus unwillingness can be expressed in the complete refusal of a man to answer the questionnaire, as well as when he gives answers which do not correspond with his genuine views. The cause of such reluctance – fear, feeling of protest, bashfulness, inconvenience, not understanding the aim of the questionnaire, etc. – can vary to a great extent. . . . The extreme expression of this is the refusal of a man to participate in a questionnaire. At first glance, there is nothing strange about such a refusal ('don't want to – *ne nado!*'), all the more so as there is always the possibility of finding another man, characterised by the same socio-demographic parameters, who agrees to answer the questionnaire with pleasure. However, in actuality such an 'avoidance' is a great danger, especially if it has some kind of definite trend or mass character.

These revealing problems had not, to my knowledge, been examined before Grushin's penetrating essay. Nor had any indication of the degree of the wish for anonymity in such research been previously given: according to Grushin, up to 25 per cent do not sign their name or they list their name saying, 'I wish you not to expose my name.' This problem is further associated with the role of the interviewer. While acknowledging that an interview is the most effective method for guaranteeing the 'minimum loss' of material, Grushin says that the interviewer might either constrain, embarrass or rush the interviewee so that, as a result, the researcher obtains the opinions of the interviewer rather than those of the interviewee.

On the whole, Grushin was able to use the material from the first seven polls – polls already tried and worked out on Soviet soil – and then instruct public opinion pollsters on ways of further improving and validating this type of research. There can be little doubt that much of his advice has been heard and digested by the Public Opinion Institute as well as by other public opinion researchers.

To Grushin's criticisms of the polls can be added the increasing Soviet criticism of public opinion research in general. Some of the defects (noted by the Soviets) arising from the 'notorious questionnaire mania' – notably the fact that the work of serious sociologists is impeded by the shoddy work produced as a result of this craze – have already been mentioned. Another outcome of this popular fascination with public opinion research is the huge quantity of material gathered. Critics complain that isolated facts from the mass of material are chosen to fit pre-conceived notions: since there is too much to process, the original hypothesis of the research is easily proven by merely eliminating those elements which do not support it. But, at the same time, the results from the research may also be interpreted too broadly; for example, if fifty people support one idea, the pollsters conclude that all of the people in the USSR follow suit.

If the pollsters have been criticised for their interpretations of the polls' results, they have also been attacked for the poor construction of the questionnaire, inadequate and inaccurate sampling methods and their polling in general.[13] Such a fundamental task as pre-testing the questionnaires is often omitted; the sample is often merely a haphazard or purposely structured collection of individuals from which further generalisations about the country at large or about a specific social group are invalid. In the final analysis, the poll is neither reliable nor sound.

In addition to the deficiencies in the actual research method, attention has focused on that which is common to most other forms of sociological research in the Soviet Union. Consider, for example, the absence of socio-demographic data. In 1966, Kantorovich argued that 'the leaning towards questionnaire methods has come about, I believe, largely because of the scarcity of published statistical data.'[14] These sentiments have been voiced many many times. Then there is the lack of co-operation between researchers in the same, or in a related, field working on similar problems. Finally, the results of many of the polls are not applied: 'solutions' may be offered, but they fall on deaf ears. Grushin, for example, reports that nothing has been done about the free-time questionnaire because of the lack of co-ordination between interested institutes. But he also indicates that some research findings have been put into practice: the *Komsomol'-skaia pravda* questionnaire about industrial design led a light industry firm to make special designs for radios and electrical equipment, and the questionnaire on holidays is being used by the trade unions.

Early dogmatic rejection of public opinion research in general has been modified. Although the original anti-public opinion research pronouncements are still being mouthed, albeit less and less frequently, new creative public opinion polling is being carried out. Now it is

105

permissible and advisable to study opinions about the concrete 'thing' (the objective) and the more abstract 'idea' (the subjective). What is more, what began in the non-academic sphere has spread to the academic. By accustoming the public to such research, the *Komsomol'skaia pravda* Institute served the best interests of academic sociologists. (It has been recently suggested that an Institute of Public Opinion, along with a number of branches in different parts of the country, be established to collate and process information and train researchers.)[15] In addition, the publication and popularisation of public opinion polls and the subsequent criticism of them have greatly improved the effectiveness of this research.

What does the growth of this type of sociological research indicate? May we not rightly draw the parallel between the expansion, improvement and acceptance of public opinion research in particular and the development of Soviet sociological research in general? Such was the case in Poland where the first public opinion institute in the socialist world was established during the renaissance of Polish sociology.[16] While the development of sociology in these two socialist countries is not parallel (e.g., sociology is more institutionalised in Poland), the Poles have indeed set an instructive example for the Soviets and have enabled the Soviets to borrow from socialist friends.

The head of the Polish Public Opinion Poll Centre, Anna Pawełczynska, noted in 1966 that her centre fulfils two parallel socio-political functions:[17]

1. as a channel of information on objective and subjective facts important to public life, thus supplying public, political and governmental institutions with the premises essential for practical decision-making, and
2. as an expression of the democratisation of public life, constituting a scientific instrument for the communication of public opinion to institutions responsible for socio-political and economic activity in various spheres.

If Soviet sociological research did not reach this two-fold stage, it was cognisant of the successful and 'freer' work the Poles were doing. Moreover, it was influenced by their research. As early as 1963, A. Kharchev, the Leningrad sociologist noted for his work on the family, described Polish progress as follows:[18]

In Polish sociological research, one meets numerous problems which would be of interest to party and government leaders as well as to science, but which in the Soviet Union are still under taboo. The subjects studied range from people's motives for joining the party, mutual relations between young and old party members, the role and the functions of the political staff, the role of traditions in army life and army education, young people's motives for entering army schools, right down to divorce and family relations. Moreover, in publishing the results of their research, the Polish sociologists present them in a comparatively (untailored) form, regardless of any political unpleasantness for the party leaders. Thus data on the prevalence of a negative attitude to Marxism or to the restriction of civic liberties, which emerged from a 1961 poll of Warsaw students, were published in their entirety in the specialized press, something which would be inconceivable for the Soviet Union at present.

The following year, the Polish Centre was praised for conducting extensive polls on fifteen to twenty subjects, the results of which were printed and sent to the appropriate party and state agencies. All in all, Polish research methods (and topics?) were first praised and then are gradually adopted.

There is no doubt that public opinion research in the Soviet Union has undergone a remarkable metamorphosis. The above study of the work of the *Komsomol'skaia pravda* Public Opinion Institute easily confirms this diagnosis. But aside from the limitations imposed by research techniques, this type of research is still restricted to certain areas of enquiry at the expense of others. The topics studied are still more or less 'safe' topics. They have the dual function of supplying information to researchers and other interested parties (e.g., the party) and permitting a channel of expression (e.g., to 'let off steam'). But to the dismay of some Soviet sociologists, this branch of sociological enquiry does not study how public opinion is shaped nor who or what shapes public opinion.[19]

7 Conclusion

Since the Twentieth Party Congress, sociology has fought for legitimation within the Soviet system of knowledge, seeking recognition and support within three distinct spheres – the academic community, the population at large and the official world.

The struggle for the right to exist as an independent academic discipline took place on several levels. On one of these, sociology had to demonstrate the necessity for a science in addition to historical materialism. After all, was not historical materialism already Marxist sociology? On another level, sociology had to emphasise that it was not an outgrowth of bourgeois sociology. Thus its roots in the Soviet past had to be stressed. Here the advocates of sociology could rely not only upon quotations about this subject from Marx and Lenin, but also upon the work of sociologists from other socialist countries.

While the discussions which began in the 1950s on sociology's right to exist have today diminished in intensity, they have not entirely ceased. Although the problem of the relationship between historical materialism and sociology has not been permanently 'solved', for all practical purposes sociology has won recognition as an independent science. The next step has been to secure the right to teach the discipline and carry out research. However, degrees in sociology have not as yet been conferred.

With regard to the question of popular acceptance, the public was first urged to participate in sociological research when the youth newspaper, *Komsomol'skaia pravda*, opened its Public Opinion Institute in 1960. The Institute began its investigations by ascertaining opinions on very general subjects, such as war, but more recently has concentrated on less abstract and more practical problems, such as the service industries. These polls have helped to accustom the public to 'sociological' methods, specifically, to questionnaires. In fact, it is probably correct to assume that sociology is equated with question-naire research in the minds of the general public.

As far as the official world is concerned, while recognition and support are hard to pinpoint, it is quite apparent that work in the ill-defined subject of sociology was again permitted in the late 1950s: the Twentieth Party Congress of 1956 and the subsequent thaw allowed sociology to take its first steps. The 1960 Party Programme in heralding the building of communism requested the help of the social scientists in its construction. And the Twenty-Third Party Congress of 1966 specifically recognised sociology as an independent discipline. Sociology is seen as an instrument which, by providing both information and analysis, helps to prevent the regime from losing contact with reality and which may help in planning and controlling society, as well as understanding it.

The general ethos within which Soviet sociology operates can best be described as one of 'problem solving'. The question as to why some areas have been studied and others have not can best be explained in this way. This is particularly so to the extent that one recognises the dual significance of this problem-solving orientation. On one level, research into non-concrete, non-utilitarian fields is rarely undertaken; research attempts to answer actual problems in concrete terms. Equally significant, however, is the fact that by encouraging a broadly empiricist concern with isolated problems of whatever significance, the orientation prevents the development of theory and research into the dynamics of the whole society. The problem-solving approach effectively prevents the development of studies concerned with the distribution of power in the Soviet Union and with such factors as the distribution of power and ideology as determinants or functions of patterns of industrialisation and social change. The problem-solving perspective would appear to be closely related to the circumstances surrounding the revival of sociology from the mid-1950s onwards. A discipline emphasising the need for fact gathering and interpretation could advance its claims within a climate of political re-orientation in which the regime sought to emphasise a break with the dogmas of the past and to establish and maintain contact with social reality. 'Concrete sociological research' is an apt title for sociology in the Soviet Union.

Although the legitimation of sociology has been achieved in broad terms, the Soviet sociologist continues to encounter certain structural obstacles. Until 1968 when it was finally given its own Institute in the Academy of Sciences, sociology remained the illegitimate offspring of philosophy. There can be no doubt that some of the continuous demands for the establishment of the Institute were related to the would-be benefits of direct monetary backing; complaints about inadequate, if at times non-existent, financing are readily ascertained.

The establishment of an Institute should also affect co-operation and/or co-ordination between sociologists themselves and between them and other social scientists. Soviet sociologists seem to call repeatedly for this which may imply that co-operation might bring better research facilities and the sharing of data and techniques. Another problem may be reduced in the near future: at present, not one periodical caters specifically to the needs of sociologists, a fact which has resulted in the appearance of articles on sociology in a wide variety of journals as well as in the daily press. There is the further problem of obtaining statistical materials: either statistics in certain 'unsafe' areas are gathered and kept secret, or they are not collected at all. Either way, the sociologists' work seems hindered.

One might of course argue that all of these constraints are minor in comparison with the limits that the over-all Soviet system imposes. Can, in fact, sociology develop within such a system? Undoubtedly, considerable if uneven development has taken place since the 1917 Revolution. This study has traced this progression. But what are the factors, peculiar to the system, which limit the sociologist?

To a greater or lesser extent, the system does dictate what is to be researched, what is to be investigated. Soviet sociologists study some areas of society in great depth while they studiously avoid others. For example, the period of the cult of personality – that is, twenty or more years of Soviet history – is pointedly ignored. Other topics – in 'non-problem' areas – have to be approached by circuitous routes. Thus the role of sex is only gradually being considered in research on the family. But, on the whole, research which has critical implications for the existing social system or which would tend to imply change in directions either beyond the control of or alien to the broad goals of the regime is not undertaken. While it is quite possible that some sociological research is conducted which has not been published and which examines more sensitive areas, the amount is probably very small. The same, however, may not be true for those findings which in one way or another differ from those anticipated.

At the same time, it is virtually impossible to correlate what the sociologist actually does or does not study with what he is or is not permitted to investigate. But once he decides on an area of research – either because 1. he was directed or encouraged to study that topic, 2. he knew that the area was previously studied and hence was acceptable, 3. he would be financed for his research, 4. he would be able to improve his academic position, or 5. he found it intrinsically interesting, etc. – the researcher then faces the question of how to investigate the problem. If certain methods or approaches are considered to be non-acceptable either on empirical grounds or for ideological reasons, then the researcher must presumably follow a more or less prescribed course of action. But this type of restraint is increasingly becoming less operative. It is at the editorial level of both journals and publishing houses that the work of the sociologist may be constrained. But once again it is difficult to know what has been edited out of or added to his work and on what grounds the omissions and additions occur. Moreover, one does not know what type of material is not published, and specifically, on what grounds. Another constraint is access or lack of access to 'bourgeois' work in the libraries. Finally, while the researcher may be limited in his choice of research, his methodological approach and the outlets for publication, the ultimate influence of his research may be inconsequential; certain research findings would not be implemented because, among other reasons, they would affect vested interests.

Other 'intangible' constraints on the Soviet sociologist include the ghosts of the past. The cult of personality has left its mark. 'The fear of responsibility, a fear surviving from the times when unthinking "quotationitis" often substituted for serious research, still lingers. . . .'[1] This can certainly explain a large, but decreasing, number of relatively innocuous and useless pieces of work which are supposedly sociological in nature but are, in fact, mere 'stringings together' of quotations from classical sources. The role of Soviet history in shaping present-day sociology cannot be ignored.

What role does Marxism-Leninism play in shaping sociological research? Soviet social theorists would be the first to stress that social science – and hence sociology – is not value free. The researcher is a member of a society and consequently reflects the norms and values of that society. The result is that 'Marxist sociology and Marxist ideology are internally and indissolubly bound together'[2] and that 'sociology is party science. The world outlook of the scientist, his social and political sympathies, his social position affect the methodology and even the method of research and, consequently, the results.'[3] But do they? This argument appears to amount to little more than that the system determines the areas from within which questions of sociological research may be approached. Any alternative view is dependent on the position that there is a specifically identifiable and distinctive Soviet sociology. Little evidence can be adduced to support such a position. This is to recognise that Soviet sociology is distinctive in a national rather than in an intellectual, specifically Marxist, way.

Soviet sociologists have not reached that point – in their writing, at least – at which they seem to question or criticise Marxism directly. In fact, the position stated by N. Preobrazhenskii in 1922 is still valid:[4]

Marxists may argue in part about the theory of method(s), still more about the means of its application; their concrete works

111

may be completely different in content . . ., but they do not argue and do not compete with each other in the sphere of the basic position of Marxism.

Just when they will argue about 'the basic position of Marxism' is a moot question. The possibility that Marxism in the form of a critical approach to social analysis will become institutionalised in the Soviet Union is extremely remote. It is possible, however, that with more and more empirical research, certain aspects of Marxism-Leninism may be questioned – accepted, discarded or modified – and new theories advanced. The beginnings of this are evident in the discussion of social stratification. The present empirical trend in Soviet sociology may lead generally to a more theoretical orientation of the discipline, or more probably, the empirical emphasis of today may simply continue to expand.

In the broadest sense, the future of the discipline is very much tied up with the atmosphere inside the Soviet Union. As a barometer, the practice of sociology indicates the degree to which the Soviet Union will permit an examination of existing social conditions. If, in the future, all areas of intellectual enquiry are restricted – if, for example, a more Stalinist policy is re-introduced – then there can be no doubt that sociology will be similarly limited. In fact, in the period of a general tightening up since 1967, research carried out by *Komsomol'skaia pravda*'s Public Opinion Institute seems negligible. Given the fact that sociology was one of the last disciplines to gain recognition after twenty or more years of silence, it would hardly be surprising if it were not one of the first to be curtailed.

Soviet sociology is a discipline attempting to develop within the context of a particular society. The ideological orientation of the Soviet regime clearly has produced a particular set of problems for the development of 'an independent sociology'. Broadly speaking, these problems are manifested in two ways: in the form of questions as to the possible relationship between this ideological basis and any conceivable sociology, and in the form of a perceived threat to the regime from the development of the discipline. From the discussion of the structural and ideological factors above, it is clear that the latter may have greater specific significance for sociology's continued development. Nevertheless, this should not obscure the fact that Soviet sociology does perform functions, face obstacles and share problems common to sociologies throughout the world.

Glossary

Apparat: system/machinery of administration; staff, personnel of the system/machinery of administration; the organisation

Byt: daily life; (mode of) life; customs; habit

Gorkom: urban committee, usually of the party

Gosplan: State Planning Commission

ITR (inzhenerno-tekhnicheskie rabotniki): engineering and technical personnel, with a higher or secondary technical education, engaged in technical management of industry or transport

Kollektiv: collective; group; team; the (whole) body of employees, etc.

Krai: territory; an administrative subdivision of the RSFSR usually including autonomous *oblasti*

Narod: the people of a state; nation(ality); national group; (common) people; folk

Narodnost': nation(ality); ethnic national group(ing); nationalism; national characteristics

Oblast': region; an administrative sub-division of a Union Republic

Partiinost': 'Party-mindedness'; partisanship seeing things and acting as one committed to realising the future as envisioned by the party; group feeling; commitment

Raikom: district committee of the party

Raion: district; administrative area within *oblast'*, *krai* or republic

Sovkhoz: state farm

Sovnarkhoz: Regional Economic Council

Tekhnikum: specialised secondary school/institute, with two to four year courses, including general education, normally from age fourteen

113

Vuz: Higher educational establishment, a university or institute with degree courses

Zakonomernost': order; regularity; sequence; pattern; conformity to systematic/established law of nature or society

Appendix I
Time budget research

A. **Time budget blank for workers and office workers**

I. General information about the respondent and his family.
    Data from the enquiry——— Number of time budget——
    Shift – day, evening, night

1. Republic, *krai, oblast'*
   City, workmen's settlement
   Branch of industry
2. Where he works (name of enterprise, institution, organisation)
3. Sex
4. Age (completed years)
5. Education:
   Up to third grade
   Elementary
   Seventh year
   General secondary school
   Special secondary school
   Higher, incomplete
   Higher
6. Where one studies:
   At day educational institutions or schools
   At night educational institutions
   By correspondence (educational institutions)
   Course for raising qualifications and schools of progressive
   methods
   Other forms of study (network of party education, of
   universities of culture, and others)
7. In what capacity does one work (position or specific duties)

8. For non-workers, indicate the source of his means of subsistence:
   Pension
   Stipend
   Dependent on others
   Other sources of his means of subsistence
9. Wage category (for a worker), number of grades in the wage category
10. Average per cent of fulfilling production norms (for piecework) during the past month:
    up to 100 per cent
    100–105 per cent
    105–110 per cent
    110–125 per cent
    125 per cent and more
11. Over-all length of service, . . .
    according to speciality
12. Extra wages for the past month
13. General daily income, on the average, for one member of the family for————month, 196—
14. Of all the members of the family (present)
    Of those:
    Workers
    Housewives
    Pensioners (non-workers)
    Children:
    up to one year old
    from one to six
    from seven to eleven
    adolescents from twelve to fifteen
    other members of the family
15. Number of children found in children's institutions
    Of these:
    In kindergartens and nurseries
    In school (including schools which stay open late)
    In boarding school
16. Size of the living space, on the average, for one member of the family
17. Family occupies (figure encompasses the family circle):
    Separate flat
    One room in a common flat
    Two or more rooms in a common flat
    A part of a room
    Dormitory
    Private house
    Private flat

18. Presence in the flat of communal comforts (figures encompass the family circle):
       Central heating
       Stove heating
       Sanitation
       Water supply
       Hot water
       Bath and shower
       Refuse disposal
       Gas
19. Presence in the family of cultural-*byt* inventory (figures encompass the family circle):
       Sewing machine
       Washing machine
       Refrigerator
       Vacuum cleaner
       Radio receiver
       Television
       Bicycle
       Motorcycle, scooter
       Private passenger car
20. Use of the enterprise's public eating facilities by members of the family:
       Regularly, two or three times a day
       Regular, once a day
       Every now and then
21. Number of books in personal library:
       Belles lettres
       Special
       Political

B. Distribution of time – sample time budget

Different Time Expenditures   *Working Days   Rest Day*

I. Working Time
    1. Time of actual work (fixed – contracted time)
    2. Time for actual work (over-time)
    3. Wasted time and non-productive working time
    4. Regulated breaks in work (industrial gymnastics, time for nursing mothers, etc.)
    5. Start and finish of shift

117

II. Non-working time, connected with work in production
    6. Eating
    7. Waiting in queues in the dining room or buffet
    8. Going to the dining room or buffet and returning
    9. Leisure and other time expenditures
    10. Time to take care of oneself before and after the shift (undressing, dressing, washing)
Moving to the place of work and returning
    11. Walking to and from the transportation stop
    12. Waiting for transportation
    13. Riding to work and back
    14. Walking to work and back

III. Housework
Shopping for non-food products
    15. Time on the way to and from the store
    16. Staying in the store (without waiting in queues)
    17. Waiting in queues
Shopping for food products
    18. Time on the way to and from the store
    19. Staying in the store (without waiting in queues)
    20. Waiting in queues
    21. Time shopping in the market place (excluding travel to and from)
Food preparation
    22. Lighting the stove, carrying the ashes, bringing firewood and coal
    23. Carrying the water (such water that was not for food preparation, if there is no water supply)
    24. Preparing or warming up the dinner, lunch or breakfast
    25. Washing the dishes (after having all the food for the day)
Care of the premises, the furniture and *byt* apparatus
    26. Tidying up the premises (washing and polishing the floors, making the bed)
    27. Tidying up the yard (rubbish, snow)

28. Repairing the flat, the furniture, *byt* apparatus and other work of taking care of the premises

Care of clothing, footwear, linen (washing)

29. Washing and ironing (besides nappies)
30. Repairing shoes and clothing
31. Cleaning clothes and footwear

Use of everyday (*byt*) service enterprises

32. Visiting the laundry
33. Visiting the workshops for repairing and cleaning clothes and shoes
34. Visiting the workshops repairing furniture and *byt* apparatus
35. Visiting the clothing and shoe workshops
36. Visiting the hiring places

Looking after the children

37. Taking care of the unweaned babies, day and night (feeding, bathing, changing nappies, rocking to sleep and washing)
38. Washing, dressing, feeding and putting the other (weaned) children to bed
39. Taking the children to the kindergarten, to the school or the day-crèche
40. Visiting the children's hospitals and consultations
41. Working in subsidiary economy (taking care of cattle, birds, gardens and vegetable gardens)

Other types of housework

42. Knitting, sewing, making domestic articles
43. Storing up fuel (supply, sawing up)
44. Other types of housework

IV. Looking after oneself

45. Dressing, washing, combing one's hair and shaving at home
46. Washing at home
47. Time for (medical) treatment at home
48. Time to and from the medical establishment
49. Time waiting at the medical establishment
50. Consultation time at the doctor's
51. Time to and from the bath and the shower
52. Waiting in queues at the bath and the shower
53. Using the bath and the shower

54. Time to and from the hairdresser
55. Waiting in queues at the hairdresser
56 Time for immediate service at the hairdresser

V. Physiological needs
Time for food (besides lunch break)
57. Time expended on eating at home
58. Time on the way to the dining room, the café, the tea room and back again
59. Waiting in queues at a dining room, a café and a tea room
60. Time for eating in a dining room, a café and a tea room
Sleep
61. Sleeping during the day
62. Sleeping at night

VI. Free time
Upbringing of children
63. Checking the school tasks, participation in preparing the children's lessons, reading, conversations and training in labour skills
64. Strolling and playing with the children
65. Visiting gatherings of relatives and meeting with teachers
Study and raising qualifications
66. Preparation for studies and reading special literature at home and in libraries
67. Studies in educational institutions (schools, academies, *tekhnikumy* [specialised secondary schools], institutes, etc.) without time for the journey
68. Studies at industrial-technical courses, at schools of progressive methods and at dress-making courses (without time for the journey)
69. Time for the journey to educational institutions, courses, reading rooms and libraries
70. Studies in the network of party education
Social work
71. Preparation and reading of reports, of lectures in the network of party education, of industrial and technical courses, of schools of progressive methods

72. Participation in meetings, sessions, conferences, etc.
73. Participation in mass Sunday work
74. Fulfilment of other public missions

Creative activity and amateur work
75. Invention and rationalisation
76. Literary creativity, painting, sculpting
77. Participation in amateur talent activities
78. Photography, radio amateurism
79. Other types of amateur work

Physical culture and sport
80. Physical exercises, other than at production
81. Amateur occupation with sports and sporting games (volleyball, football, hunting, fishing, skating, etc.)
82. Pursuits at athletic schools and sections, participation in competitions

Leisure and entertainment
83. Reading newspapers
84. Reading magazines and *belles lettres*
85. Attending lectures and discussions
86. Listening to the radio
87. Looking at programmes on television
88. Going to the cinema
89. Going to theatres
90. Going to concert halls, clubs, Houses of Culture
91. Going to museums and exhibitions
92. Going to parks, gardens, stadiums, mass outdoor fêtes, walking without children
93. Singing, playing on musical instruments at home
94. House table games (dominoes, chess, checkers, lotto, cards, etc.)
95. Receiving guests and visiting relatives and friends
96. Inactive leisure
97. Other types of leisure

VII. Other time expenditures
98. Visiting institutions for personal business (savings banks, district and executive committees, post offices, militia, etc.)
99. Unallocated time

121

TOTAL
Besides this, time expenditures
            (under the conditions of a simultaneous outlay of time,
            taken into account by other items)
Reading newspapers
Reading books and magazines
Listening to radio and television broadcasts

Date of Completion
Signature of registrar

Appendix II
Komsomol'skaia pravda
public opinion polls

I. What do the Soviet people think? How do they appraise the present correlation of the forces of peace and war?

(*Komsomol'skaia pravda:* 19 May 1960)

1. Will mankind succeed in averting a war?
2. On what do you base your belief?
3. What must be done above all to strengthen peace?

II. How has your standard of living changed?

(*Komsomol'skaia pravda*: 7 October 1960)

1. How has your living standard changed in recent years?
   (Risen, Remained the same, Declined)
2. In what way is this manifested? To what do you first and foremost attribute this?
3. Which problem do you consider to be most urgent (underline):
   Shortening of the working day
   Increase in the output of consumer goods
   Housing construction
   Improvement in *byt* services
   Increase in food output
   Higher wages
   Expansion of the number of children's institutions
4. What do you suggest for the quickest solution to the problem you have indicated above?

III. What do you think about your generation?

(*Komsomol'skaia pravda:* 6 January 1961)

1. What do you think of your generation? Does it please you, and are you satisfied with its pursuits? (Yes or No)
2. On what do you base your statement?
3. In your opinion, what traits are the strongest in Soviet young people? Where are they most clearly in evidence?
4. In your opinion, are there any negative characteristics common among young people? If your answer is yes, what are they?
5. What justification do you have for your opinion?
6. Which of the following, in your opinion, is more typical of your peers (underline one):
   Purposefulness – A lack of goals
7. Do you personally have a goal in life?
   (Yes, No, Have not thought about it)
8. What is it?
9. What must you do to achieve it?
10. What have you already done?
11. Do you think you will achieve this goal?
    (Yes, No, Don't know)
12. On what do you base your conviction?

IV. What do you think about the scouts of the future?

Part One (*Komsomol'skaia pravda:* 16 August 1961)

1. What do you see as the very strongest aspects of the life of the collectives of communist labour (in production, relations between people, culture, daily life, etc.)?
2. Which aspects of the development of the movement do you consider to be the most long-term?
3. The most important task of each komsomol is to join actively in the fight for communist labour. With which of the following problems do you connect, in the first place, the further mass spread of the movement?
   interest in new techniques
   raising education and culture
   improvement of professional mastery
   growth of consciousness
   possibly, what other problem?

4. From your point of view, what are the shortcomings which occur in the competition for communist labour?

5. What is your opinion about the existing procedure of acquiring honorary titles by the collectives? Are any changes needed in this procedure?

6. In what way should the wide mass of workers take part in awarding honorary titles? In your opinion, who ought to have the right of the deciding vote?

7. In your opinion, may a man be deprived of an honorary title? If yes, in which cases?

Part Two (*Komsomol'skaia pravda:* 23 September 1961)

1. What causes you the greatest difficulty in the struggle for the rank of collective of communist labour? What do you consider your most important achievement?

2. What new features distinguish your collective's labour? (in regard to productive relations, creativity, consciousness, working without reward, etc.)

3. What changes occurred in your life (culture, *byt*, relations between people, etc.) since the time when you chose by precept 'to live in a communist way'?

4. To what degree and in what way does your collective influence the life of other people (patronage, educational work, help in work, etc.)? What, in your opinion, deserves wide dissemination from this experience?

5. From your point of view, which shortcomings occur in the competition for communist labour?

6. Same as 3 of Part One

7. In what forms, in your opinion, will the movement for communist labour be developed in the future?

8. What is your opinion about the existing system of awarding honorary titles to collectives? Does this system need any changes?

9. Same as 6 of Part One

10. Same as 7 of Part One

V. What is your opinion of the young family?

(*Komsomol'skaia pravda:* 10 December 1961)

1. In your opinion, what are the strongest traits characterising the Soviet family?

2. What do you value most in your own family?

3. From what still-existing survivals of the past, in your opinion, is it necessary for young families to free themselves?

4. What features in the upbringing of children in the Soviet family do you consider the best and most advanced?

5. In your opinion, what difficulties in the upbringing of children do families encounter at the present time?

6. What ways would you suggest for overcoming these difficulties?

7. Which of the following would be the most important in eliminating the vestiges of woman's inferior position in everyday life? (Underline)

> Expansion of public forms of satisfying the needs of the family (personal service shops, enterprises of public eating, etc.)
>
> Lessening the woman's labour at production (emancipation from heavy work, night shifts, etc.)
>
> Expansion of the network of children's institutions (crèches, kindergartens, boarding schools, schools keeping open late, etc.)
>
> Participation of husband, of children in carrying out housework
>
> Lightening housework by means of mechanisation
>
> Possibly, any other problem

8. In your opinion, how well prepared are young married people to create a family? How does a lack of preparation manifest itself?

9. In your opinion, is the existing marriage procedure in need of changes? If so, what changes?

10. Are changes needed in the existing procedure for the dissolution of a marriage?

11. How do you explain the break-up of young families?

12. What measures can you suggest for strengthening the young family?

Moscow University students: In the name of what are you studying?

(*Komsomol'skaia pravda:* 1 September 1962)

1. Which of the motives prompted you to devote yourself to your chosen speciality:

> tradition of the family
> romanticism of the profession
> the relative ease of the job

the desire to acquire popularity and glory
sense of mission
high pay for the given profession
striving to move in cultured society
impossibility to study your calling
not thought of it
possibly, what other kind of motive

2. What aim do you place before yourself in your work?
3. Will you succeed in attaining it?

yes
no
don't know

4. What are you keen on besides your speciality? (literature, art, technology, social work, sports, etc.)
5. On completion of university, where and how do you intend to use the knowledge you have received?
6. Could something hinder your intentions? If yes, precisely what?

VI. How do you spend your free time?

(*Komsomol'skaia pravda:* 4 January 1963)

1. How much time, on the average, do you spend each day on the following:
   a. Your main work (in the case of students, your studies)
   b. Supplementary work to earn money
   c. Everyday needs (housework, shopping for food and other items, making use of communal and service institutions, etc.)
   d. In transit from home to place of work (each way)
   e. Evening or correspondence study at educational institutions
   f. Care of children
   g. Sleep
2. What do you do with the remaining free time? (How much time do you give to volunteer work, reading, sports, etc.? How often do you go to the cinema, the theatre, sports events, etc.?)
3. What do you do on your day off?
4. What would you like most of all to do with your free time?
5. What keeps you from spending your free time as you would like to (underline):

Lack of time

Lack of the necessary conditions – amateur arts circles, sports groups, organised evening entertainment, etc.
Lack of cultural institutions
Lack of personal means
Fatigue after work
Inability to organise your time
Other reasons

6. What are the most important ways you see for making better use of leisure time?

VII. To Mars, with what?

(Komsomol'skaia pravda: 1 March 1963)

What should be carried in a rocket that is sent to Mars?

1. Photographs of what news event of the century should be placed in the capsule?
2. What document of importance for the history of mankind should we place in the capsule?
3. An account of what great man of our epoch?
4. A portrait of which person whose exploit has glorified the twentieth century?
5. A description of what outstanding scientific discovery of modern times?
6. A model of what technological invention?
7. What modern implement of labour?
8. What object of everyday life most typical of our times?
9. What sports equipment should we place in the capsule?
10. What work of literature?
11. What score of what musical work?
12. What feature film?
13. A reproduction of what painting or sculpture?
14. A model of what work of architecture?
15. There is still one empty space in the capsule. Suggest your own exhibit. What should it tell the Martians about life on earth?

VIII. Let's project – televisions, radios, etc.

(Komsomol'skaia pravda: 26 June 1964)

1. What type of television would you prefer?
    a. Table

    b. On legs
    c. Portable
    d. Hinged (hung) in the corner
    e. Mounted in sectional furniture
    f. Furnished with earphones
    g. With a revolving screen
    h. With a screen (by the diagonals)
        35 centimetres 47 centimetres 59 centimetres and
        more
    If you wish, propose its construction.

2. Do you need remote control?

    Television   Yes   No
    Radio receiver   Yes   No

3. Do you need an automatic record changer on the record-player?
                                  Yes   No

4. What exterior decoration do you prefer?
    a. Polished, dull
    b. Natural colours of light, red warm wood
    c. Plastics, coloured plastics (bright or muted tone)

5. Which brands do you have:
    Television
    Radio-receiver
    Record-player
    Tape recorder

6. What do you like about them?
    Exterior
    Loudness
    Position of controls
    Other technical data

7. What do you not like that we need to change?

IX. An innovation demands a name

(*Komsomol'skaia pravda:* 28 October 1964)

Please supply names for the following:
    Television
    Wireless set – radio receiver
    Radio-gramophone, radiogram
    Tape recorder – radio
    Magnetic tape recorder
    Record-player
    Dynamics of a relaying system

K

APPENDIX II

Children and words

(*Komsomol'skaia pravda:* 2 August 1964)

Twenty-five out of the fifty words which were listed:

Altar' – altar
Baryshnik – profiteer
Bespridannitsa – dowerless girl
Biurokrat – bureaucrat
Goven'e – preparation for receiving the sacrament
Gol' perekatnaia – utter destitution
Domovoi – house spirit
Edinolochnik – private peasant
Katsap – (Polish) a Great Russian
Kustar' – homeworker (producer for the market); handicraft worker
Lapotnik – dealer in, maker of, bast shoes; primitive person (obsolete)
Mireod – peasant employer of labour; land grabber, usurer
Nakhlebnik – parasite
Podkulachnik – kulak follower or adherer
Podkhalim – yes-man, lickspittle
Seredniak – a middle peasant with own modest resources, but not employing labour
Sklochnitsa – squabbler, troublemaker
Skopidom – miser
Spetsy – specialist (especially of those remaining in the USSR after 1917 but distrusted by the authorities)
Sutiaga – litigious person
Tolkuchka – second-hand merchant
Troitsa – Trinity (holiday – Whitsun)
Khanzha – sanctimonious hypocrite
Khokhol – nickname of the Little Russians

X. How do you rate the service industries?

(*Komsomol'skaia pravda:* 20 November 1964)

1. What, in your opinion, are the basic deficiencies in different spheres of service?

Rate the following services:

Trade
Communal eating
Transport
Medical network (hospitals, pharmacies, sanatoria and others)

Combines (integrated works) of every-day services (workshops, laundries, hairdressers, hotels and others)

Cultural establishments (theatres, cinemas, clubs, libraries
and others)

Sports centres (stadia, sports halls, swimming pools and
others)

Communications enterprises (post, telegraph, telephone)

Rate the services listed above *according to:*

Unnecessary expenditures of time (because of a shortage of
service points, duration of fulfilment of orders, etc.)

Inconvenient hours of service

Unsatisfactory organisation of supplies

Work of poor quality, poor fulfilment of orders

Low calibre of service personnel

2. What services which you do not have the opportunity of using
would you like to use?

3. In your opinion, the basic reasons for the deficiencies which you
have noted include?

4. What do you value most of all in the existing work of the services?

5. What would you suggest to improve the system of services?

XI. Komsomol members about the komsomol

(*Komsomol'skaia pravda:* 26 April 1966)

1. Which trends in the komsomol's work ought to be developed
first and foremost?
   a. Participation in the management of the affairs of society
   b. Participation in solving economic questions
   c. Championing the interests and defending the rights of
   youth
   d. Education of youth

2. With what questions is your komsomol organisation primarily
concerned?

3. What do you consider to be the greatest success and the greatest
failure in the action of your organisation?

4. How has the komsomol helped and what role did it play in
attaining your life plans?

5. Have you ever raised any questions before your organisation?
   If not, why not?
   If yes, were you satisfied by their conclusions?

131

a. Are changes needed in the present practice of admission into the komsomol? If yes, precisely what?

b. Are changes needed in the present system of reports and elections in the komsomol? If yes, precisely what?

6. What are the main qualities that a present-day komsomol leader should possess?

XII. Holidays – How can you best spend them?

Part One (*Komsomol'skaia pravda*: 23 June 1966)

1. In your opinion, what are the basic positive aspects of the organisation of the annual holiday of our country's population?

2. In your opinion, what are the basic inadequacies in the organisation of the holiday?

3. On the whole, how do you evaluate the organisation of the annual holiday?

   Good   Satisfactory   Poor

4. Which categories of people have the best organised leisure and which the worst (age, occupation, social position, etc.)?

   In what ways is this manifested?

5. Which types of holiday do you consider the most valuable?
   - those promoting the strengthening of health and morals, raising culture and developing relations between people (Underline any one)
   - staying in houses of rest, sanitoria, pensions, etc.
   - staying in places of rest under your own steam (without passes)
   - tourism (walking, by water, etc.) journeys
   - excursions, trips to cities
   - staying at home, at a dacha, in a village with relatives
   - staying at a sports camp, in homes for fishermen and hunters, etc.
   - journeys with youth groups (detachments) to construction, to *sovkhoz*, kolkhoz, etc.

   Explain why you think this.

6. What, in your opinion, can play a decisive role in improving the holiday of workers today? (mark any one)
   - extending the construction of rest houses, tourist camps and centres, hotels, etc., bettering the organisation of leisure
   - increasing income (as a means of carrying out leisure)

- raising the culture of leisure, the ability to organise it wisely
- increasing the duration of holidays

7. In your opinion, which areas of leisure should be developed today in the first place? (underline any one)
   - traditional zones of leisure (Crimea, Caucasus, Pre-Baltic, suburban regions of large centres)
   - new, still unopened zones of leisure

   If the latter, then which regions do you have in mind?

8. What do you consider to be most expedient:

   to preserve the existing tradition of having a holiday once a year, or

   to change it, dividing (according to desire) a holiday in two sections?

9. According to established tradition, the majority of the people of our country take a holiday exclusively in the summer or at the beginning of the autumn. Do you think this is right, and why does this occur? Should we change the present tradition? If yes, then what, in your opinion, must be done for the development of leisure at other times of the year?

10. In your opinion, what today limits most of all the possibility of parents and children having a holiday together?

    What ways do you propose for the solution of the problem?

11. What do you consider to be the basic problems in the organisation of the leisure of youth, aged fifteen to eighteen?

    What do you propose to do in this direction?

12. Which conditions must we create in the first place in order to guarantee the subsequent development of mass tourism in our country?

XII. How would you like to spend your holiday?

Part Two (*Komsomol'skaia pravda*: 29 July 1966)

1. What do you think a good rest should give to a healthy man? (indicate by order of importance)
   - remove tiredness, give strength for further work
   - strengthen health, toughen physically
   - expand the horizon (views), get new knowledge
   - distract from usual cares
   - increase number of acquaintances, connections with interesting people

2. What, in your opinion, has the most significance for the realisation of good and valuable leisure (underline):
   material possibilities or the ability of a man to rest

3. In your opinion, when we plan the future leisure of the population, which group(s) of holiday makers must we have in mind, first and foremost?
   - leisure with the family
   - leisure in the company of friends, colleagues, professional colleagues
   - leisure with unknown company
   - leisure alone

4. In view of the working out of measures on the subsequent improvement of the organisation of leisure in the country, which types of leisure – in your opinion – should be shown preference?
   leisure by travelling with a free travel warrant or without a free travel warrant
   leisure in one place or by transferring from one place to another

5. In view of the development of the material base of leisure, to what should we today turn our main attention? (underline any one)
   - construction of many-storeyed buildings of a city type
   - construction of small homes (cottages) for several people
   - construction of light, prefabricated little homes
   - construction of tents, camps

6. What do you think? Is it necessary to attract the (monetary) means of the population for the extension of the material base of leisure? (underline)
   Yes   No   Don't know
   If yes, how do you introduce this?

7. Why do you suppose that tourism received such wide development especially in the last years, and how?

8. In your opinion, the further spread of mass tourism in our country depends on the development of what kind of transportation? (underline)
   Depends on:
   Public transportation (rail, sea, bus and other communications)   OR   Individual transportation (increase number of personal cars, scooters, launches and others)

9. What kind of role in the choice of place and means of leisure do the existing sources of information play today? (Indicate by order of importance)

– advertising prospectus
– radio and television
– advice of friends and acquaintances
– special information, books, pictures, atlases
– newspaper and magazine articles
– artistic literature, films

10. What can you suggest for improving information about different types of leisure?

XIII. The reader about himself and about the newspaper

(*Komsomol'skaia pravda:* 12 October 1966)

1. How did you become acquainted with our newspaper?
    – subscribed at home
    – read the newspaper subscribed to by your institution
    – bought it at a kiosk
    – read it at a street display stand
    – read it at your neighbour's, acquaintance's
    – read it at a library, club, recreation and reading room

2. For how many years have you subscribed to the newspaper?

3. Do you intend to subscribe to *Komsomol'skaia pravda* in 1967?
    Yes   No
    On what is your decision based?

4. How regularly do you read the paper?
    Daily
    Several times a week
    Only on Saturdays and Sundays
    Irregularly

5. Which sections of our paper interest you most of all?
    (mark by degree of importance – not more than three)
    – problems of youth, of komsomol life
    – economics, questions of industry and agriculture
    – propaganda of Leninism, problems of theory, analysis of practical activity
    – sports
    – international life
    – science and technology
    – materials on historical-revolutionary, military-patriotic themes
    – questions of morals and *byt*
    – culture, literature, art
    – problems of secondary and higher education

6. Which other newspapers do you subscribe to and read regularly?

7. Are other newspapers on the same plane as *Komsomol'skaia pravda*, or do they answer your needs better?

8. What do you see as the strong aspects of *Komsomol'skaia pravda?*

9. Which materials under the regular headings of the newspaper do you more or less read regularly? Which practically never? 49 choices were listed here (e.g., letters to the editor, etc.) The Public Opinion Institute was listed in sixteenth place.

10. How much time, on the average, do you usually spend reading our newspaper during the day?

	Work days	Sundays
10–15 minutes		
15–30 minutes		
30 minutes to one hour		
More than one hour		

11. Is this time adequate for you to read everything that you would like to read in the paper?

	Work days	Sundays
Yes		
No		

Abbreviations

CDSP	*Current Digest of the Soviet Press*
Fil Nauki	*Filosofskie nauki (Nauchnye doklady vysshei shkoly)*
Vestnik AN SSSR	*Vestnik Akademii Nauki SSSR*
Vestnik LGU	*Vestnik Leningradskogo Universiteta:* Seriia Ekonomiki, Filosofii, Prava
Vestnik MGU	*Vestnik Moskovskogo Universiteta:* Seriia VIII – Ekonomika, Filosofiia
Vop Fil	*Voprosy filosofii*

Notes

Chapter 1   Historical background

[1]M. M. Kovalevskii, 'Sotsiologiia na zapadei v Rossii', *Novye idei v sotsiologii*, St Petersburg, 1913, I, pp. 3–4.

[2]V. I. Klushin, *Bor'ba za istoricheskii materializm v Leningradskom gosudarstvennom universitete (1918–1925 gody)*, Leningrad, 1970, pp. 11–12.

[3]See J. F. Hecker, *Russian Sociology: A Contribution to the History of Sociological Thought and Theory*, London, 1934, 299 pp.; V. M. Khvostov, *Osnovye Sotsiologii: Uchenie o zakonomernosti obshchestvennykh protsessov*, Moscow, 1920, 91 pp.; and P. A. Sorokin, 'Russian sociology in the twentieth century', *Publications of the American Sociological Society*, XXI, December, 1926, pp. 57–69.

[4]N. G. Voronov, *Osnovaniia sotsiologii*, Moscow, 1912, p. 1.

[5]The themes of the four published books were: 1. Sociology. Its subject and present state; 2. Sociology and Psychology; 3. What is progress?; 4. Genetical Sociology. Contributors were both Russian and non-Russian sociologists.

[6]For a discussion of the first ten years of philosophy and sociology see I. Luppol, 'Filosofiia v SSSR za desiat let', *Obshchestvennye nauki SSSR 1917–1927*, V. P. Volgin, G. O. Gordon and I. K. Luppol (eds), Moscow, 1928, pp. 5–24.

[7]It should be noted that although bourgeois concepts were criticised, they were still discussed and different points of view were aired.

[8]V. I. Klushin, 'Sotsiologiia v Petrogradskom universitete (1920–1924)', *Vestnik LGU*, no. 5, 1964, p. 70.

[9]Pitirim Sorokin, *Leaves from a Russian Diary (1917–1922)*, London, 1925, p. 225. He tells how, for example, he had to lecture in the dark. It is not made clear whether he lectured this way because there was no electric power or because he was scared.

[10]K. M. Takhtarev, *Sravnitel'naia istoriia razvitiia chelovecheskogo obshchestva i obshchestvennykh form: chast' pervaia*, Leningrad, 1924, p. 6.

[11]Klushin, *Vestnik LGU*, no. 5, 1964, p. 71 and his *Bor'ba za* . . ., chap. 2.

[12]See Klushin's article and book for further discussion of the disputes.
[13]B. A. Chagin, 'Razvitie sotsiologicheskoi mysli v SSSR v 20-e gody', *Fil Nauki*, no. 5, 1967, p. 102.
[14]*Ibid.*
[15]M. A. Dynnik *et al.* (eds), *Istoriia filosofii, VI*, book 1, Moscow, 1965, p. 221.
[16]See A. Gouldner's discussion of this term in *The Coming Crisis of Western Sociology*, London, 1971.
[17]Compare the argument of Peter Winch's *The Idea of a Social Science and its Relation to Philosophy*, London, 1960 and the ensuing debate.
[18]See 'Diskussiia o marksistskom ponimanii sotsiologii', *Istorik Marksist*, no. 12, 1929, pp. 189–213.
[19]B. A. Chagin, *Ocherk istorii sotsiologicheskoi mysli v SSSR*, Leningrad, 1971, p. 166.
[20]*Ibid.*, p. 175.
[21]The following discussion is based upon the generally agreed view as it emerges from: G. M. Andreeva, *Sovremennaia burzhuaznaia empiricheskaia sotsiologiia: kriticheskii ocherk*, Moscow, 1965, p. 294; P. N. Fedoseev, 'Marksistskaia sotsiologiia, ee zadachi i perspektivy', *Vestnik AN SSSR*, no. 7, 1966, p. 3: 'Predislovie', *Sotsiologiia v SSSR*, I, G. V. Osipov (ed.), Moscow, 1966, pp. 3–4; S. P. Trapeznikov, 'Razvitie obshchestvennykh nauk i povyshenie ikh roli v kommunisticheskom stroitel'stve', *Vop Fil*, no. 11, 1967, p. 19; V. A. Iadov, 'O chem govorit opyt organizatsii i provedeniia konkretnykh sotsial'nykh issledovanii v Leningrade', *Fil Nauki*, no. 2, 1965, pp. 157–60; Chagin, *Ocherk istorii. . . .*
[22]V. Kantorovich, 'Sotsiologiia i literatura', *Novy mir*, no. 12, 1967, p. 149.
[23]Klushin, *Vestnik LGU*, no. 5, 1964, p. 76.
[24]M. B. Mitin, 'K voprosu', *Revoliutsiia i kul'tura*, no. 19–20, 1930, p. 37, cited by David Joravsky, *Soviet Marxism and Natural Science: 1917–1932*, New York, 1961, p. 258.
[25]G. V. Osipov, *Sovremennaia burzhuaznaia sotsiologiia*, Moscow, 1964, p. 29.
[26]B. A. Grushin, 'Sotsiologiia i sotsiologi', *Literaturnaia gazeta*, 25 September 1965, p. 1.
[27]See M. Cole and I. Maltzman (eds) *A Handbook of Contemporary Soviet Psychology*, London, 1969, p. 6.
[28]Chagin, *Ocherk istorii . . .*, p. 179.
[29]G. Aleksandrov, 'O nekotorykh zadachakh obshchestvennykh nauk v sovremennykh usloviiakh', *Bol'shevik*, no. 14, 1945, p. 23.
[30]For a discussion of Soviet views of bourgeois sociology, see chapter 2.
[31]Chagin, *Ocherk istorii . . .*, pp. 186, 189.

Chapter 2   Soviet and bourgeois sociology

[1]B. A. Grushin, 'Sotsiologiia i sotsiologi', *Literaturnaia gazeta*, 25 September 1965, p. 1.
[2]For a recent statement of this position, see the criticism of Iu. A. Levada for either attempting to separate historical materialism (or rather, all-

sociological theory) from Marxist sociology or create an alternative theory. First see Levada's 'Lektsii po sotsiologii' in *Informatsionnyi biulleten nauchnogo soveta AN SSSR po problemam konkretnykh sotsial'nykh issledovanii* (Moscow, 1969) nos 20–1. For criticism, see 'O Lektsiakh po sotsiologii Iu. A. Levady', *Vestnik MGU: Seriia Filosofiia*, no. 3, 1970, pp. 95–6 and B. E. Kozlovskii and Iu. A. Sychev, 'Obsuzhdenie kursa lektsii Iu. A. Levady po sotsiologii', *Fil Nauki*, no. 3, 1970, pp. 178–85.

[3]A. G. Zdravomyslov, *Metodologiia i protsedura sotsiologicheskikh issledovanii*, Moscow, 1969, p. 16.

[4]See the following for an overall discussion of the problem: V. P. Rozhin, 'O predmete marksistskoi sotsiologii', *Voprosy marksistskoi sotsiologii*, V. P. Rozhin (ed.), Leningrad, 1962, pp. 3–6; A. Verbin and A. Furman, *Mesto istoricheskogo materializma v sisteme nauk*, Moscow, 1965, pp. 141–3; B. A. Grushin, *Mneniia o mire i mir mnenii*, Moscow, 1967, pp. 3–8.

[5]'Formation' is the translation for the Russian *formatsiia*, meaning stage or structure, especially as it refers to a social system. Hence, stage of social development.

[6]A. I. Verbin, V. Zh. Kelle, and M. Ia. Koval'zon, 'Istoricheskii materializm i sotsiologiia', *Vop Fil*, no. 5, 1968, p. 154.

[7]G. V. Osipov, *Sovremennaia burzhuaznaia sotsiologiia*, Moscow, 1964, pp. 373–4.

[8]Some maintain that this second distinction refers only to communist formation and the third to individual social groups within this formation. Therefore, other formations (e.g., capitalism) are not studied.

[9]A. M. Kovalev, 'Eshche raz o sotsiologii marksizma i nauchnom kommunizme', *Fil Nauki*, no. 1, 1967, pp. 112–13.

[10]D. I. Chesnokov, 'K voprosu o sootnoshenii obshchestvennykh nauk,' *Metodologicheskie voprosy obshchestvennykh nauk*, D. I. Chesnokov et al. (eds), Moscow, 1966, p. 38.

[11]F. Konstantinov and V. Kelle, *Historical Materialism – the Marxist Sociology*, Moscow, 1965, p. 17.

[12]A. G. Zdravomyslov and M. T. Petrov, 'Trudy V. I. Lenina – klassicheskii obrazets marksistskogo konkretnogo sotsial'nogo issledovaniia', *Fil Naukt*, no. 2, 1963, p. 3.

[13]See, for example, A. M. Rumiantsev and G. V. Osipov, 'Marksistskaia sotsiologiia i konkretnye sotsial'nye issledovaniia', *Vop Fil*, no. 6, 1968, p. 7.

[14]V. Shliapentokh, *Sotsiologiia dlia vsekh*, Moscow, 1970, p. 45 and N. F. Naumova, 'Nravstvennye antonomii sovremennoi burzhuaznoi sotsiologii', *Vop Fil*, no. 2, 1970, p. 112.

[15]The corollary to this is bourgeois sociology's function as detractor of socialism, communism and Marxist sociology.

[16]G. V. Osipov et al., 'Marksistskaia sotsiologiia i mesto v nei konkretnikh sotsiologicheskikh issledovanii', *Fil Nauki*, no. 5, 1962, pp. 21–32.

[17]N. V. Novikov, *Kritika sovremennoi burzhuaznoi 'Nauki o sotsial'nom povedenii'*, Moscow, 1966, p. 71.

[18]One Soviet critic has criticised fellow Marxist writers for confusing

bourgeois philosophical beliefs with bourgeois sociological beliefs. See G. M. Andreeva, 'Priemy i metody empiricheskikh issledovanii v sovremennoi burzhuaznoi sotsiologii', *Voprosy organizatsii i metodiki konkretno-sotsiologicheskikh issledovanii*, G. K. Ashin *et al.* (eds), Moscow, 1963, p. 90. Also M. P. Baskin's 'Krizis burzhuaznoi ideologii', *Sovremennaia burzhuaznaia sotsiologiia*, by G. V. Osipov, Moscow, 1964, p. 20.

19'Strukturno-funkstional'naia shkola', *Sotsiologiia v SSSR*, II, G. V. Osipov (ed.), Moscow, 1966, p. 505.

20D. M. Ugrinovich, 'O predmete marksistskoi sotsiologii', in *Ocherki metodologii poznaniia sotsial'nykh iavlenii*, D. M. Ugrinovich, O. V. Larmin, and A. K. Uledov (eds), Moscow, 1970, p. 31.

21*Ibid.*, p. 29.

22If this is a change in the position, this would parallel changes in the acceptance of 'bourgeois' methods described in chapter 3.

23I. M. Popova, 'Mesto i rol' sotsial'noi psikhologii v Amerikanskii sotsiologii', *Vestnik MGU*, no. 5, 1960, pp. 44–57.

24G. V. Osipov, 'Nekotorye cherty i osobennosti burzhuaznoi sotsiologii XX veka', *Vop Fil*, no. 8, 1962, pp. 120–31.

25M. N. Rutkevich and L. N. Kogan, 'O metodakh konkretno-sotsiologicheskogo issledovaniia', *Vop Fil*, no. 3, 1961, pp. 123–33.

26G. M. Andreeva, 'Metodologicheskie osnovy burzhuaznoi empiricheskoi sotsiologii', *Metodologicheskie voprosy obshchestvennykh nauk*, D. I. Chesnokov *et al.* (eds), Moscow, 1966, p. 99.

27'Sotsiologiia', *Kratkii slovar' po filosofii*, I. V. Blauberg (ed.), Moscow, 1966, pp. 278–80.

28See, for example, V. S. Semenov and M. N. Gretskii, 'Marksistsko-leninskaia nauka v nastuplenii', *Fil Nauki*, no. 2, 1971, p. 163.

29G. Sjoberg (ed.), *Ethics, Politics and Social Research*, London, 1969.

Chapter 3   The theory of research

1V. A. Iadov, 'Prestizh v opasnosti', *Literaturnaia gazeta*, 28 February 1968, p. 11.

2V. V. Mshvenieradze and G. V. Osipov, 'Osnovny napravleniia i problematika konkretnykh sotsial'nykh issledovanii', *Sotsiologiia v SSSR*, I, G. V. Osipov (ed.), Moscow, 1966, p. 57.

3P. N. Fedoseev, 'Marksistskaia sotsiologiia, ee zadachi i perspektivy', *Vestnik AN SSSR*, no. 7, 1966, p. 7.

4*Zakonomernost'* – order; regularity; pattern; conformity to systematic/ established law of nature or society.

5A. M. Rumiantsev, 'Vstupaiushchemu v mir nauki', *Komsomol'skaia pravda*, 8 June 1967, p. 3. (Rumiantsev's italics).

6B. A. Grushin, 'Sotsiologiia i sotsiologi', *Literaturnaia gazeta*, 25 September 1965, p. 2.

7See G. M. Andreeva's discussion in 'Metodologicheskaia rol' teorii na raznykh etapakh sotsial'nogo issledovaniia', *Vop Fil*, no. 7, 1964, p. 16.

8V. A. Iadov, 'Ob ustanovlenii faktov v konkretnom sotsiologicheskom issledovanii', *Fil Nauki*, no. 5, 1966, pp. 28–38. Also discussed in Iadov's

Metodologiia i protsedury sotsiologicheskikh issledovanii, Tartu, 1968, pp. 20–32. See also G. M. Andreeva and E. P. Nikitin's proposals for a series of hierarchically organised levels for explaining laws ('Metod ob'iasneniia v sotsiologii', *Sotsiologiia v SSSR*, vol. II, Moscow, 1966, pp. 124–44).

[9]Iadov, *Fil Nauki*, no. 5, 1966, p. 37.

[10]V. A. Iadov, 'Rol' metodologii v opredelenii metodov i tekhniki konkretnogo sotsiologicheskogo issledovaniia', *Vop Fil*, no. 10, 1966, pp. 27–37.

[11]Iadov fails to mention one other early 'method', namely, the role of scientific and theoretical conferences. These conferences are usually listed as one of the primary methods of research.

[12]Iadov, *Vop Fil*, no. 10, 1966, p. 33.

[13]A. M. Rumiantsev and G. V. Osipov, 'Marksistskaia sotsiologiia i konkretnye sotsial'nye issledovaniia', *Vop Fil*, no. 6, 1968, p. 7.

[14]V. N. Shubkin, 'Kolichestvennye metody v sotsiologii', *Vop Fil*, no. 3, 1967, p. 38. Also see Shubkin's *Sotsiologicheskie opyty*, Moscow, 1970, pp. 66–7.

[15]A. G. Zdravomyslov, *Metodologiia i protsedura sotsiologicheskikh issledovanii*, Moscow, 1969, pp. 44, 47.

Chapter 4   The sociologists

[1]V. N. Shubkin, 'Sotsiologiia: Problemy i perspektivy', *Pravda*, 13 March 1966, p. 3.

[2]A. Aleksandrov, 'Slovo o sotsiologii', *Literaturnaia gazeta*, 21 April 1966, p. 2.

[3]V. A. Iadov, 'Sotsiologiia: Problemy i fakty—otvetstvennost' ', *Literaturnaia gazeta*, 12 November 1966, p. 2.

[4]E. V. Beliaev et al., 'Vsesoiuznyi simpozium sotsiologov', *Vop Fil*, no. 10, 1966, p. 156.

[5]Iadov, *Literaturnaia gazeta*, 12 November 1966, p. 2.

[6]V. Mikhailov and V. Perevedentsev, 'Bol'shie ozhidaniia', *Literaturnaia gazeta*, 14 June 1967, p. 18.

[7]M. F. Ovsiannikov and Iu. A. Petrov, 'O sostoianii dissertatsionnoi raboty po filosofii v 1964–5 uchebnom godu', *Vop Fil*, no. 2, 1966, pp. 138–40; M. F. Ovsiannikov and Iu. A. Petrov, 'O dissertatsionnoi rabote po filosofii v 1965–6 uchebnom godu', *Vop Fil*, no. 1, 1967, pp. 150–3; M. F. Ovsiannikov and Iu. A. Petrov, 'O dissertatsionnoi rabote po filosofii v 1966–7 uchebnom godu', *Vop Fil*, no. 11, 1967, pp. 131–6; V. G. Afanas'ev and Iu. A. Petrov, 'O dissertatsionnykh rabotakh po filosofii v 1967–8 uchenbom godu', *Vop Fil*, no. 1, 1969, pp. 145–52; A. G. Afanas'ev and Iu. A. Petrov, 'O dissertatsionnykh rabotakh po filosofii i sotsiologii v 1968–9 uchenbom godu', *Vop Fil*, no. 12, 1969, pp. 140–6; and A. S. Bogomolov and Iu. A. Petrov, 'O dissertatsionnykh rabotakh po filosofii v 1969–70 uchebnom godu', *Vop Fil*, no. 1, 1971, pp. 140–5. The following discussion was compiled from these reports.

[8]A. Rumiantsev, T. Timofeev, and Iu. Sheinin, 'Dlia progress nauki i truda', *Izvestiia*, 12 May 1966, p. 3.

⁹G. V. Osipov, 'Teoriia i praktika sovetskoi sotsiologii', *Sotsial'nye issledovaniia*, no. 5, 1970, p. 22.

¹⁰George Fischer, 'Sociology', *Science and Ideology in Soviet Society*, George Fischer (ed.), New York, 1967, p. 11.

¹¹*Tass* report, 11 May 1965.

¹²L. L. Gremiako, V. Ia. El'meev, and D. A. Kerimov, 'Institut sotsial'nykh issledovanii', *Vop Fil*, no. 8, 1966, p. 146.

¹³Much of the following discussion is based on V. A. Iadov's 'O chem govorit opyt organizatsii i provedeniia konkretnykh sotsial'nykh issledovanii v Leningrade', *Fil Nauki*, no. 2, 1965, pp. 157–60. More recently, see the article by B. G. Anan'ev and A. S. Pashkov, 'Kompleksnoe issledovanie sotsial'nykh problem', *Chelovek i obshchestvo*, no. 8, 1971, pp. 3–15.

¹⁴See V. V. Kim and K. N. Liubutin, 'Razvitie filosofskikh issledovanii v Sverdlovske', *Fil Nauki*, no. 6, 1967, pp. 125–9.

¹⁵See E. S. Lazutkin, 'Ekonomiko-sotsiologicheskie issledovaniia', *Vop Fil*, no. 3, 1966, pp. 120–8. Also O. V. Belykh *et al.*, 'Ob opyte konkretnykh sotsial'nykh issledovanii', *Fil Nauki*, no. 3, 1966, pp. 139–48. The latter is relevant for all of the centres of sociological research.

¹⁶R. S. Rusakov and V. D. Karchemnik, 'O rabote Instituta istorii, filologii i filosofii SO AN SSSR v 1969 godu', *Izvestiia sibirskogo otdeleniia Akademii nauk SSSR*, no. 6, 1970, pp. 153–6.

¹⁷R. A. Anufrieva and V. A. Vasilenko, 'Sotsiologiia na Ukraine i ee perspektivy', *Vop Fil*, no. 9, 1967, pp. 159–61.

¹⁸V. Vol'skii, 'Partiinaia zhizn': krugozor rukovoditelia', *Pravda*, 17 January 1967, p. 2.

¹⁹Iu. S. Meleshchenko, Iu. P. Smirnov, and A. G. Kharchev, 'Sotsiologicheskie issledovaniia i partiinaia rabota', *Chelovek i obshchestvo*, no. 3, 1968, p. 84, and R. I. Kosolapov and P. I. Simush, 'Partiinaia rabota i konkretnye sotsiologicheskie issledovaniia', *Ideologicheskaia rabota partiinykh organizatsii*, A. M. Korolev and S. I. Mosiagin (eds), Moscow, 1969, pp. 234–56.

²⁰V. N. Malin, 'Za nauchnyi podkhod k partiino-ideologicheskoi rabote', *Problemy nauchnogo kommunizma*, no. 2, Moscow, 1968, p. 7.

²¹Meleshchenko *et al.*, *Chelovek i obshchestvo*, no. 3, 1968, p. 81, and V. Provotorov, 'Sotsiologicheskie issledovaniia v partiinoi rabote', *Partiinaia zhizn'*, no. 19, 1967, p. 36.

²²M. I. Zhabskii and P. K. Lenik, 'Sotsiologicheskoe issledovanie massovogo retsipienta iskusstva', *Vestnik MGU*, no. 4, 1967, p. 85.

²³See the discussion by Ia. S. Kapeliush and A. I. Prigozhin, 'Sobranie sovetskoi sotsiologicheskoi assotsiatsii', *Vop Fil*, no. 6, 1966, pp. 157–60, as well as 'Sessiia sotsiologov', *Pravda*, 23 November 1967, p. 6.

²⁴A. G. Zdravomyslov, *Metodologiia i protsedura sotsiologicheskikh issledovanii*, Moscow, 1969, p. 3.

²⁵V. S. Semenov, 'VI vsemirnii sotsiologicheskii kongress', *Vop Fil*, no. 8, 1967, pp. 121–32.

²⁶In addition to V. S. Semenov, the following have written about the VIth Congress: G. M. Andreeva, 'O VI mezhdunarodnom kongresse sotsiologov', *Vestnik MGU*, no. 1, 1967, pp. 65–72; M. T. Iovchuk,

143

'Mezhdunarodnyi forum sotsiologov', *Vestnik AN SSSR*, no. 2, 1967, pp. 68–74; I. S. Kon and V. A. Iadov, 'Na VI vsemirnom sotsiologicheskom kongresse', *Fil Nauki*, no. 1, 1967, pp. 162–6.

27 Karel Makha and Iulius Strinka, 'Filosofskie publikatsii v Chekhoslovakii v 1960–63 godakh', *Vop Fil*, no. 1, 1965, pp. 178–81, and K. Zagurskii, 'Pol'skaia literatura po sotsiologii 1960–64 gg', *Vop Fil*, no. 4, pp. 178–82.

28 V. V. Vodzinskaia and V. A. Iadov, 'U Pol'skikh sotsiologov', *Fil Nauki*, no. 3, 1963, pp. 133–7.

29 M. Kaleb, 'Pervaia obshchegosudarstvennaia konferentsiia Chekhoslovatskikh sotsiologov', *Vop Fil*, no. 6, 1967, pp. 149–52.

30 M. B. Belov, '*Voprosy filosofii* na Cherepovetskom metallurgicheskom zavode', *Vop Fil*, no. 11, 1965, pp. 161–2.

31 L. I. Seleskeridi, 'Chitatel'skaia konferentsiia v Tbilisi', *Vop Fil*, no. 4, 1966, pp. 172–4.

Chapter 5   Areas of research

1 P. Fedoseev, 'Marksistskaia sotsiologiia i konkretnye sotsiologicheskie issledovaniia', *Partiinaia zhizn*, no. 20, 1967, p. 37.

2 B. A. Grushin, quoted in 'Sila i slabosti molodoi nauki', *Literaturnaia gazeta*, 6 August 1966, p. 2. The participants' quote is also from this source.

3 For a more detailed analysis of time budget research, see my doctoral dissertation entitled 'The development of sociological studies in communist states: the case of the USSR', University of London, 1970, chapter 7. For a detailed bibliography of time budget research, see B. T. Kolpakov and V. D. Patrushev, *Biudzhet vremeni gorodskogo naseleniia*, Moscow, 1971.

4 G. A. Prudenskii (ed.), *Vnerabochee vremia trudiashchikhsia*, Novosibirsk, 1961, 254 pp. The actual questionnaires were included in the appendix.

5 See B. Kolpakov and G. Prudenskii, 'Opyt izmereniia vnerabochego vremeni trudiashchikhsiia', *Vop Fil*, no. 9, 1964, pp. 27–34; G. S. Petrosian, *Vnerabochee vremia trudiashchikhsia v SSSR*, Moscow, 1965, 194 pp.; and G. S. Petrosian, 'Natsional' no-etnograficheskie razlichiia, osobennosti byta i vnerabochee vremia trudiashchikhsia', *Fil Nauki*, no. 2, 1969, pp. 73–7.

6 See an outline of the competing positions prepared by Petrosian, *Vnerabochee vremia . . .*, pp. 21–2.

7 See the preliminary report by Alexander Szalai, 'The multinational comparative time budget research project: a venture in international research cooperation', *American Behavioral Scientist*, vol. 10, no. 4, December 1966, pp. 1–31.

8 Figure by inference from V. I. Zanin, 'Biudzhet rabochego vremeni', *Sotsialnye issledovaniia: problemy biudzheta vremeni trudiashchikhsia*, vol. 6, V. I. Bolgov, (ed.), Moscow, 1970, p. 157.

9 R. E. F. Smith, *A Russian-English Dictionary of Social Science Terms*, London, 1962, p. 136.

[10]V. D. Patrushev, 'Biudzhet vremeni gorodskogo naseleniia sotsialisti-cheskikh i kapitalisticheskikh stran', *Fil Nauki*, no. 5, 1968, p. 53, and G. S. Petrosian, *Fil Nauki*, no. 2, 1969, p. 73.

[11]V. A. Artemov and B. P. Kutyrev, 'Biudzhet vremeni i sotsial'no-ekonomicheskoe planirovaniia', *Fil Nauki*, no. 6, 1969, p, 184.

[12]L. Leont'ev, 'Sotsiologiia i ekonomicheskaia nauka', *Literaturnaia gazeta*, 26 May 1966, p. 2.

[13]See the comprehensive section V entitled 'Sotsial'nye problemy truda i dosuga' in *Sotsiologiia v SSSR*, vol. 2, G. V. Osipov, (ed.), Moscow, 1966, pp. 5–267. Many of these essays are translated in G. V. Osipov (ed.), *Industry and Labour in the USSR*, London, 1966. See almost any issue of *Chelovek i obshchestvo* and *Sotsial'nye issledovaniia*, as well as any of the collections on sociology in general.

[14]Osipov (ed.), *Sotsiologiia v SSSR*, vol. 2, p. 9.

[15]V. N. Shubkin, 'Molodezh' vstupaet v zhizn' ', *Vop Fil*, no. 5, 1965, pp. 57–70; article in N. V. Novikov *et al.* (eds), *Sotsial'nye issledovaniia*, vol. 1, Moscow, 1965, pp. 118–39; 'Kolichestvennye metody v sotsio-logicheskikh issledovaniiakh problem trudoustroistva i vybora professii', *Kolichestvennye metody v sotsiologii*, A. G. Aganbegian, G. V. Osipov, and V. N. Shubkin (eds), Moscow, 1966, pp. 168–231; 'Ob ustoichivosti otsenok privlekatel'nosti professii', *Sotsiologicheskie issledovaniia: Voprosy metodologii i metodiki*, R. V. Ryvkina (ed.), Novosibirsk, 1966, pp. 247–67; and *Sotsiologicheskie opyty*, Moscow, 1970, pp. 151–251.

[16]Shubkin, *Vop Fil*, no. 5, 1965, pp. 57–8.

[17]A. G. Zdravomyslov and V. A. Iadov, 'Opyt konkretnogo issledovaniia otnosheniia k trudu', *Vop Fil*, no. 4, 1964, pp. 72–84; article by the same authors in *Sotsiologiia v SSSR*, vol. 2, G. V. Osipov (ed.), Moscow, 1966, pp. 187–207. The book with all of the results of the research was published as A. G. Zdravomyslov, V. P. Rozhin, and V. A. Iadov (eds), *Chelovek i ego rabota*, Moscow, 1967. See also two Soviet reviews of the book: T. Zaslavskaia, V. Shliapentokh, and V. Shubkin, 'Sotsiolog i ego rabota', *Izvestiia*, 10 October 1967, p. 4, and N. F. Naumova, 'Sotsio-logiia truda, ee uspekhi i problemy', *Vop Fil*, no. 7, 1968, pp. 130–3.

[18]A. G. Zdravomyslov and V. A. Iadov, 'Effect of vocational distinctions on the attitude to work', *Industry and Labour in the USSR*, G. V. Osipov (ed.), London, 1966, p. 114.

[19]Joan Woodward, *Management and Technology*, HMSO, London, 1958.

[20]See, for example, the John H. Goldthorpe *et al.* thesis in volume 1 of *The Affluent Worker: Industrial Attitudes and Behaviour*, Cambridge, 1968.

[21]See, for example, Zaslavskaia, Shliapentokh and Shubkin, *Izvestiia*, 10 October 1967, p. 4.

[22]E. Antosenkov (ed.), *Opyt issledovaniia peremeny truda v promysh-lennosti: po rezul'tatam ekonomicheskogo i sotsiologicheskogo obsle-dovaniia tekuchesti rabochikh kadrov*, Novosibirsk, 1969, and E. Antosenkov, *Labour Turnover in USSR National Economy: Socio-Economic Nature and Principles of Control*, Novosibirsk, 1970, 15 pp.

[23]Ibid., pp. 5–6.

[24]See his *Migratsiia naseleniia i trudovye problemy Sibiri*, Novosibirsk,

1966; *Narodonaselenie i ekonomika*, Moscow, 1967; and 'Migratsiia naseleniia i ispol'zovanie trudovykh resursov', *Voprosy ekonomiki*, no. 9, 1970, pp. 35-43.
25T. I. Zaslavakaia, *Migratsiia sel'skogo naseleniia*, Moscow, 1970, 348 pp.
26L. Gordon and B. Levin, 'Nekotorye sotsial'no-bytovye posledstviia piatidnevki v bol'shikh i malykh gorodakh', *Voprosy ekonomiki*, no. 4, 1968, pp. 138-42.
27G. Sviridov, 'Iz praktiki konkretnykh sotsiologicheskikh issledovanii', *Partiinaia zhizn'*, no. 16, 1970, pp. 35-8.
28I. I. Kravchenko and E. T. Faddeev, 'O sotsial'noi strukture sovetskogo obshchestva', *Vop Fil*, no. 5, 1966, pp. 143-54, and K. L. Potaenko and M. L. Tsegoeva, 'Izmeneniia sotsial'noi struktury sovetskogo obshchestva', *Fil Nauki*, no. 3, 1966, pp. 133-8. Some Soviet writers trace this back to a statement first seen in an article by F. Konstantinov and V. Kelle, 'Istoricheskii materializm—marksistskaia sotsiologiia', *Kommunist*, no. 1, 1965, p. 17.
29V. S. Semenov, Moscow Home Service, 31 May 1966.
30*Ibid.*
31For references, see the authors listed individually below.
32See his 'O poniatii intelligentsii kak sotsial'nogo sloia sotsialisticheskogo obshchestva', *Fil Nauki*, no. 4, 1966, pp. 20-8; 'Izmenenie sotsial'noi struktury sovetskogo obshchestva i intelligentsiia', *Sotsiologiia v SSSR*, vol. 1, G. V. Osipov (ed.), Moscow, 1966, pp. 391-413; *Izmenenie sotsial'noi struktury sovetskogo obshchestva*, Moscow, 1966; 'Sotsial'nye istochniki popolneniia sovetskoi intelligentsii', *Vop Fil*, no. 6, 1967, pp. 15-23; 'O kriteriakh sotsial'nykh razlichii i ikh primenenii k intelligentsii', in *Protsessy izmeneniia sotsial'noi struktury v sovetskom obshchestve*, M. N. Rutkevich (ed.), Sverdlovsk, 1967, pp. 76-88; 'Problemy izmeneniia sotsial'noi struktury sovetskogo obshchestva', *Fil Nauki*, no. 3, 1968, pp. 44-52; 'V.I. Lenin i problemy razvitiia intelligentsii', in *Doklady k VII mezhdunarodnomy sotsiologicheskomu kongressu*, O. N. Zhemanov (ed.), Sverdlovsk, 1970, pp. 3-13; 'Protsessy sotsial'nykh peremeshchenii i poniatie "sotsial'noi mobil'nosti" ', *Fil Nauki*, no. 5, 1970, pp. 14-21.
33Iu. V. Arutunian: 'Sotsial'naia struktura sel'skogo naseleniia', *Vop Fil*, no. 5, 1966, pp. 51-61; 'Konkretno-sotsial'noe issledovanie sela', *Vop Fil*, no. 10, 1966, pp. 166-9; 'Sotsial'nye aspekty kul'turnogo rosta sel'skogo naseleniia', *Vop Fil*, no. 9, 1968, pp. 114-31; *Opyt sotsiologicheskogo izucheniia sela*, Moscow, 1968; 'Rural sociology' and 'Rural social structure' in *Town, Country and People*, G. V. Osipov (ed.), London, 1969, pp. 218-48; *Sotsial'naia struktura sel'skogo naseleniia*, Moscow, 1971.
34Arutunian, *Vop Fil*, no. 5, 1966, p. 52. Also in 'Rural Social Structure', in *Town, Country and People*, p. 235.
35O. I. Shkaratan: 'Sotsial'naia struktura sovetskogo rabochego klassa', *Vop Fil*, no. 1, 1967, pp. 28-39; 'Rabochii klass sotsialisticheskogo obshchestva v epokhu nauchnotekhnicheskii revoliutsii', *Vop Fil*, no. 11, 1968, pp. 14-25; 'Problemy sotsial'noi struktury sovetskogo goroda', *Fil Nauki*, no. 5, 1970, pp. 22-31; *Problemy sotsial'noi struktury*

rabochego klassa, Moscow, 1970. For Arutunian and Shkaratan, see also V. A. Provotorov, 'Obuzhdenie problem sotsial'noi strukury obshchestva', *Fil Nauki*, no. 1, 1966, pp. 145–8, and O. V. Belykh *et al.*, 'Ob opyte konkretnykh sotsial'nykh issledovanii', *Fil Nauki*, no. 3, 1966, pp. 139–48.

³⁶Shkaratan, *Vop Fil*, no. 1, 1967, p. 33.

³⁷Shkaratan, *Problemy sotsial'noi* . . . , p. 4.

³⁸A. G. Kharchev, *Brak i sem'ia v SSSR*, Moscow, 1964, p. 325.

³⁹I. S. Kon, 'Tsennoe issledovanie', *Fil Nauki*, no. 1, 1965, p. 120.

⁴⁰Some of the findings which appear in this book were previously published in an article entitled, 'O nekotorykh rezul'tatakh issledovaniia motivov braka v SSSR', *Fil Nauki*, no. 4, 1963, pp. 47–58.

⁴¹Kon, *Fil Nauki*, no. 1, 1965, p. 120.

⁴²I. Mindlin also reviewed the book. See 'Staroe v novom', *Novyi mir*, no. 12, 1964, pp. 260–2.

⁴³A. G. Kharchev, 'Marriage motivation studies' in *Town, Country and People*, G. V. Osipov (ed.), London, 1969, p. 73.

⁴⁴See N. V. Ustinovich, 'Sotsializm i sem'ia', *Vop Fil*, no. 7, 1967, pp. 137–40 and M. A. Kirillova and M. G. Pantratova, 'Simpozium sotsiologov po issledovaniiu problem sem'i i byta', *Fil Nauki*, no. 4, 1967, pp. 198–9. Also N. Solov'ev, Iu. Lazauskas, and Z. Iankova (eds), *Problemy byta, braka i sem'i*, Vil'nius, 1970, 247 pp.

⁴⁵I. Kasiukov and A. Mendeleev, 'Nuzhen li talant sem'ianinu?', *Nedelia*, no. 12, 1967, p. 18.

⁴⁶*Ibid.*

⁴⁷See the conclusion in N. G. Iurkevich, *Sovetskaia sem'ia: Funktsii i usloviia stabil'nosti*, Minsk, 1970.

⁴⁸Z. Iankova, 'O bytovykh roliakh rabotaiushchei zhenshchiny (k probleme osyshchestvleniia fakticheskogo ravenstva zhenshchiny s muzhchinoi) in *Problemy byta, braka i sem'i* by N. Solov'ev, Iu. Lazauskas, and Z. Iankova (eds), Vil'nius, 1970, pp. 42–9.

⁴⁹V. Besedina and T. Mamonova, 'Sprosim nashikh muzhchin', *Komsomol'skaia pravda*, 27 May 1966, p. 2.

⁵⁰A. I. Pimenova, 'Sem'ia i perspektivy razvitiia obschestvennogo truda zhenshchin pri sotsializme', *Fil Nauki*, no. 3, 1966, pp. 35–44.

⁵¹See the section devoted to social problems of the city and village in the second volume of *Sotsiologiia v SSSR*, G. V. Osipov (ed.), Moscow, 1966, pp. 267–337. For a bibliography on studies of urbanisation see D. N. Pevzner, *Sotsiologicheskie issledovaniia goroda*, Moscow, 1967, mimeographed.

⁵²B. Khorev, 'Kakoi gorod nuzhen?', *Literaturnaia gazeta*, 2 April 1969, p. 12.

⁵³O. S. Pchelintsev, 'Problemy razvitiia bol'shikh gorodov', *Sotsiologiia v SSSR*, vol. 2, G. V. Osipov (ed.), Moscow, 1966, p. 284.

⁵⁴V. Perevedentsev, 'Spornoe mnenie: Goroda i gody', *Literaturnaia gazeta*, 26 February 1969, p. 12.

⁵⁵Khorev, *Literaturnaia gazeta*, 2 April 1969, p. 12.

⁵⁶L. N. Kogan and V. I. Loktev, 'Sociological aspects of the modelling

of towns', *Town, Country and People*, G. V. Osipov (ed.), London, 1969, pp. 107–8.

57N. Aitov, 'Na perekrestke mnenii: Gorod–proportsii razvitiia', *Izvestiia*, 17 February 1972, p. 5.

58See B. Michael Frolic, 'The Soviet study of Soviet cities', *Journal of Politics*, vol. 32, no. 3, 1970, pp. 675–95.

59*Ibid.* For one example, see E. Levina and E. Syrkina, 'Razmyshleniia o mikroraione', *Zvezda*, no. 10, 1966, pp. 150–6.

60I have used the unpublished master's thesis of Peter H. Solomon, Jr., for the background of this discussion. See his 'Soviet criminology: the effects of post-Stalin politics on a social science', Columbia University, 1967.

61M. D. Shagorodskii, 'Prichiny i profilaktika prestupnosti', *Voprosy marksistskoi sotsiologii*, V. P. Rozhin (ed.), Leningrad, 1962, p. 96. (Italics mine.)

62*Ibid.* (Italics by Shagorodskii.)

63S. S. Ostroumov and V. E. Chugunov, 'Izuchenie lichnosti prestupnika po materialam kriminologicheskikh issledovanii', *Sovetskoe gosudarstvo i pravo*, no. 9, 1965, p. 101.

64See the discussion (and disapproval) of this by B. S. Utevskii, 'Sotsiologicheskie issledovaniia i kriminologiia', *Vop Fil*, no. 2, 1964, pp. 46–51.

65One commentator has criticised those who first correlate an insufficiently high level of education with crime and then complain that the absence of higher or secondary education is a negative phenomenon. V. N. Kudriavtsev, *Prichinnost' v kriminologii*, Moscow, 1968, p. 80.

66Ustinovich, *Vop Fil*, no. 7, 1967, p. 139.

67B. D. Ovchinnikov, 'Sostnoshenie sotsial'nogo i biologicheskogo v sviazi s problemoi prestupnosti', *Vestnik LGU*, no. 23, 1969, pp. 142–50. For a classification of motives for crime, see P. S. Dagel, 'Klassifikatsiia motivov prestupleniia i ee kriminologicheskoe znachenie', *Nekotorye voprosy sotsiologii i prava*, L. A. Petrov (ed.), Irkutsk, 1967, pp. 265–74.

68V. Kudriavtsev, 'Analiz plius tekhnika', *Izvestiia*, 30 September 1966, p. 3.

69G. M. Minkovskii, 'Nekotorye prichiny prestupnosti nesovershennoletnikh v SSSR i mery ee preduprezhdeniia', *Sovetskoe gosudarstvo i pravo*, no. 5, 1966, pp. 84–93.

70'Antiobshchestvennye iavleniia, ikh prichiny i sredstva bor'by s nimi', *Kommunist*, no. 12, 1966, pp. 58–68.

71See V. N. Kudriavtsev, 'Problemy prichinnosti v kriminologii', *Vop Fil*, no. 10, 1971, pp. 76–87.

72V. Kudriavtsev, 'Prestupnost': Sootnoshenie sotsial'nogo i biologicheskogo: Dano li pri rozhdenii', *Literaturnaia gazeta*, 29 November 1967, p. 12.

73A. I. Klibanov, 'Piat'desiat let nauchnogo issledovannia religioznogo sektantstva', *Voprosy nauchnogo ateizma*, no. 4, 1967, pp. 349–84.

74A good review of the literature on this subject may be found in E. G. Filimonov, 'Problemy konkretno-sotsiologicheskikh issledovanii religioznosti v sovetskoi literature (1961–66)', *Konkretnye issledovaniia sovremennykh religioznykh verovanii*, A. I. Klibanov *et al.* (eds), Moscow, 1967, pp. 217-42.

[75]See the first conference on the psychology of religion as reported by P. A. Lopatkin and M. A. Popova, 'Problemy psikhologiia religii', *Vop Fil*, no. 7, 1969, pp. 150-5.

[76]G. L. Andreev *et al.*, 'Nauchnyi ateizm za 50 let', *Vop Fil*, no. 12, 1967, pp. 37-47.

[77]D. M. Aptekman, 'Prichiny zhivuchesti religioznogo obriada kreshcheniia v sovremennykh usloviiakh', *Vop Fil*, no. 3, 1965, pp. 83-9.

[78]I. N. Iablokov, 'Ob opyte konkretnogo issledovaniia religioznosti', *Vestnik MGU*, no. 4, 1967, pp. 27-35.

[79]L. N. Mitrokhin, 'Methods of research into religion', *Town, Country and People*, G. V. Osipov (ed.), London, 1969, pp. 182-201.

[80]N. Andrianov, 'Puti k istine: zametki ob ateisticheskoi propagande', *Pravda*, 7 September 1970, p. 2.

Chapter 6   Public opinion research

[1]A. K. Uledov, 'O filosofskoi metodologii i konkretnykh metodikh sotsial'no-psikhologicheskogo issledovaniia', *Metodologicheskie voprosy obshchestvennykh nauk*, D. I. Chesnokov *et al.* (eds), Moscow, 1966, pp. 66-7.

[2]V. N. Shubkin, 'O konkretnykh issledovaniiakh sotsial'nykh protsessov', *Kommunist*, no. 3, 1965, p. 55.

[3]Iu. A. Sherkovin, 'Obshchestvennoe mnenie v sovetskom obshchestve', *Vop Fil*, no. 11, 1964, p. 175.

[4]Hugh Lunghi, 'Opinion probe in Russia', European Service General News Talk, 26 May 1960, p. 4.

[5]B. A. Erunov, *Sila obshchestvennogo mneniia*, Leningrad, 1964, pp. 31 and 53.

[6]B. A. Grushin, *Svobodnoe vremia: Aktual'nye problemy*, Moscow, 1967, 174 pp.

[7]See a report of the conference by Iu. K., 'V statisticheskoi sektsii Moskovskogo doma uchenykh', *Vestnik statistiki*, no. 6, 1961, pp. 82-4. The third poll was omitted from the discussion.

[8]The results of the third poll were presented in a lengthy book in 1962. See B. A. Grushin and V. Chikin, *Ispoved' pokoleniia*, Moscow, 1962, 248 pp.

[9]M. Kh. Igitkhanian, 'Dukhovnyi oblik sovetskoi molodezhi', *Vop Fil*, no. 6, 1963, pp. 75-85.

[10]B. A. Grushin, 'K probleme kachestvennoi reprezentatsii v vyborochnom oprose', *Opyt i metodika konkretnykh sotsiologicheskikh issledovanii*, G. E. Glezerman and V. G. Afanas'eva (eds), Moscow, 1965, pp. 61-107.

[11]*Ibid.*, p. 77.

[12]*Ibid.*, p. 99.

[13]See the recent discussion by A. G. Zdravomyslov in *Metodologiia i protsedura sotsiologicheskikh issledovanii*, Moscow, 1969, pp. 114-37.

[14]V. Kantorovich, 'Rodstvennaia nam nauka', *Literaturnaia gazeta*, 5 May 1966, pp. 1-2 and 14 May 1966, pp. 1-2.

[15]A. I. Prigozhin, 'Metodologicheskie problemy issledovaniia obshchest-vennogo mneniia', *Vop Fil*, no. 2, 1969, p. 73. At present, there is a section of public opinion in the Academy of Sciences' Institute of Concrete Social Research.

[16]For a discussion of Polish public opinion research, see the *Polish Sociological Bulletin* (Semi-Annual of the Polish Sociological Association), especially work by Z. Gostowski (no. 1[13], 1966; no. 2[20], 1969; no. 2[22], 1970), W. Wisniewski (no. 2[14], 1966), and K. Lutynska (no. 2[20], 1969; no. 2[22], 1970).

[17]Anna Pawełcznyska, 'Principles and problems of public opinion research in Poland', *Empirical Sociology in Poland*, Warsaw, 1966, p. 14.

[18]A. Kharchev, 'Sotsiologicheskie issledovaniia v Pol'she', *Vop Fil*, no. 6, 1963, p. 149.

[19]Prigozhin, *Vop Fil*, no. 2, 1969, p. 70.

Chapter 7   Conclusion

[1]S. Kovalev, 'Voprosy teorii: trebovaniia zhizni i obshchestvennye nauki', *Pravda*, 6 May 1966, p. 3.

[2]F. V. Konstantinov, 'Voprosy teorii: filosofiia revoliutsionnoi epokhi', *Pravda*, 24 July 1967, p. 3.

[3]V. Shliapentokh, *Sotsiologiia dlia vsekh*, Moscow, 1970, p. 43.

[4]N. Preobrazhenskii, 'Blizhaishie zadachi Sotsialisticheskoi Akademii', *Vestnik Sotsialisticheskoi Akademii*, no. 1, 1922, p. 6.

Bibliography

AFANAS'EV, V. G., GOLUBEV, A. N., and PETROV, I. G. (eds) *Problemy nauchnogo kommunizma: Konkretnye sotsiologicheskie issledovaniia i ideologicheskaia deiatel'nost'* (*Problems of Scientific Communism: Concrete Sociological Research and Ideological Activity*), no. 2, Moscow, 1968.

AFANAS'EV, V. G. and PETROV, IU. A. 'O dissertatsionnykh rabotakh po filosofii v 1967/68 uchebnom godu' ('On dissertations in philosophy for the 1967–8 academic year'), *Vop Fil*, no. 1, 1969.

——'O dissertatsionnykh rabotakh po filosofii i sotsiologii v 1968/69 uchebnom godu' ('On dissertations in philosophy and sociology for the 1968–9 academic year'), *Vop Fil*, no. 12, 1969.

AGANBEGIAN, A. G., OSIPOV, G. V., and SHUBKIN, V. N. (eds) *Kolichestvennye metody v sotsiologii* (*Quantitative Methods in Sociology*), Moscow, 1966.

AITOV, N. 'Na perekrestke mnenii: Gorod – proportsii razvitiia' ('At the crossroads of opinions: the city – proportions of development'), *Izvestiia*, 17 February 1972. Translated by the *CDSP*, vol. 24, no 7, 1972.

ALEKSANDROV, A. 'Slovo o sotsiologii' ('A word about sociology'), *Literaturnaia gazeta*, 21 April 1966. Translated by the *CDSP*, vol. 23, no. 17, 1966.

ALEKSANDROV, G. 'O nekotorykh zadachakh obshchestvennykh nauk v sovremennykh usloviiakh' ('On several tasks of the social sciences in contemporary conditions'), *Bol'shevik*, no. 14, 1945.

ANAN'EV, B. G., EL'MEEV, V. IA., and KERIMOV, D. A. (eds) *Chelovek i obshchestvo* (*Man and Society*), vol. 2, Leningrad, 1967.

ANAN'EV, B. G. and KERIMOV, D. A. (eds) *Chelovek i obshchestvo* (*Man and Society*), vol. 1, Leningrad, 1966; vol. 3, Leningrad, 1968; vol. 4, Leningrad, 1969; vol. 5, Leningrad, 1969; vol. 6: *Chelovek i obshchestvo: Sotsial'nye problemy molodezhi* (*Man and Society: Social Problems of Youth*), Leningrad, 1969.

ANAN'EV, B. G., KERIMOV, D. A., and PASHKOV, A. S. (eds) *Chelovek i obshchestvo: Problemy sotsial'nogo planirovaniia* (*Man and Society: Problems of Social Planning*), vol. 7, Leningrad, 1970.

ANAN'EV, B. G. and PASHKOV, A. S. 'Kompleksnoe issledovanie sotsial'nykh problem' ('Complex research of social problems'), *Chelovek i obshchestvo*, vol. 8, Leningrad, 1971.

ANAN'EV, B. G. and SPIRIDONOV, L. I. (eds) *Chelovek i obshchestvo: Problemy sotsializatsii individa (Man and Society: Problems of Socialization of the Individual)*, vol. 9, Leningrad, 1971.

ANDREEV, G. L., *et al.* 'Nauchnyi ateizm za 50 let' ('Scientific atheism for fifty years'), *Vop Fil*, no. 12, 1967.

ANDREEVA, G. M. 'Priemy i metody empiricheskikh issledovanii v sovremennoi burzhuaznoi sotsiologii' ('Modes and methods of empirical research in contemporary bourgeois sociology'), *Voprosy organizatsii i metodiki konkretno-sotsiologicheskikh issledovanii*, G. K. Ashin *et al.* (eds), Moscow, 1963.

——'Metodologicheskaia rol' teorii na raznykh etapakh sotsial'nogo issledovaniia' ('Methodological role of theory at different stages of social research'), *Vop Fil*, no. 7, 1964.

——*Sovremennaia burzhuaznaia empiricheskaia sotsiologiia: kriticheskii ocherk (Contemporary Bourgeois Empirical Sociology: Critical Essay)*, Moscow, 1965.

——'Metodologicheskie osnovy burzhuaznoi empiricheskoi sotsiologii' ('Methodological bases of bourgeois empirical sotsiology'), *Metodologicheskie voprosy obshchestvennykh nauk*, D. I. Chesnokov *et al.* (eds), Moscow, 1966.

——'O VI mezhdunarodnom kongresse sotsiologov' ('On the Sixth World Congress of Sociologists'), *Vestnik MGU*, no. 1, 1967.

——'O sootnoshenii mikro- i makrosotsiologii' ('About the correlation of micro- and macro-sociology'), *Vop Fil*, no. 7, 1970.

ANDREEVA, G. M. and NIKITIN, E. P. 'Metod ob''iasneniia v sotsiologii' ('Method of explanation in sociology'), *Sotsiologiia v SSSR*, vol. 1, G. V. Osipov (ed.), Moscow, 1966. Translated by *Soviet Sociology*, vol. 5, no. 1, 1966.

ANDRIANOV, N. 'Puti k istine: zametki ob ateisticheskoi propagande' ('Paths to truth: notes on atheist propaganda'), *Pravda*, 7 September 1970. Translated by the *CDSP*, vol. 22, no. 37, 1970.

'Antiobshchestvennye iavleniia, ikh prichiny i sredstva bor'bu s nimi' ('Anti-social phenomena, their causes and means of struggle with them'), *Kommunist*, no. 12, 1966. Translated by the *CDSP*, vol. 18, no. 36, 1966.

ANTOSENKOV, E. *Labour Turnover in USSR National Economy: Socio-economic Nature and Principles of Control*, Novosibirsk, 1970.

ANTOSENKOV, E. (ed.) *Opyt issledovaniia peremeny truda v promyshlennosti: po rezul'tatam ekonomicheskogo i sotsiologicheskogo obsledovaniia tekuchesti rabochikh kadrov (The Experience of Research on Labour Turnover in Industry: according to Results of an Economic and Sociological Enquiry into the Turnover of Working Cadres)*, Novosibirsk, 1969.

ANUFRIEVA, R. A. and VASILENKO, V. A. 'Sotsiologiia na Ukraine i ee perspektivy' ('Sociology in the Ukraine and its prospects'), *Vop Fil*, no. 9, 1967.

APTEKMAN, D. M. 'Prichiny zhivuchesti religioznogo obriada kreshcheniia v sovremennykh usloviiakh' ('Causes of the vitality of the ceremony of baptism under modern conditions'), *Vop Fil*, no. 3, 1965. Translated by *Soviet Sociology*, vol. 4, no. 2, 1965.

ARTEMOV, V. A. 'O nekotorykh metodakh analiza biudzhetov vremeni trudiashchikhsia' ('On several methods of analysis of working people's time budgets'), *Sotsiologicheskie issledovaniia: Voprosy metodologii i metodiki*, R. V. Ryvkina (ed.), Novosibirsk, 1966.

ARTEMOV, V. A., *et al. Statistika biudzhetov vremeni trudiashchikhsia (Statistics of Time Budgets of Working People)*, Moscow, 1967.

ARTEMOV, V. A. and KUTYREV, B. P. 'Biudzhet vremeni i sotsial'no-ekonomicheskoe planirovanie' ('Time budget and socio-economic planning'), *Fil Nauki*, no. 6, 1969.

ARUTIUNIAN, IU. V. 'Sotsial'naia struktura sel'skogo naseleniia' ('Social structure of the rural population'), *Vop Fil*, no. 5, 1966. Translated by the *CDSP*, vol. 18, no. 25, 1966.

——'Konkretno-sotsial'noe issledovanie sela' ('Concrete social research of the village'), *Vop Fil*, no. 10, 1966.

——*Opyt sotsiologicheskogo izucheniia sela (The Experience of a Sociological Study of the Village)*, Moscow, 1968.

——'Sotsial'nye aspekty kul'turnogo rosta sel'skogo naseleniia' ('Social aspects of the cultural growth of the rural population'), *Vop Fil*, no. 9, 1968.

——'Rural sociology' and 'Rural social structure', *Town, Country and People*, G. V. Osipov (ed.), London, 1969.

——*Sotsial'naia struktura sel'skogo naseleniia (Social Structure of the Rural Population)*, Moscow, 1971.

ASHIN, G. K., *et al.* (eds) *Voprosy organizatsii i metodiki konkretno-sotsiologicheskikh issledovanii (Questions of the Organization and Method of Concrete Sociological Research)*, Moscow, 1963.

BAIKOVA, V. G., DUCHAL, A. S., and ZEMTSOV, A. A. *Svobodnoe vremia i vsestoronnee razvitie lichnosti (Free Time and the All-round Development of the Individual)*, Moscow, 1965.

BASKIN, M. P. 'Krizis burzhuaznoi sotsiologii – otrazhenie degradatsii burzhuaznoi ideologii' ('Crisis of bourgeois sociology – a reflection of the degradation of bourgeois ideology'), *Sovremennaia burzhuaznaia sotsiologiia*, G. V. Osipov (ed.), Moscow, 1964.

BELIAEV, E. V., *et al.* 'Izuchenie biudzheta vremeni trudiashchikhsia kak odin iz metodov konkretno-sotsiologicheskogo issledovaniia' ('The study of the time budget of working people as one of the methods of concrete sociological research'), *Vestnik LGU*, no. 23, 1961. Translated by *Soviet Sociology*, vol. 1, no. 1, 1962.

——'Vsesoiuznyi simpozium sotsiologov' ('All-Union symposium of sociologists'), *Vop Fil*, no. 10, 1966.

BELOV, M. V. '*Voprosy filosofii* na Cherepovetskom metallurgicheskom zavode' ('*Voprosy filosofii* at Cherepovetsk metallurgical factory'), *Vop Fil*, no. 11, 1965.

BELYKH, O. V., *et al.* 'Ob opyte konkretnykh sotsial'nykh issledovanii' ('On the experience of concrete social research'), *Fil Nauki*, no. 3, 1966.

BESEDINA, V. and MAMONOVA, T. 'Sprosim nashikh muzhchin' ('We ask our men'), *Komsomol'skaia pravda*, 27 May 1966. Translated by the *CDSP*, vol. 18, no. 29, 1966.

BLAUBERG, I. V. and NAUMOVA, N. F. (eds) *Sotsial'nye issledovaniia: teoriia i metody* (*Social Research: Theory and Methods*), vol. 5, Moscow, 1970.

BOGOMOLOV, A. S. and PETROV, IU. A. 'O dissertatsionnykh rabotakh po filosofii v 1969–70 uchebnom godu' ('On dissertations in philosophy for the 1969–70 academic year'), *Vop Fil*, no. 1, 1971.

BOLGOV, V. I. 'Kategoriia vremeni v sotsial'nom izmerenii i planirovanii i problema ekonomii vremeni' ('The category of time in social measuring and planning and the problem of the economics of time'), *Sotsial'nye issledovaniia: problemy biudzheta vremeni trudiashchikhsia*, vol. 6, Moscow, 1970.

BOLGOV, V. I. (ed.) *Sotsial'nye issledovaniia: problemy biudzheta vremeni trudiashchikhsia*, vol. 6, Moscow, 1970.

BUKHARIN, NIKOLAI. *Historical Materialism: A System of Sociology*, New York, 1925.

CHAGIN, B. A. 'Razvitie sotsiologicheskoi mysli v SSSR v 20-e gody' ('Development of sociological thought in the USSR in the 1920s'), *Fil Nauki*, no. 5, 1967.

——*Ocherk istorii sotsiologicheskoi mysli v SSSR* (*Sketch of the History of Sociological Thought in the USSR*), Leningrad, 1971.

CHESNOKOV, D. I. *Istoricheskii materializm i sotsial'nye issledovaniia* (*Historical Materialism and Social Research*), Moscow, 1967.

CHESNOKOV, D. I., et al. (eds) *Metodologicheskie voprosy obshchestvennykh nauk* (*Methodological Questions of the Social Sciences*), Moscow, 1966.

DAGEL', P. S. 'Klassifikatsiia motivov prestupleniia i ee kriminologicheskoe znachenie' ('Classification of motives of crime and its criminological significance'), *Nekotorye voprosy sotsiologii i prava*, L. A. Petrov (ed.), Irkutsk, 1967.

'Diskussiia o marksistskom ponimanii sotsiologii' ('Discussion about the Marxist concept of sociology'), *Istorik marksist*, no. 12, 1929.

DOBRYNINA, V. I. (ed.) *Molodezh' i trud* (*Youth and Labour*), Moscow, 1970.

DYNNIK, M. A., et al. (eds) *Istoriia filosofii* (*History of Philosophy*), vol. 6, books one and two, Moscow, 1965.

ERUNOV, B. A. *Sila obshchestvennogo mneniia* (*The Force of Public Opinion*), Leningrad, 1964.

FEDOSEEV, P. N. 'Marksistskaia sotsiologiia, ee zadachi i perspektivy' ('Marxist sociology, its tasks and prospects'), *Vestnik AN SSSR*, no. 7, 1966.

——'Marksistskaia sotsiologiia i konkretnye sotsiologicheskie issledovaniia' ('Marxist sociology and concrete sociological research'), *Partiinaia zhizn'*, no. 20, 1967. Translated by the *CDSP*, vol. 19, no. 48, 1967.

——'Sotsiologicheskie issledovaniia v SSSR' ('Sociological research in the USSR'), *Sotsial'nye issledovaniia*, vol. 2, Moscow, 1968.

FILIMONOV, E. G. 'Problemy konkretno-sotsiologicheskikh issledovanii religioznosti v sovetskoi literature (1961–66)' ('Problems of concrete sociological research of religiosity in Soviet literature: 1961–6'), *Konkretnye issledovaniia sovremennykh religioznykh verovanii*, A. I. Klibanov et al. (eds), Moscow, 1967.

FISCHER, GEORGE. 'Sociology', *Science and Ideology in Soviet Society*, G. Fischer (ed.), New York, 1967.

FROLIC, B. MICHAEL. 'The Soviet study of Soviet cities', *Journal of Politics*, vol. 32, no. 3, 1970.

FURMAN, D. E. 'Diskussiia o strukture marksistskoi sotsiologicheskoi teorii' ('A discussion about the structure of Marxist sociological theory'), *Vestnik MGU*, no. 5, 1968.

GLEZERMAN, G. E. and AFANAS'EV, V. G. (eds) *Opyt i metodika konkretnykh sotsiologicheskikh issledovanii* (*The Experience and System of Rules of Concrete Sociological Research*), Moscow, 1965.

GORDON, L. and LEVIN, B. 'Nekotorye sotsial'no-bytovye posledstviia piatidnevki v bol'shikh i malykh gorodakh' ('Several socio-*byt* consequences of the five-day week in large and small cities'), *Voprosy ekonomiki*, no. 4, 1968. Translated by *Soviet Sociology*, vol. 7, no. 4, 1969.

GREMIAKO, L. L., EL'MEEV, V. IA., and KERIMOV, D. A. 'Institut sotsial'nykh issledovanii' ('Institute of social research'), *Vop Fil*, no. 8, 1966.

GRUSHIN, B. A. 'Institut obshchestvennogo mneniia *Komsomol'skoi pravdy*' ('*Komsomol'skaia pravda*'s Public Opinion Institute'), *Voprosy organizatsii i metodika konkretno-sotsiologicheskikh issledovanii*, G. K. Ashin *et al.* (eds), Moscow, 1963.

——'K probleme kachestvennoi reprezentatsii v vyborochnom orposc' ('To the problem of qualitative representation in questionnaires'), *Opyt i metodika konkretnykh sotsiologicheskikh issledovanii*, G. E. Glezerman and V. G. Afanas'ev (eds), Moscow, 1965.

——'Sotsiologiia i sotsiologi' ('Sociology and sociologists'), *Literaturnaia gazeta*, 25 September 1965. Translated in the *CDSP*, vol. 17, no. 40, 1965.

——*Svobodnoe vremia: Aktual'nye problemy* (*Free Time: Actual Problems*), Moscow, 1967.

——*Mneniia o mire i mir mnenii* (*Opinion about the World and the World of Opinion*), Moscow, 1967.

GRUSHIN, B. and CHIKIN, V. *Ispoved' pokoleniia* (*Confession of a generation*), Moscow, 1962.

HECKER, JULIUS F. *Russian Sociology: A Contribution to the History of Sociological Thought and Theory*, London, 1934.

IABLOKOV, I. N. 'Ob opyte konkretnogo issledovaniia religioznosti' ('On the experience of concrete research of religiosity'), *Vestnik MGU*, no. 4, 1967.

IADOV, V. A. 'O chem govorit opyt organizatsii i provedeniia konkretnykh sotsial'nykh issledovanii v Leningrade' ('What the experience of the organization and execution of concrete social research in Leningrad indicates'), *Fil Nauki*, no. 2, 1965. Translated by the *CDSP*, vol. 17, no. 31, 1965.

——'Sotsiologiia: Problemy i fakty: Otvetstvennost' ' ('Sociology: problems and facts: responsibility'), *Literaturnaia gazeta*, 12 November 1966. Translated by the *CDSP*, vol. 18, no. 48, 1966.

——'Ob ustanovlenii faktov v konkretnom sotsiologicheskom issledovanii' ('On ascertaining facts in concrete sociological research'), *Fil Nauki*, no. 5, 1966.

——'Rol' metodologii v opredelenii metodov i tekhniki konkretnogo sotsiologicheskogo issledovaniia' ('The role of methodology in determining methods and techniques of concrete sociological research'), *Vop Fil*, no. 10, 1966.

——*Metodologiia i protsedury sotsiologicheskikh issledovanii (Methodology and Procedures of Sociological Research)*, Tartu, 1968.

IANKOVA, Z. 'O bytovykh roliakh rabotaiushchei zhenshchiny (k probleme osushchestvleniia fakticheskogo ravenstva zhenshchiny s muzhchinoi)' ('About domestic roles of working women: to the problem of the realization of factual equality of women with men'), *Problemy byta, braka i sem'i*, N. Solov'ev, Iu. Lazauskas and Z. Iankova (eds), Vil'nius, 1970.

IANOV, A. 'Vremia vzroslet' ' ('Time to mature'), *Komsomol'skaia pravda*, 2 June 1967. Translated by the *CDSP*, vol. 19, no. 25, 1967.

IGITKHANIAN, M. KH. 'Dukhovnyi oblik sovetskoi molodezhi' ('The spiritual image of Soviet youth'), *Vop Fil*, no. 6, 1963. Translated by the *CDSP*, vol. 15, no. 39, 1963.

IKONNIKOVA, S. N. and LISOVSKII, V. T. *Molodezh' o sebe, o svoikh sverstnikakh (Youth about Itself, about its Coevals)*, Leningrad, 1969.

IOVCHUK, M. T. 'Mezhdunarodnyi forum sotsiologov' (International forum of sociologists'), *Vestnik AN SSSR*, no. 2, 1967.

IOVCHUK, M. T., *et al.* (eds) *Marksistsko-leninskaia filosofiia i sotsiologiia v SSSR i evropeiskikh sotsialisticheskikh stranakh (Marxist-Leninist Philosophy and Sociology in the USSR and European Socialist Countries)*, Moscow, 1965.

IURKEVICH, N. G. *Sovetskaia sem'ia: Funktsii i usloviia stabil'nosti (The Soviet Family: Functions and Conditions of Stability)*, Minsk, 1970.

K., IU. 'V statisticheskoi sektsili Moskovskogo doma uchenykh' ('In the statistical section of the Moscow House of Scholars'), *Vestnik statistiki*, no. 6, 1961.

KACHALEVSKII, E. 'Esli videt' perspektivu: partiinaia zhizn' ' ('If one sees the long-range perspective: party life'), *Pravda*, 6 December 1971. Translated by the *CDSP*, vol. 23, no. 49, 1971.

KANTOROVICH, V. 'Rodstvennaia nam nauka' ('A science kindred to us'), *Literaturnaia gazeta*, 5 May 1966 and 14 May 1966. Translated by the *CDSP*, vol. 18, no. 26, 1966.

——'Sotsiologiia i literatura' ('Sociology and literature'), *Novyi mir*, no. 12, 1967.

KAPELIUSH, IA. S. and PRIGOZHIN, A. I. 'Sobranie sovetskoi sotsiologicheskoi assotsiatsii' ('Meeting of the Soviet Sociological Association'), *Vop Fil*, no. 6, 1966.

KASIUKOV, I. and MENDELEEV, A. 'Nuzhen li talant sem'ianinu?' ('Must a family man have talent?'), *Nedelia*, no. 12, 1967. Translated by the *CDSP*, vol. 19, no. 13, 1967.

KELLE, V. ZH. 'O nekotorykh napravleniiakh razvitiia istoricheskogo materializma' ('On several directions of the development of historical materialism'), *Vop Fil*, no. 10, 1967.

KHARCHEV, A. G. 'O nekotorykh razultatakh issledovaniia motivov braka v SSSR' ('On several results of research on motives for marriage in the

USSR'), *Fil Nauki*, no. 4, 1963. Translated by *Soviet Review*, vol. 5, no. 2, 1964.

——'Sotsiologicheskie issledovaniia v Pol'she' ('Sociological research in Poland'), *Vop Fil*, no. 6, 1963.

——*Brak i sem'ia v SSSR* (*Marriage and the Family in the USSR*), Moscow, 1964.

——'Marriage motivation studies', *Town, Country and People*, G. V. Osipov (ed.), London, 1969.

KHOREV, B. 'Kakoi gorod nuzhen?' ('What kind of city is needed?'), *Literaturnaia gazeta*, 2 April 1969. Translated by the *CDSP*, vol. 21, no. 14, 1969.

KHVOSTOV, V. M. *Osnovy sotsiologii. Uchenie o zakonomernosti obshchestvennykh protsessov* (*The Bases of Sociology. A Study of the 'zakonomernosti' of Social Processes*), Moscow, 1920.

KIM, V. V. and LIUBUTIN, K. N. 'Razvitie filosofskikh issledovanii v Sverdlovske' ('Development of philosophical research in Sverdlovsk'), *Fil Nauki*, no. 6, 1967.

KIRILLOVA, M. A. and PANKRATOVA, M. G. 'Simpozium sotsiologov po issledovaniiu problem sem'i i byta' ('Symposium of sociologists on the study of the problems of the family and *byt*'), *Fil Nauki*, no. 4, 1967.

KLIBANOV, A. I. 'Piat'desiat let nauchnogo issledovaniia religioznogo sektantstva' ('Fifty years of scientific study of religious sectarianism'), *Voprosy nauchnogo ateizma*, no. 4, Moscow, 1967. Translated by *Soviet Sociology*, vol. 8, no. 3–4, 1970.

KLOPOV, E. V. 'Biudzhet vremeni i sotsial'noe planirovanie' ('Time budget and social planning'), *Vop Fil*, no. 9, 1969.

KLUSHIN, V. I. 'Sotsiologiia v Petrogradskom universitete (1920–24)' ('Sociology in Petrograd University – 1920–4'), *Vestnik LGU*, no. 5, 1964.

——*Bor'ba za istoricheskii materializm v Leningradskom gosudarstvennom universitete* (*1918–25 gody*) (*The Fight for Historical Materialism in Leningrad State University – 1918–25*), Leningrad, 1970.

KOGAN, L. N., (ed.) *Molodezh', ee interesy, stremleniia, idealy* (*Youth, its Interests, Aspirations, Ideals*), Moscow, 1969.

KOGAN, L. N. and LOKTEV, V. I. 'Sociological aspects of the modelling of towns', *Town, Country and People*, G. V. Osipov (ed.), London, 1969.

KOLBANOVSKII, V. V. and SLESAREV, G. A. 'Obshchee sobranie sovetskoi sotsiologicheskoi assotsiatsii' ('General meeting of the Soviet Sociological Association'), *Vop Fil*, no. 5, 1961.

KOLPAKOV, B. T. and PATRUSHEV, V. D. *Biudzhet vremeni gorodskogo naseleniia* (*Time Budget of the Urban Population*), Moscow, 1971.

KOLPAKOV, B. and PRUDENSKII, G. 'Opyt izmereniia vnerabochego vremeni trudiashchikhsia' ('The experience of the measurement of working people's non-working time'), *Voprosy ekonomiki*, no. 9, 1964.

Komsomol'skaia pravda: Polls listed in chronological order, by topic:

Peace and war
'Institut obshchestvennogo mneniia *Komsomol'skoi pravdy*' ('*Komsomol'-skaia pravda*'s Public Opinion Institute'), 19 May 1960.
'Udastsia li chelovechestvu predotvratit' voinu? Da! otvechaet tridtsatyi

meridian' ('Will mankind succeed in preventing war? Yes! answered the thirtieth meridian'), 19 May 1960.
How has your standard of living changed?
'Kak izmenilsia uroven' vashei zhizni?' ('How has your standard of living changed?'), 7 October 1960.
Grushin, B. and Chikin, V. 'O chem rasskazali ankety' ('What the questionnaires tell'), 7 October 1960.
What do you think about your generation?
'Chto vy dumaete o svoem pokolenii?' ('What do you think about your generation?'), 6 January 1961; 11 January 1961.
'Molodoe pokolenie o samom sebe' ('The young generation about itself'), 26 January 1961.
Grushin, B. and Chikin, V. 'Ispoved' pokoleniia' ('Confessions of a generation'), 21 July 1961; 22 July 1961.
Scouts of the future
'Chto vy dumaete o razvedchikakh budushchego?' ('What do you think about the scouts of the future?'), 16 August 1961; 23 August 1961; 30 August 1961; 23 September 1961.
Grushin, B. and Chikin, V. 'Razvedka i nastuplenie' ('Reconnaissance and attack'), 14 September 1962.
What is your opinion about the young family?
'Vashe mnenie o molodoi sem'e?' ('What is your opinion about the young family?'), 10 December 1961; 17 December 1961; 24 December 1961; 6 January 1962.
Verza, Olga 'The twelve problems of a young family', *Moscow News*, 1 February 1964.
Grushin, B. ' "Poeziia" i "proza" semeinoi zhizni' ('The poetry and prose of family life'), 9 July 1964.
Moscow University students
'My razdvinem granitsy poznaniia' ('We are extending the boundaries of understanding'), 1 September 1962.
How do you spend your free time?
'Kak vy provodite svobodnoe vremia?' ('How do you spend your free time?'), 4 January 1963; 11 January 1963; 20 January 1963.
'Zhit' nel'zia "prosto – naprosto" ' ('It is simply impossible to live!'), 25 January 1963.
Shalaev, A. 'Prizvanie – grazhdanin' ('A vocation – citizen'), 17 February 1963.
Gromova, T. 'A poka zhdu . . .' ('I'm still waiting'), 27 March 1963.
Dolinina, N. 'Kogda uchitel' smotrit na chasy' ('When a teacher looks at his watch'), 26 May 1963.
Peremyslov, A. 'Kommuny doma prorastaiut' ('Communal house projects get bigger and bigger'), 7 June 1963.
Polianichko, V. 'Prikhodite v dom schastlivykh' ('Come to the house of the lucky ones'), 21 August 1963.
Egorov, A. 'Podnimite perchatku, Il'ia Il'ich!' ('Pick up the gauntlet, Il'ia Il'ich!'), 24 November 1963.
Gromova, T. and Ronina, G. 'Kogda vremia zaniato nami' ('When we are busy'), 27 December 1963.

'Iskusstvo zhit' – v imenii tsenit' vremia' ('The art of living – is the ability to value time'), 8 January 1964.

'Tol'ko vpered, za begushchim dnem!' ('Ever onwards, day by day!'), 30 January 1964.

Gromova, T. and Ronina, G. 'Starsheklassnik posle urokov' ('Senior pupils after class'), 18 June 1965.

Grushin, B. 'Kak vy provodite svobodnoe vremia?' ('How do you spend your free time?'), 24 February 1966; 25 February 1966; 26 February 1966.

To Mars, with what?
'Na Mars – s chem?' ('To Mars, with what?'), 1 March 1963; 17 March 1963; 12 April 1963.

'Oktiabr' kosmos mir' ('The October Revolution, the cosmos and peace'), 18 June 1963.

Oganov, B. and Chikin, V. 'O vremeni i o sebe' ('About time and about oneself'), 20 October 1963; 22 October 1963; 23 October 1963; 24 October 1963.

Let's project – televisions, radios, etc.
'Proektiruem sami' ('Let's project'), 26 June 1964; 10 July 1964; 28 October 1964.

An innovation demands a name
'Novinka prosit im'ia' ('An innovation demands a name'), 28 October 1964; 13 November 1964.

'Novinka – luchshee im'ia' ('Innovation – the best name'), 12 November 1965.

Children and words
'1000 detei o piatidesiati slovakh' ('1000 children on fifty words'), 2 August 1964.

Kassil', Lev. 'Ikh glazami' ('Through their eyes'), 2 August 1964.

Gromova, T. and Ronina, G. 'Ot deviati do desiati . . .' ('From nine to ten'), 2 August 1964.

——'Otnesemsia ser'ezno!' ('Let's treat it seriously!'), 2 August 1964.

Service industries
'Khorosho li vas obsluzhivaiut?' ('How do you rate the service industries?'), 20 November 1964.

Kliamkin, I. 'Motor torgovli' ('Motive force of trade'), 7 January 1965.

Il'ina, N. 'Ushla na bazu, tseluiu, obnimaiu . . .' ('I went to the store, I kiss and embrace . . .'), 19 February 1965.

Tsipis, Ia. and Tishchenkov, E. 'Mashina izuchaet spros' ('The machine studies the demand'), 27 February 1965.

'Kakoi nam nuzhen servis' ('What kind of service do we need?'), 27 February 1965.

Iun', O. 'I liubo, o . . . dorogo' ('It's a real pleasure, but so dear!'), 30 March 1965.

'346 interv'iu v prilavke' ('346 interviews at the counter'), 21 April 1965.

Struev, A. I. '10 voprosov o prilavke' ('10 questions about the counter'), 14 December 1965.

Tarasov, N. N. 'Na vkus, na tsvet i po neobkhodimosti' ('To taste, to colour, and according to necessity'), 5 January 1966.

Artem'ev, S. P. 'I mechty na dorogakh' ('With all we do, let's not forget our dreams'), 27 January 1966.
Komsomol members about the komsomol
Grushin, B. 'Komsomol'tsy o komsomole' ('Komsomol members about the komsomol'), 26 April 1966.
'Komsomol'tsy o komsomole' ('Komsomol members about the komsomol'), 17 May 1966.
Ronina, G. 'Slishkom malo znaiu . . .' ('I know too little'), 13 September 1966.
Holidays – how can you best spend them and how would you like to spend them?
'Vremia otpuskov. Kak luchshe provesti ego?' ('Holiday time – how can you best spend it?'), 23 June 1966; 30 June 1966; 8 July 1966; 20 July 1966.
'Kak vy khotite provesti svoi otpusk?' ('How would you like to spend your holiday?'), 29 July 1966.
'V zime svoe ocharovanie' ('Winter too has its charm'), 22 September 1966.
Shelomov, N. 'Industriia otdykha' ('The industry of leisure'), 27 September 1966.
'Otdykh – zdorov'e – trud' ('Leisure, health, labour'), 23 November 1966.
Komsomol'skaia pravda reader about himself and the newspaper
'Chitatel' o sebe i o gazete' ('The reader about himself and about the newspaper'), 12 October 1966.
Naming children
'Piat' voprosov papam i mamam' ('Five questions for fathers and mothers'), 10 September 1967; 17 September 1967; 29 September 1967.
'Kak vybiraiut imena' ('How names are chosen'), 31 December 1967.
KON, I. S. 'O rabote sotsiologicheskogo seminara' ('On the work of the sociology seminar'), *Vestnik LGU*, no. 1, 1960. Translated by the *Soviet Review*, vol. 1, no. 1, 1960.
——'Tsennoe issledovanie' ('Valuable research'), *Fil Nauki*, no. 1, 1965. Translated by the *CDSP*, vol. 17, no. 19, 1965.
KON, I. S. and IADOV, V. A. 'Na VI vsemirnom sotsiologicheskom kongresse' ('At the Sixth World Congress of Sociology'), *Fil Nauki*, no. 1, 1967.
KONSTANTINOV, F. 'Voprosy teorii: Filosofiia revoliutsionnoi epokhi' ('Questions of theory: philosophy of the revolutionary epoch'), *Pravda*, 24 July 1967. Translated by the *CDSP*, vol. 19, no. 30, 1967.
KONSTANTINOV, F. and KELLE, V. 'Istoricheskii materializm – marksistkaia sotsiologiia' ('Historical materialism – Marxist sociology'), *Kommunist*, no. 1, 1965. Translated by the *CDSP*, vol. 17, no. 8, 1965.
KONSTANTINOV, F. and KELLE, V. *Istoricheskii materializm – marksistkaia sotsiologiia* (*Historical Materialism – Marxist Sociology*), Moscow, 1965.
KONSTANTINOV, F. V., OSIPOV, G. V., and SEMENOV, V. S., (eds) *Marksistkaia i burzhuaznaia sotsiologiia segodnia* (*Marxist and Bourgeois Sociology Today*), Moscow, 1964.
KOSOLAPOV, R. I. and SIMUSH, P. I. 'Partiinaia rabota i konkretnye sotsiologicheskie issledovaniia' ('Party work and concrete sociological research'), *Ideologicheskaia rabota partiinykh organizatsii*, A. M. Korolev and S. I. Mosiagin (eds), Moscow, 1969.

KOVALEV, A. M. 'Eshche raz o sotsiologii marksizma i nauchnom kommunizme' ('Once more about the sociology of Marxism and scientific communism'), *Fil Nauki*, no. 1, 1967.

——'O sootnoshenii istoricheskogo materializma, nauchnogo kommunizma i konkretnykh issledovanii' ('About the correlation of historical materialism, scientific communism and concrete research'), *Vestnik MGU*, no. 2, 1969.

KOVALEV, S. 'Voprosy teorii: Trebovaniia zhizni i obshchestvennye nauki' ('Questions of theory: Life's demands and the social sciences'), *Pravda*, 6 May 1966. Translated by the *CDSP*, vol. 18, no. 18, 1966.

KOVALEVSKII, M. M. 'Sotsiologiia na zapade i v Rossii' ('Sociology in the West and in Russia'), *Novye idei v sotsiologii*, vol. 1, M. M. Kovalevskii and E. V. deRoberty (eds), St Petersburg, 1913.

KOVALEVSKII, M. M. and DEROBERTY, E. V. *Novye idei v sotsiologii* (*New Ideas in Sociology*), vols 1 to 4, St Petersburg, 1913–14.

KOZLOVSKII, V. E. and SYCHEV, IU. A. 'Obsuzhdenie kursa lektsii Iu. A. Levady po sotsiologii' ('Discussion of the lecture course by Iu. A. Levada on sociology'), *Fil Nauki*, no. 3, 1970.

KRAVCHENKO, I. I. and FADDEEV, E. T. 'O sotsial'noi strukture sovetskogo obshchestva' ('On the social structure of Soviet society'), *Vop Fil*, no. 5, 1966.

KRAVCHENKO, I. I. and TRUBITSYN, O. N. 'Problemy izmeniia sotsial'noi struktury sovetskogo obshchestva' ('Problems of the change of the social structure of Soviet society'), *Vop Fil*, no. 6, 1972.

KUDRIAVTSEV, V. 'Analiz plius tekhnika' ('Analysis plus technique'), *Izvestiia*, 30 September 1966. Translated by the *CDSP*, vol. 18, no. 39, 1966.

——'Prestupnost': Sootnoshenie sotsial'nogo i biologicheskogo: dano li pri rozhdenii?' (Crime: Correlation of the social and the biological: Are you born with it?'), *Literaturnaia gazeta*, 29 November 1967. Translated by the *CDSP*, vol. 19, no. 49, 1967.

——*Prichinnost' v kriminologii* (*Crime in Criminology*), Moscow, 1968.

——'Problemy prichinnosti v kriminologii' ('Problems of crime in criminology'), *Vop Fil*, no. 10, 1971.

KUGEL', S. A. 'Izmenenie sotsial'noi struktury sotsialisticheskogo obshchestva pod vozdeistviem nauchno-tekhnicheskoi revoliutsii' ('Change of the social structure of socialist society under the influence of the scientific-technical revolution'), *Vop Fil*, no. 3, 1969.

KURYLOV, A. K., SMOL'KOV, V. G., and SHTRAKS, G. M., (eds) *Iz opyta konkretnykh sotsiologicheskikh issledovanii* (*From the Experience of Concrete Sociological Research*), Moscow, 1969.

LAZUTKIN, E. S. 'Ekonomiko-sotsiologicheskie issledovaniia' ('Economic and sociological research'), *Vop Fil*, no. 3, 1966.

LEONT'EV, L. 'Sotsiologiia i ekonomicheskaia nauka' ('Sociology and economics'), *Literaturnaia gazeta*, 26 May 1966. Translated by the *CDSP*, vol. 18, no. 26, 1966.

LEVADA, IU. A. 'Lektsii po sotsiologii' ('Lectures on sociology'), *Informatsionnyi biulleten' nauchnogo soveta AN SSSR po problemam konkretnykh sotsial'nykh issledovanii*, nos 20–1, Moscow, 1969.

161

M

LEVINA, E. and SYRINA, E. 'Razmyshleniia o mikroraione' ('Reflections on the microdistrict'), *Zvezda*, no. 10, 1966. Translated by the *CDSP*, vol. 19, no. 3, 1967.

LISAVTSEV, E., MASLIN, V., and OVCHINNIKOV, N. 'Na nauchnoi osnove – sotsial'nye issledovaniia v praktiku partiinoi raboty' ('On a scientific basis – social research applied to party work'), *Pravda*, 11 May 1965. Translated by the *CDSP*, vol. 17, no. 19, 1965.

Liste des Participants, Supplément II du Bulletin d'Information no. 3 (Sixième Congrès mondial de sociologie), Geneva, 1966.

LOPATKIN, P. A. and POPOVA, M. A. 'Problemy psikhologii religii' ('Problems of the psychology of religion'), *Vop Fil*, no. 7, 1969.

LUPPOL, I. 'Filosofiia v SSSR za desiat' let' ('Philosophy in the USSR for ten years'), *Obshchestvennye nauki SSSR* (1917–27), by V. P. Volgin, G. O. Gordon, and I. K. Luppol, Moscow, 1928.

MAKHA, K. and STRINKA, IU. 'Filosofskie publikatsii v Chekhoslovakii v 1960–63 godakh' ('Philosophical publications in Czechoslovakia in 1960–3'), *Vop Fil*, no. 1, 1965.

MALIN, B. N. 'Za nauchnyi podkhod k partiino-ideologicheskoi rabote' ('For a scientific approach to party-ideological work'), *Problemy nauchnogo kommunizma*, no. 2, Moscow, 1968.

MASLOV, P. P. 'Modelirovanie v sotsiologicheskikh issledovaniakh' ('Modelling in sociological research'), *Vop Fil*, no. 3, 1962.

MELESHCHENKO, IU. S., SMIRNOV, IU. P., and KHARCHEV, A. G. 'Sotsiologicheskie issledovaniia i partiinaia rabota' ('Sociological research and party work'), *Chelovek i obshchestvo*, vol. 3, Leningrad, 1968.

MIKHAILOV, V. and PEREVEDENTSEV, V. 'Bol'shie ozhidaniia' ('Great expectations'), *Literaturnaia gazeta*, 14 June 1967. Translated by the *CDSP*, vol. 19, no. 25, 1967.

MINDLIN, I. 'Staroe v novom' ('The old in the new'), *Novyi mir*, no. 12, 1964. Translated by the *CDSP*, vol. 17, no. 8, 1965.

MIN'KOVSKII, G. M. 'Nekotorye prichiny prestupnosti nesovershennoletnikh v SSSR i mery ee preduprezhdeniia' ('Some causes of juvenile delinquency in the USSR and measures to prevent it'), *Sovetskoe gosudarstvo i pravo*, no. 5, 1966. Translated by the *CDSP*, vol. 18, no. 30, 1966.

MITROKHIN, L. N. 'Methods of research into religion', *Town, Country and People*, G. V. Osipov (ed.), London, 1969.

MSHVENIERADZE, V. V. and OSIPOV, G. V. 'Osnovnye napravleniia i problematika konkretnykh sotsial'nykh issledovanii' ('The basic trends and problems of concrete social research'), *Sotsiologiia v SSSR*, vol. 1, G. V. Osipov (ed.), Moscow, 1966. Translated by *Soviet Sociology*, vol. 5, no. 1, 1966.

NARSKII, I. S. 'Ob istoricheskom materializme kak marksistskoi sotsiologii' ('On historical materialism as Marxist sociology'), *Vop Fil*, no. 4, 1959.

NAUMOVA, N. F. 'Sotsiologiia truda, ee uspekha i problemy' ('Sociology of labour, its successes and problems'), *Vop Fil*, no. 7, 1968.

——'Nravstvennye antinomii sovremennoi burzhuaznoi sotsiologii' ('Moral antimony of contemporary bourgeois sociology'), *Vop Fil*, no. 2, 1970.

NOVIKOV, N. V. *Kritika sovremennoi burzhuaznoi 'Nauki o sotsial'nom povedenii'* (*Critique of Contemporary Bourgeois 'Science of Social Behaviour'*), Moscow, 1966.

NOVIKOV, N. V., OSIPOV, G. V., and IANKOVA, Z. A. (eds) *Sotsial'nye issledovaniia* (*Social Research*), vol. 2, Moscow, 1968.

NOVIKOV, N. V., OSIPOV, G. V., and SLESAREV, G. A. (eds) *Sotsial'nye issledovaniia* (*Social Research*), vol. 1, Moscow, 1965.

'*O lektsiakh po sotsiologii* Iu. A. Levady' ('On *Lectures on Sociology* by Iu. A. Levada'), *Vestnik MGU: seriia filosofiia*, no. 3, 1970.

'O sozdanii Sovetskoi sotsiologicheskoi assotsiatsii' ('On the creation of the Soviet Sociological Association'), *Vop Fil*, no. 8, 1958.

OKULOV, A. F., *et al.* (eds) *Voprosy nauchnogo ateizma: pobedy nauchno-ateisticheskogo mirovozzreniia v SSSR za 50 let* (*Questions of Scientific Atheism: Victories of a Scientific Atheist World-view in the USSR for fifty years*), no. 4, Moscow, 1967.

OSIPOV, G. V. 'Nekotorye cherty i osobennosti burzhuaznoi sotsiologii' ('Several characteristics and features of bourgeois sociology'), *Vop Fil*, no. 8, 1962. Translated by the *CDSP*, vol. 14, no. 42, 1962.

——*Sovremennaia burzhuaznaia sotsiologiia* (*Contemporary Bourgeois Sociology*), Moscow, 1964.

——'Teoriia i praktika sovetskoi sotsiologii' ('Theory and practice of Soviet sociology'), *Sotsial'nye issledovaniia: teoriia i metody*, vol. 5, Moscow, 1970.

——(ed.) *Sotsiologiia v SSSR* (*Sociology in the USSR*), vols. 1 and 2, Moscow, 1966.

——(ed.) *Industry and Labour in the USSR*, London, 1966.

——'Sotsiologiia kak nauka' ('Sociology as a science'), *Sotsial'nye issledovaniia*, vol. 2, Moscow, 1968.

——(ed.) *Town, Country and People*, London, 1969.

OSIPOV, G. V., *et al.* (eds) *Rabochii klass i tekhnicheskii progress: Issledovanie izmenenii v sotsial'noi strukture rabochego klassa* (*The Working Class and Technical Progress: Research on the Change in the Social Structure of the Working Class*), Moscow, 1965.

OSIPOV, G. V., KHARCHEV, A. G., and IANKOVA, Z. A. (eds) *Sotsial'nye issledovaniia: problemy braka, sem'i i demografii* (*Social Research: Problems of Marriage, the Family and Demography*), vol. 4, Moscow, 1970.

OSIPOV, G. V. and SZCZEPANSKI, IA. (eds) *Sotsial'nye problemy truda i proizvodstva* (*Social Problems of Labour and Production*), Moscow, 1969.

OSIPOV, G. V., ZIMANOV, S. Z., and SALIEV, A. 'Plany filosofskikh i sotsiologicheskikh issledovanii' ('Plans of philosophical and sociological research'), *Vop Fil*, no. 2, 1969.

OSTROUMOV, S. S. and CHUGUNOV, V. E. 'Izuchenie lichnosti prestupnika po materialam kriminologicheskikh issledovanii' ('Study of the criminal personality from materials of criminological research'), *Sovetskoe gosudarstvo i pravo*, no. 9, 1965. Translated by the *Soviet Review*, vol. 7, no. 2, 1966.

OVCHINNIKOV, B. D. 'Sootnoshenie sotsial'nogo i biologicheskogo v sviazi s problemoi prestupnosti' ('The correlation of the social and the biological in connection with the problem of crime'), *Vestnik LGU*, no. 23, 1969.

OVSIANNIKOV, M. F. and PETROV, IU. A. 'O sostoinaii dissertatsionnoi raboty po filosofii v 1964–65 uchebnom godu' ('On the state of dissertations in philosophy in the 1964–5 academic year'), *Vop Fil*, no. 2, 1966.

——'O dissertatsionnoi rabote po filosofii v 1965–66 uchebnom godu' ('On dissertations in philosophy in the 1965–6 academic year'), *Vop Fil*, no. 1, 1967.

——'O dissertatsionnoi rabote po filosofii v 1966–67 uchebnom godu' ('On dissertations in philosophy in the 1966–7 academic year'), *Vop Fil*, no. 11, 1967.

PASHKOV, A. S. (ed.) *Chelovek i obshchestvo* (*Man and Society*), vol. 8, Leningrad, 1971.

PATRUSHEV, V. D. 'Ob izuchenii biudzheta vremeni trudiashchikhsia' ('On the study of working people's time budgets'), *Vestnik statistiki*, no. 11, 1966. Translated by *Soviet Sociology*, vol. 1, no. 1, 1962.

——'Biudzhet vremeni gorodskogo naseleniia sotsialisticheskikh i kapitalisticheskikh stran' ('Time budgets of the urban population of socialist and capitalist countries'), *Fil Nauki*, no. 5, 1968.

——'O prakticheskom ispol'zovanii dannykh biudzhetov vremeni' ('On the practical use of time budget data'), *Sotsial'nye issledovaniia: Problemy biudzheta vremeni trudiashchikhsia*, vol. 6, Moscow, 1970.

PAWEŁCZYNSKA, ANNA. 'Principles and problems of public opinion research in Poland', *Empirical Sociology in Poland*, J. Szczepanski (ed.), Warsaw, 1966.

PCHELINTSEV, O. S. 'Problemy razvitiia bol'shikh gorodov' ('Problems of the development of large cities'), *Sotsiologiia v SSSR*, vol. 2, G. V. Osipov (ed.), Moscow, 1966. Translated by the *Soviet Review*, vol. 7, no. 4, 1966–7.

PEREVEDENTSEV, V. I. *Migratsiia naseleniia i trudovye problemy Sibiri* (*Migration of the Population and Labour Problems in Siberia*), Novosibirsk, 1966. Translated by *Soviet Sociology*, beginning with vol. 7, no. 3, 1968–9.

——*Narodonaselenie i ekonomika* (*Human Population and the Economic System*), Moscow, 1967.

——'Spornoe mnenie: Goroda i gody' ('Controversial opinion: cities and years'), *Literaturnaia gazeta*, 26 February 1969. Translated by the *CDSP*, vol. 21, no. 9, 1969.

——'Migratsiia naseleniia i ispol'zovanie trudovykh resursov' ('Population migration and the use of labour resources'), *Voprosy ekonomiki*, no. 9, 1970. Translated by *Problems of Economics*, vol. 13, no. 11, 1971.

PETROSIAN, G. S. *Vnerabochee vremia trudiashchikhsia v SSSR* (*Non-working Time of Working People in the USSR*), Moscow, 1965.

——'Natsional'no-etnograficheskie razlichiia, osobennosti byta i vnerabochee vremia trudiashchikhsia' ('National-ethnographic differences, features of *byt* and non-working time of working people'), *Fil Nauki*, no. 2, 1969.

PIMENOVA, A. L. 'Sem'ia i perspektivy razvitiia obshchestvennogo truda zhenshchin pri sotsializme' ('The family and the prospects of the development of women's social labour under socialism'), *Fil Nauki*, no. 3, 1966.

POPOVA, I. M. 'Mesto i rol' sotsial'noi psikhologii v Amerikanskoi sotsiologii' ('The place and role of social psychology in American sociology'), *Vestnik MGU*, no. 5, 1960. Translated by the *Soviet Review*, vol. 2, no. 8, 1961.

POTAENKO, K. L. and TSEGOEVA, M. L. 'Izmeneniia sotsial'noi struktury sovetskogo obshchestva' ('Change in the social structure of Soviet society'), *Fil Nauki*, no. 3, 1966.

PRIGOZHIN, A. I. 'Metodologicheskie problemy issledovaniia obshchestvennogo mneniia' ('Methodological problems of public opinion research'), *Vop Fil*, no. 2, 1969.

PROVOTOROV, V. A. 'Obsuzhdenie problem sotsial'noi struktury obshchestva' ('Discussion of the problems of social structure'), *Fil Nauki*, no. 1, 1966.

——'Sotsiologicheskie issledovaniia v partiinoi rabote' ('Sociological research in party work'), *Partiinaia zhizn'*, no. 19, 1967.

PRUDENSKII, G. A. (ed.) *Vnerabochee vremia trudiashchikhsia (Non-working Time of Working People)*, Novosibirsk, 1961.

RACHKOV, P. A., UGRINOVICH, D. M., and ULEDOV, A. K. (eds) *O strukture marksistskoi sotsiologicheskoi teorii (About the Structure of Marxist Sociological Theory)*, Moscow, 1970.

RAZUMOVSKII, I. 'Filosofiia i iuridicheskaia teoriia' ('Philosophy and juridical theory'), *Pod znamenem marksizma*, no. 12, 1926.

ROZHIN, V. P. 'O predmete marksistskoi sotsiologii' ('On the subject of Marxist sociology'), *Voprosy marksistskoi sotsiologii*, V. P. Rozhin (ed.), Leningrad, 1962.

——'Razvivat' konkretnye sotsiologicheskie issledovaniia' ('To develop concrete sociological research'), *Vestnik MGU*, no. 5, 1966.

——(ed.) *Voprosy marksistsoi sotsiologii (Questions of Marxist Sociology)*, Leningrad, 1962.

RUMIANTSEV, A. M. 'Vstupaiushchemu v mir nauki' ('To those entering the world of science'), *Komsomol'skaia pravda*, 8 June 1967. Translated by the *CDSP*, vol. 19, no. 30, 1967.

RUMIANTSEV, A., BURLATSKII, F., and OSIPOV, G. 'Konkretnye sotsial'nye issledovaniia: zadachi, perspektivy' ('Concrete social research: tasks and prospects'), *Izvestiia*, 8 June 1968. Translated by the *CDSP*, vol. 20, no. 24, 1968.

RUMIANTSEV, A. M. and OSIPOV, G. V. 'Marksistskaia sotsiologiia i konkretnye sotsial'nye issledovaniia' ('Marxist sociology and concrete social research'), *Vop Fil*, no. 6, 1968.

RUMIANTSEV, A., TIMOFEEV, T., and SHEININ, IU. 'Dlia progressa nauki i truda' ('For progress of science and labour'), *Izvestiia*, 12 May 1966. Translated by the *CDSP*, vol. 18, no. 19, 1966.

RUSAKOV, R. S. and KARCHEMNIK, V. D. 'O rabote Instituta istorii, filologii i filosofii SO AN SSSR v 1969 godu' ('On the work of the Institute of History, Philology and Philosophy of the SO AN USSR in 1969'), *Izvestiia sibirskogo otdeleniia Akademii nauk SSSR*, no. 6, 1970.

RUTKEVICH, M. N. 'Izmenenie sotsial'noi struktury sovetskogo obshchestva i intelligentsiia' ('Change in the social structure of Soviet society and the intelligentsia'), *Sotsiologiia v SSSR*, vol. 1, G. V. Osipov (ed.), Moscow, 1966.

——'O poniatii intelligentsii kak sotsial'nogo sloia sotsialisticheskogo obshchestva' ('On the notion of the intelligentsia as a social layer of socialist society'), *Fil Nauki*, no. 4, 1966.

——*Protsessy izmeneniia sotsial'noi struktury v sovetskom obshchestve* (*Processes of Change of the Social Structure of Soviet Society*), Sverdlovsk, 1967.

——'Sotsial'nye istochniki popolneniia sovetskoi intelligentsii' ('Social sources of replenishment of the Soviet intelligentsia'), *Vop Fil*, no. 6, 1967. Translated by the *CDSP*, vol. 19, no. 35, 1967.

——'O kriteriiakh sotsial'nykh razlichii i ikh primenenii k intelligentsii' ('About the criteria of social differences and their application to the intelligentsia'), *Protsessy izmeneniia sotsial'noi struktury v sovetskom obshchestve*, M. N. Rutkevich (ed.), Sverdlovsk, 1967.

——'Problemy izmeneniia sotsial'noi struktury sovetskogo obshchestva' ('Problems of change of the structure of Soviet society'), *Fil Nauki*, no. 3, 1968.

——'Protsessy sotsial'nykh peremeshchenii i poniatie "sotsial'noi mobil'nost"' ('Processes of social movement and the concept of "social mobility"'), *Fil Nauki*, no. 5, 1970.

——'V. I. Lenin i problemy razvitiia intelligentsii' ('V. I. Lenin and the problems of the development of the intelligentsia'), *Doklady k VII mezhdunarodnomy sotsiologicheskomu kongressu*, O. N. Zhemanov (ed.), Sverdlovsk, 1970.

RUTKEVICH, M. N. and FILIPPOV, F. P. *Sotsial'nye peremeshcheniia* (*Social Movements*), Moscow, 1970.

RUTKEVICH, M. N. and KOGAN, L. N. 'O metodakh konkretno-sotsiologicheskogo issledovaniia' ('On the methods of concrete sociological research'), *Vop Fil*, no. 3, 1961. Translated by the *Soviet Review*, vol. 3, no. 11, 1962.

——'Marksistskaia sotsiologiia, sotsial'noe prognozirovanie i planirovanie' ('Marxist sociology, social forecasting and planning'), *Fil Nauki*, no. 3, 1971.

RYVKINA, R. V. 'Rol' i znachenie eksperimenta v obshchestvennykh naukakh' ('Role and significance of the experiment in the social sciences'), *Vop Fil*, no. 5, 1964.

——(ed.) *Sotsiologicheskie issledovaniia: voprosy metodologii i metodiki* (*Sociological Research: Questions of Methodology and Methods*), Novosibirsk, 1966.

SAMSONOV, IU. B. 'Vsesoiuznoe soveshchanie sotsiologov' ('All-Union conference of sociologists'), *Vop Fil*, no. 10, 1967.

SELESKERIDI, L. I. 'Chitatel'skaia konferentsiia v Tbilisi' ('Readers' conference in Tbilisi'), *Vop Fil*, no. 4, 1966.

SEMENOV, V. S. *Moscow Home Service*, 31 May 1966.

——'VI vsemirnyi sotsiologicheskii kongress' ('Sixth World Congress of Sociology'), *Vop Fil*, no. 8, 1967.

——'Novye iavleniia v sotsial'noi strukture sovetskogo obshchestva'

('New phenomena in the social structure of Soviet society'), *Fil Nauki*, no. 4, 1972.

SEMENOV, V. S. and GRETSKII, M. N. 'Marksistsko-Leninskaia nauka v nastuplenii' ('Marxist-Leninist science on the offensive'), *Fil Nauki*, no. 2, 1971.

SENNIKOVA, L. I. and TRUBINTSYN, O. N. 'Izmenenie sotsial'noi struktury sovetskogo obshchestva' ('Change of the social structure of Soviet society'), *Fil Nauki*, no. 4, 1972.

'Sessia sotsiologov' ('Session of sociologists'), *Pravda*, 23 November 1967. Translated by the *CDSP*, vol. 19, no. 47, 1967.

SHARGORODSKII, M. D. 'Prichiny i profilaktika prestupnosti' ('Causes and prevention of crime'), *Voprosy marksistskoi sotsiologii*, V. P. Rozhin (ed.), Leningrad, 1962. Translated by the *Soviet Review*, vol. 5, no. 3, 1964.

SHERKOVIN, IU. A. 'Obshchestvennoe mnenie v sovetskom obshchestve' ('Public opinion in Soviet society'), *Vop Fil*, no. 11, 1964.

SHKARATAN, O. I. 'Sotsial'naia struktura sovetskogo rabochego klassa' ('Social structure of the Soviet working class'), *Vop Fil*, no. 1, 1967. Translated by the *CDSP*, vol. 19, no. 12, 1967.

——'Rabochii klass sotsialisticheskogo obshchestva v epokhu nauchno-tekhnicheskoi revoliutsii' ('The working class in socialist society in the epoch of scientific and technical revolution'), *Vop Fil*, no. 11, 1968.

——'Problemy sotsial'noi struktury sovetskogo goroda' ('Problems of the social structure of the Soviet city'), *Fil Nauki*, no. 5, 1970.

——*Problemy sotsial'noi struktury rabochego klassa* (*Problems of the Social Structure of the Working Class*), Moscow, 1970.

SHLIAPENTOKH, V. *Sotsiologiia dlia vsekh* (*Sociology for Everyone*), Moscow, 1970.

SHUBKIN, V. N. 'Molodezh' vstupaet v zhizn' ' ('Youth enters life'), *Vop Fil*, no. 5, 1965. Translated by the *CDSP*, vol. 17, no. 30, 1965.

——'Nekotorye voprosy adaptatsii molodezhi k trudu' ('Several questions of adaptation of youth to labour'), *Sotsial'nye issledovaniia*, vol. 1, Moscow, 1965.

——'O konkretnykh issledovaniiakh sotsial'nykh protsessov' ('On concrete research of social processes'), *Kommunist*, no. 3, 1965. Translated by the *CDSP*, vol. 17, no. 17, 1965.

——'Ob ustoichivosti otsenok privlekatel'nosti professii' ('On the stability of an assessment of the attractiveness of certain professions'), *Sotsiologicheskie issledovaniia: voprosy metodologii i metodiki*, R. V. Ryvkina (ed.). Novosibirsk, 1966.

——'Sotsiologiia: Problemy i perspektivy' ('Sociology: problems and prospects'), *Pravda*, 13 March 1966. Translated by the *CDSP*, vol. 18, no. 11, 1966.

——'Kolichestvennye metody v sotsiologii' ('Quantitative methods in sociology'), *Vop Fil*, no. 3, 1967.

——*Sotsiologicheskie opyty: Metodologicheskie voprosy sotsial'nykh issledovanii* (*Sociological Experiences: Methodological Questions of Social Research*), Moscow, 1970.

'Sila i slabosti molodoi nauki' ('Strength and weaknesses of a young science'), *Literaturnaia gazeta*, 6 August 1966. Translated by the *CDSP*, vol. 18, no. 32, 1966.

'Sobranie sovetskoi sotsiologicheskoi assotsiatsii' ('Meeting of the Soviet Sociological Association'), *Vop Fil*, no. 6, 1966. Translated by the *CDSP*, vol. 18, no. 32, 1966.

SOLOMON, PETER H., Jr. 'Soviet criminology: the effects of post-Stalin politics on a social science', unpublished Master's dissertation, Columbia University, 1967.

SOLOV'EV, N., LAZAUSKAS, IU. and IANKOVA, Z. *Problemy byta, braka i sem'i* (*Problems of Byt, Marriage and the Family*), Vil'nius, 1970.

SOROKIN, P. A. *Leaves from a Russian Diary* (*1917–22*), London, 1925.

——'Russian sociology in the twentieth century', *Publications of the American Sociological Society*, vol. 21, 1926.

'Sotsiologiia' ('Sociology'), *Kratkii slovar' po filosofii*, I. V. Blauberg (ed.), Moscow, 1966.

STEPANIAN, TS. A. and SEMENOV, V. S. (eds) *Klassy, sotsial'nye sloi i gruppy v SSSR* (*Classes, social strata and groups in the USSR*), Moscow, 1968

——(eds) *Problemy izmeneniia sotsial'noi struktury sovetskogo obshchestva* (*Problems of the Change of the Social Structure of Soviet Society*), Moscow, 1968.

STRUMILIN, S. G. *Problemy ekonomiki truda* (*Problems of the Economics of Labour*), Moscow, 1957.

——*Rabochii den' i kommunizm* (*Work Day and Communism*), Moscow, 1959.

SUVOROV, L. N. 'Marksistskaia sotsiologiia i konkretnye sotsial'nye issledovaniia' ('Marxist sociology and concrete social research'), *Fil Nauki*, no. 3, 1963.

SVIRIDOV, G. 'Iz praktiki konkretnykh sotsiologicheskikh issledovanii' ('From the work of concrete sociological research'), *Partiinaia zhizn'*, no. 16, 1970.

SZALAI, A. 'The multinational comparative time budget research project: a venture in international research cooperation', *American Behavioral Scientist*, vol. 10, no. 4, 1966.

TAKHTAREV, K. M. *Sravnitel'naia istoriia razvitiia chelovecheskogo obshchestva i obshchestvennykh form: chast' pervaia* (*Comparative History of the Development of Human Society and Social Forms: Part One*), Leningrad, 1924.

TRAPEZNIKOV, S. P. 'Razvitie obshchestvennykh nauk i povyshenie ikh roli v kommunisticheskom stroitel'stve' ('Development of the social sciences and raising their role in communist construction'), *Vop Fil*, no. 11, 1967.

UGRINOVICH, D. M. 'Religiia kak predmet sotsiologicheskogo issledovaniia' ('Religion as a subject for sociological research'), *Ocherki metodologiia poznaniia sotsial'nykh iavlenii*, D. M. Ugrinovich, O. V. Larmin, and A. K. Uledov (eds), Moscow, 1970.

——'O predmete marksistskoi sotsiologii' ('On the subject of Marxist sociology'), *Ocherki metodologii poznaniia sotsial'nykh iavlenii*, D. M. Ugrinovich, O. V. Larmin, and A. K. Uledov (eds), Moscow, 1970.

UGRINOVICH, D. M., LARMIN, O. V., and ULEDOV, A. K. (eds), *Ocherki metodologii poznaniia sotsial'nykh iavlenii* (*Essays on the Methodology of Knowledge of Social Phenomena*), Moscow, 1970.

ULEDOV, A. K. 'O filosofskoi metodologii i konkretnykh metodakh sotsial'no-psikhologicheskogo issledovaniia: na materialakh izucheniia obshchestvennogo mneniia' ('On philosophical methodology and concrete methods of socio-psychological research: on materials of studying public opinion'), *Metodologicheskie voprosy obshchestvennykh nauk*, D. I. Chesnokov *et al.* (eds), Moscow, 1966.

USTINOVICH, N. V. 'Sotsializm i sem'ia' ('Socialism and the family'), *Vop Fil*, no. 7, 1967.

UTEVSKII, B. S. 'Sotsiologicheskie issledovaniia i kriminologiia' ('Sociological research and criminology'), *Vop Fil*, no. 2, 1964.

VERBIN, A. and FURMAN, A. *Mesto istoricheskogo materializma v sisteme nauk* (*The Place of Historical Materialism in the System of Sciences*), Moscow, 1965.

VERBIN, A. I., KELLE, V. ZH., and KOVAL'ZON, M. IA. 'Istoricheskii materializm i sotsiologiia' ('Historical materialism and sociology'), *Vop Fil*, no. 5, 1958.

VODZINSKAIA, V. V. and IADOV, V. A. 'U Pol'skikh sotsiologov' ('Among Polish sociologists'), *Fil Nauki*, no. 3, 1963.

VOL'FSON, S. IA. *Sotsiologiia braka i sem'i* (*Sociology of Marriage and the Family*), Moscow, 1928.

——*Sem'ia i brak v ikh istoricheskom ravzitii* (*Family and Marriage in their Historical Development*), Moscow, 1937.

VOLOVIK, L. A. (ed.) *Sotsiologiia i ideologiia* (*Sociology and Ideology*), Moscow, 1969.

VOL'SKII, V. 'Partiinaia zhizn': krugozor rukovoditelia' ('Party life: the leader's outlook'), *Pravda*, 17 January 1967. Translated by the *CDSP*, vol. 19, no. 3, 1967.

VORONOV, N. G. *Osnovaniia sotsiologii* (*The Foundations of Sociology*), Moscow, 1912.

ZANIN, V. I. 'Biudzhet rabochego vremeni' ('Budget of working time'), *Sotsial'nye issledovaniia: problemy biudzheta vremeni trudiashchikhsia*, vol. 6, Moscow, 1970.

ZASLAVSKAIA, T. I. (ed.) *Migratsiia sel'skogo naseleniia* (*Migration of the Rural Population*), Moscow, 1970.

ZASLAVSKAIA, T., SHLIAPENTOKH, V. and SHUBKIN, V. 'Sotsiolog i ego rabota' ('The sociologist and his work'), *Izvestiia*, 10 October 1967. Translated by the *CDSP*, vol. 19, no. 41, 1967.

ZDRAVOMYSLOV, A. 'Sotsiologiia: otkrytiia i vozmozhnosti kak razvivat' novuiu otrasl' znaniia' ('Sociology: discoveries and possibilities to develop a new sphere of knowledge'), *Sovetskaia rossiia*, 21 May 1964. Translated by the *CDSP*, vol. 16, no. 2, 1964.

——*Metodologiia i protsedura sotsiologicheskikh issledovanii* (*Methodology and Procedures of Sociological Research*), Moscow, 1969.

ZDRAVOMYSLOV, A. and IADOV, V. 'Opyt konkretnogo issledovaniia otnosheniia k trudu' ('Experience of concrete research on attitudes toward labour'), *Vop Fil*, no. 4, 1964. Translated by the *CDSP*, vol. 16, no. 24, 1964.

——(eds) *Trud i razvitie lichnosti* (*Labour and the Development of the Individual*), Leningrad, 1965.

——'Effect of vocational distinctions on the attitude to work', *Industry and Labour in the USSR*, G. V. Osipov (ed.), London, 1966.

ZDRAVOMYSLOV, A. G., ROZHIN, V. P., and IADOV, V. A. (eds), *Chelovek i ego rabota* (*Man and his Work*), Moscow, 1967.

ZHABSKII, M. I. and LENIK, P. K. 'Sotsiologicheskoe issledovanie massovogo retsipienta iskusstva' ('Sociological research of the influence of art on the masses'), *Vestnik MGU*, no. 4, 1967.

ZHEMANOV, O. N. (ed.) *Doklady k VII mezhdunarodnomu sotsiologicheskomu kongressu* (*Reports to the Seventh World Congress of Sociology*), Sverdlovsk, 1970.

ZVORYKIN, A. A. 'Istoricheskii materializm kak obshchesotsiologicheskikh teoriia i konkretnye sotsiologicheskie issledovaniia' ('Historical materialism as all-sociological theory and concrete sociological research'), *Fil Nauki*, no. 6, 1963.

170

Index

International Library of Sociology

Edited by
John Rex
University of Warwick

Founded by
Karl Mannheim

as The International Library of Sociology
and Social Reconstruction

*This Catalogue also contains other Social Science
series published by Routledge*

Routledge & Kegan Paul   London and Boston

68-74 Carter Lane London EC4V 5EL
9 Park Street Boston Mass 02108

Contents

● *Books so marked are available in paperback*
All books are in Metric Demy 8vo format (216 × 138mm approx.)

GENERAL SOCIOLOGY

Belshaw, Cyril. The Conditions of Social Performance. *An Exploratory Theory. 144 pp.*

Brown, Robert. Explanation in Social Science. *208 pp.*

● Rules and Laws in Sociology.

Cain, Maureen E. Society and the Policeman's Role. *About 300 pp.*

Gibson, Quentin. The Logic of Social Enquiry. *240 pp.*

Gurvitch, Georges. Sociology of Law. *Preface by Roscoe Pound. 264 pp.*

Homans, George C. Sentiments and Activities: *Essays in Social Science. 336 pp.*

Johnson, Harry M. Sociology: *a Systematic Introduction. Foreword by Robert K. Merton. 710 pp.*

Mannheim, Karl. Essays on Sociology and Social Psychology. *Edited by Paul Keckskemeti. With Editorial Note by Adolph Lowe. 344 pp.*

Systematic Sociology: *An Introduction to the Study of Society. Edited by J. S. Erös and Professor W. A. C. Stewart. 220 pp.*

Martindale, Don. The Nature and Types of Sociological Theory. *292 pp.*

● **Maus, Heinz.** A Short History of Sociology. *234 pp.*

Mey, Harald. Field-Theory. *A Study of its Application in the Social Sciences. 352 pp.*

Myrdal, Gunnar. Value in Social Theory: *A Collection of Essays on Methodology. Edited by Paul Streeten. 332 pp.*

Ogburn, William F., and **Nimkoff, Meyer F.** A Handbook of Sociology. *Preface by Karl Mannheim. 656 pp. 46 figures. 35 tables.*

Parsons, Talcott, and **Smelser, Neil J.** Economy and Society: *A Study in the Integration of Economic and Social Theory. 362 pp.*

● **Rex, John.** Key Problems of Sociological Theory. *220 pp.*

Urry, John. Reference Groups and the Theory of Revolution.

FOREIGN CLASSICS OF SOCIOLOGY

● **Durkheim, Emile.** Suicide. *A Study in Sociology. Edited and with an Introduction by George Simpson. 404 pp.*

Professional Ethics and Civic Morals. *Translated by Cornelia Brookfield. 288 pp.*

● **Gerth, H. H.,** and **Mills, C. Wright.** From Max Weber: *Essays in Sociology. 502 pp.*

Tönnies, Ferdinand. Community and Association. *(Gemeinschaft und Gesellschaft.) Translated and Supplemented by Charles P. Loomis. Foreword by Pitirim A. Sorokin. 334 pp.*

SOCIAL STRUCTURE

Andreski, Stanislav. Military Organization and Society. *Foreword by Professor A. R. Radcliffe-Brown. 226 pp. 1 folder.*

Coontz, Sydney H. Population Theories and the Economic Interpretation. *202 pp.*

Coser, Lewis. The Functions of Social Conflict. *204 pp.*

Dickie-Clark, H. F. Marginal Situation: *A Sociological Study of a Coloured Group. 240 pp. 11 tables.*

Glass, D. V. (Ed.). Social Mobility in Britain. *Contributions by J. Berent, T. Bottomore, R. C. Chambers, J. Floud, D. V. Glass, J. R. Hall, H. T. Himmelweit, R. K. Kelsall, F. M. Martin, C. A. Moser, R. Mukherjee, and W. Ziegel. 420 pp.*

Glaser, Barney, and **Strauss, Anselm L.** Status Passage. *A Formal Theory. 208 pp.*

Jones, Garth N. Planned Organizational Change: *An Exploratory Study Using an Empirical Approach. 268 pp.*

Kelsall, R. K. Higher Civil Servants in Britain: *From 1870 to the Present Day. 268 pp. 31 tables.*

König, René. The Community. *232 pp. Illustrated.*

● **Lawton, Denis.** Social Class, Language and Education. *192 pp.*

McLeish, John. The Theory of Social Change: *Four Views Considered. 128 pp.*

Marsh, David C. The Changing Social Structure of England and Wales, 1871-1961. *288 pp.*

Mouzelis, Nicos. Organization and Bureaucracy. *An Analysis of Modern Theories. 240 pp.*

Mulkay, M. J. Functionalism, Exchange and Theoretical Strategy. *272 pp.*

Ossowski, Stanislaw. Class Structure in the Social Consciousness. *210 pp.*

SOCIOLOGY AND POLITICS

Hertz, Frederick. Nationality in History and Politics: *A Psychology and Sociology of National Sentiment and Nationalism. 432 pp.*

Kornhauser, William. The Politics of Mass Society. *272 pp. 20 tables.*

Laidler, Harry W. History of Socialism. *Social-Economic Movements: An Historical and Comparative Survey of Socialism, Communism, Co-operation, Utopianism; and other Systems of Reform and Reconstruction. 992 pp.*

Mannheim, Karl. Freedom, Power and Democratic Planning. *Edited by Hans Gerth and Ernest K. Bramstedt. 424 pp.*

Mansur, Fatma. Process of Independence. *Foreword by A. H. Hanson. 208 pp.*

Martin, David A. Pacificism: *an Historical and Sociological Study. 262 pp.*

Myrdal, Gunnar. The Political Element in the Development of Economic Theory. *Translated from the German by Paul Streeten. 282 pp.*

Wootton, Graham. Workers, Unions and the State. *188 pp.*

FOREIGN AFFAIRS: THEIR SOCIAL, POLITICAL AND ECONOMIC FOUNDATIONS

Mayer, J. P. Political Thought in France from the Revolution to the Fifth Republic. *164 pp.*

CRIMINOLOGY

Ancel, Marc. Social Defence: *A Modern Approach to Criminal Problems. Foreword by Leon Radzinowicz. 240 pp.*

Cloward, Richard A., and **Ohlin, Lloyd E.** Delinquency and Opportunity: *A Theory of Delinquent Gangs. 248 pp.*

Downes, David M. The Delinquent Solution. *A Study in Subcultural Theory. 296 pp.*

Dunlop, A. B., and **McCabe, S.** Young Men in Detention Centres. *192 pp.*

Friedlander, Kate. The Psycho-Analytical Approach to Juvenile Delinquency: *Theory, Case Studies, Treatment. 320 pp.*

Glueck, Sheldon, and **Eleanor.** Family Environment and Delinquency. *With the statistical assistance of Rose W. Kneznek. 340 pp.*

Lopez-Rey, Manuel. Crime. *An Analytical Appraisal. 288 pp.*

Mannheim, Hermann. Comparative Criminology: *a Text Book. Two volumes. 442 pp. and 380 pp.*

Morris, Terence. The Criminal Area: *A Study in Social Ecology. Foreword by Hermann Mannheim. 232 pp. 25 tables. 4 maps.*

● **Taylor, Ian, Walton, Paul,** and **Young, Jock.** The New Criminology. *For a Social Theory of Deviance.*

SOCIAL PSYCHOLOGY

Bagley, Christopher. The Social Psychology of the Epileptic Child. 220 pp.

Barbu, Zevedei. Problems of Historical Psychology. *248 pp.*

Blackburn, Julian. Psychology and the Social Pattern. *184 pp.*

● **Brittan, Arthur.** Meanings and Situations. *224 pp.*

● **Fleming, C. M.** Adolescence: Its Social Psychology. *With an Introduction to recent findings from the fields of Anthropology, Physiology, Medicine, Psychometrics and Sociometry. 288 pp.*

● The Social Psychology of Education: *An Introduction and Guide to Its Study. 136 pp.*

Homans, George C. The Human Group. *Foreword by Bernard DeVoto. Introduction by Robert K. Merton. 526 pp.*

Social Behaviour: *its Elementary Forms. 416 pp.*

Klein, Josephine. The Study of Groups. *226 pp. 31 figures. 5 tables.*

Linton, Ralph. The Cultural Background of Personality. *132 pp.*

Mayo, Elton. The Social Problems of an Industrial Civilization. *With an appendix on the Political Problem. 180 pp.*

Ottaway, A. K. C. Learning Through Group Experience. *176 pp.*

Ridder, J. C. de. The Personality of the Urban African in South Africa. *A Thematic Apperception Test Study. 196 pp. 12 plates.*

● **Rose, Arnold M.** (Ed.). Human Behaviour and Social Processes: *an Interactionist Approach. Contributions by Arnold M. Rose, Ralph H. Turner, Anselm Strauss, Everett C. Hughes, E. Franklin Frazier, Howard S. Becker, et al. 696 pp.*

Smelser, Neil J. Theory of Collective Behaviour. *448 pp.*
Stephenson, Geoffrey M. The Development of Conscience. *128 pp.*
Young, Kimball. Handbook of Social Psychology. *658 pp. 16 figures. 10 tables.*

SOCIOLOGY OF THE FAMILY

Banks, J. A. Prosperity and Parenthood: *A Study of Family Planning among The Victorian Middle Classes. 262 pp.*
Bell, Colin R. Middle Class Families: *Social and Geographical Mobility. 224 pp.*
Burton, Lindy. Vulnerable Children. *272 pp.*
Gavron, Hannah. The Captive Wife: *Conflicts of Household Mothers. 190 pp.*
George, Victor, and **Wilding, Paul.** Motherless Families. *220 pp.*
Klein, Josephine. Samples from English Cultures.
  1. Three Preliminary Studies and Aspects of Adult Life in England. *447 pp.*
  2. Child-Rearing Practices and Index. *247 pp.*
Klein, Viola. Britain's Married Women Workers. *180 pp.*
  The Feminine Character. *History of an Ideology. 244 pp.*
McWhinnie, Alexina M. Adopted Children. *How They Grow Up. 304 pp.*
Myrdal, Alva, and **Klein, Viola.** Women's Two Roles: *Home and Work. 238 pp. 27 tables.*
Parsons, Talcott, and **Bales, Robert F.** Family: Socialization and Interaction Process. *In collaboration with James Olds, Morris Zelditch and Philip E. Slater. 456 pp. 50 figures and tables.*

SOCIAL SERVICES

Bastide, Roger. The Sociology of Mental Disorder. *Translated from the French by Jean McNeil. 260 pp.*
Carlebach, Julius. Caring For Children in Trouble. *266 pp.*
Forder, R. A. (Ed.). Penelope Hall's Social Services of England and Wales. *352 pp.*
George, Victor. Foster Care. *Theory and Practice. 234 pp.*
  Social Security: *Beveridge and After. 258 pp.*
● **Goetschius, George W.** Working with Community Groups. *256 pp.*
Goetschius, George W., and **Tash, Joan.** Working with Unattached Youth. *416 pp.*
Hall, M. P., and **Howes, I. V.** The Church in Social Work. *A Study of Moral Welfare Work undertaken by the Church of England. 320 pp.*
Heywood, Jean S. Children in Care: *the Development of the Service for the Deprived Child. 264 pp.*
Hoenig, J., and **Hamilton, Marian W.** The De-Segration of the Mentally Ill. *284 pp.*
Jones, Kathleen. Mental Health and Social Policy, 1845-1959. *264 pp.*

King, Roy D., Raynes, Norma V., and Tizard, Jack. Patterns of Residential Care. *356 pp.*

Leigh, John. Young People and Leisure. *256 pp.*

Morris, Mary. Voluntary Work and the Welfare State. *300 pp.*

Morris, Pauline. Put Away: *A Sociological Study of Institutions for the Mentally Retarded. 364 pp.*

Nokes, P. L. The Professional Task in Welfare Practice. *152 pp.*

Timms, Noel. Psychiatric Social Work in Great Britain (1939-1962). *280 pp.*

●   Social Casework: *Principles and Practice. 256 pp.*

Young, A. F., and Ashton, E. T. British Social Work in the Nineteenth Century. *288 pp.*

Young, A. F. Social Services in British Industry. *272 pp.*

SOCIOLOGY OF EDUCATION

Banks, Olive. Parity and Prestige in English Secondary Education: a Study in Educational Sociology. *272 pp.*

Bentwich, Joseph. Education in Israel. *224 pp. 8 pp. plates.*

● Blyth, W. A. L. English Primary Education. *A Sociological Description.*
  1. Schools. *232 pp.*
  2. Background. *168 pp.*

Collier, K. G. The Social Purposes of Education: *Personal and Social Values in Education. 268 pp.*

Dale, R. R., and Griffith, S. Down Stream: *Failure in the Grammar School. 108 pp.*

Dore, R. P. Education in Tokugawa Japan. *356 pp. 9 pp. plates*

Evans, K. M. Sociometry and Education. *158 pp.*

Foster, P. J. Education and Social Change in Ghana. *336 pp. 3 maps.*

Fraser, W. R. Education and Society in Modern France. *150 pp.*

Grace, Gerald R. Role Conflict and the Teacher. *About 200 pp.*

Hans, Nicholas. New Trends in Education in the Eighteenth Century. *278 pp. 19 tables.*

●   Comparative Education: *A Study of Educational Factors and Traditions. 360 pp.*

Hargreaves, David. Interpersonal Relations and Education. *432 pp.*

●   Social Relations in a Secondary School. *240 pp.*

Holmes, Brian. Problems in Education. *A Comparative Approach. 336 pp.*

King, Ronald. Values and Involvement in a Grammar School. *164 pp.*
  School Organization and Pupil Involvement. *A Study of Secondary Schools.*

● Mannheim, Karl, and Stewart, W. A. C. An Introduction to the Sociology of Education. *206 pp.*

Morris, Raymond N. The Sixth Form and College Entrance. *231 pp.*

● Musgrove, F. Youth and the Social Order. *176 pp.*

● Ottaway, A. K. C. Education and Society: An Introduction to the Sociology of Education. *With an Introduction by W. O. Lester Smith. 212 pp.*

Peers, Robert. Adult Education: *A Comparative Study. 398 pp.*

Pritchard, D. G. Education and the Handicapped: *1760 to 1960. 258 pp.*
Richardson, Helen. Adolescent Girls in Approved Schools. *308 pp.*
Stratta, Erica. The Education of Borstal Boys. *A Study of their Educational Experiences prior to, and during Borstal Training. 256 pp.*

SOCIOLOGY OF CULTURE

Eppel, E. M., and **M.** Adolescents and Morality: *A Study of some Moral Values and Dilemmas of Working Adolescents in the Context of a changing Climate of Opinion. Foreword by W. J. H. Sprott. 268 pp. 39 tables.*
● **Fromm, Erich.** The Fear of Freedom. *286 pp.*
The Sane Society. *400 pp.*
Mannheim, Karl. Essays on the Sociology of Culture. *Edited by Ernst Mannheim in co-operation with Paul Kecskemeti. Editorial Note by Adolph Lowe. 280 pp.*
Weber, Alfred. Farewell to European History: *or The Conquest of Nihilism Translated from the German by R. F. C. Hull. 224 pp.*

SOCIOLOGY OF RELIGION

Argyle, Michael. Religious Behaviour. *224 pp. 8 figures. 41 tables.*
Nelson, G. K. Spiritualism and Society. *313 pp.*
Stark, Werner. The Sociology of Religion. *A Study of Christendom.*
Volume I. *Established Religion. 248 pp.*
Volume II. *Sectarian Religion. 368 pp.*
Volume III. *The Universal Church. 464 pp.*
Volume IV. *Types of Religious Man. 352 pp.*
Volume V. *Types of Religious Culture. 464 pp.*
Watt, W. Montgomery. Islam and the Integration of Society. *320 pp.*

SOCIOLOGY OF ART AND LITERATURE

Jarvie, Ian C. Towards a Sociology of the Cinema. *A Comparative Essay on the Structure and Functioning of a Major Entertainment Industry. 405 pp.*
Rust, Frances S. Dance in Society. *An Analysis of the Relationships between the Social Dance and Society in England from the Middle Ages to the Present Day. 256 pp. 8 pp. of plates.*
Schücking, L. L. The Sociology of Literary Taste. *112 pp.*

SOCIOLOGY OF KNOWLEDGE

Mannheim, Karl. Essays on the Sociology of Knowledge. *Edited by Paul Kecskemeti. Editorial Note by Adolph Lowe. 353 pp.*
Remmling, Gunter W. (Ed.). Towards the Sociology of Knowledge. *Origins and Development of a Sociological Thought Style.*
Stark, Werner. The Sociology of Knowledge: *An Essay in Aid of a Deeper Understanding of the History of Ideas. 384 pp.*

URBAN SOCIOLOGY

Ashworth, William. The Genesis of Modern British Town Planning: *A Study in Economic and Social History of the Nineteenth and Twentieth Centuries. 288 pp.*
Cullingworth, J. B. Housing Needs and Planning Policy: *A Restatement of the Problems of Housing Need and 'Overspill' in England and Wales. 232 pp. 44 tables. 8 maps.*
Dickinson, Robert E. City and Region: *A Geographical Interpretation. 608 pp. 125 figures.*
The West European City: *A Geographical Interpretation. 600 pp. 129 maps. 29 plates.*
● The City Region in Western Europe. *320 pp. Maps.*
Humphreys, Alexander J. New Dubliners: *Urbanization and the Irish Family. Foreword by George C. Homans. 304 pp.*
Jackson, Brian. Working Class Community: *Some General Notions raised by a Series of Studies in Northern England. 192 pp.*
Jennings, Hilda. Societies in the Making: *a Study of Development and Redevelopment within a County Borough. Foreword by D. A. Clark. 286 pp.*
● **Mann, P. H.** An Approach to Urban Sociology. *240 pp.*
Morris, R. N., and **Mogey, J.** The Sociology of Housing. *Studies at Berinsfield. 232 pp. 4 pp. plates.*
Rosser, C., and **Harris, C.** The Family and Social Change. *A Study of Family and Kinship in a South Wales Town. 352 pp. 8 maps.*

RURAL SOCIOLOGY

Chambers, R. J. H. Settlement Schemes in Tropical Africa: *A Selective Study. 268 pp.*
Haswell, M. R. The Economics of Development in Village India. *120 pp.*
Littlejohn, James. Westrigg: *the Sociology of a Cheviot Parish. 172 pp. 5 figures.*
Mayer, Adrian C. Peasants in the Pacific. *A Study of Fiji Indian Rural Society. 248 pp. 20 plates.*
Williams, W. M. The Sociology of an English Village: *Gosforth. 272 pp. 12 figures. 13 tables.*

SOCIOLOGY OF INDUSTRY AND DISTRIBUTION

Anderson, Nels. Work and Leisure. *280 pp.*
● **Blau, Peter M.,** and **Scott, W. Richard.** Formal Organizations: *a Comparative approach. Introduction and Additional Bibliography by J. H. Smith. 326 pp.*
Eldridge, J. E. T. Industrial Disputes. *Essays in the Sociology of Industrial Relations. 288 pp.*
Hetzler, Stanley. Applied Measures for Promoting Technological Growth. *352 pp.*
Technological Growth and Social Change. *Achieving Modernization. 269 pp.*
Hollowell, Peter G. The Lorry Driver. *272 pp.*
Jefferys, Margot, *with the assistance of Winifred Moss.* Mobility in the Labour Market: *Employment Changes in Battersea and Dagenham. Preface by Barbara Wootton. 186 pp. 51 tables.*
Millerson, Geoffrey. The Qualifying Associations: *a Study in Professionalization. 320 pp.*
Smelser, Neil J. Social Change in the Industrial Revolution: *An Application of Theory to the Lancashire Cotton Industry, 1770-1840. 468 pp. 12 figures. 14 tables.*
Williams, Gertrude. Recruitment to Skilled Trades. *240 pp.*
Young, A. F. Industrial Injuries Insurance: *an Examination of British Policy. 192 pp.*

DOCUMENTARY

Schlesinger, Rudolf (Ed.). Changing Attitudes in Soviet Russia.
2. The Nationalities Problem and Soviet Administration. *Selected Readings on the Development of Soviet Nationalities Policies. Introduced by the editor. Translated by W. W. Gottlieb. 324 pp.*

ANTHROPOLOGY

Ammar, Hamed. Growing up in an Egyptian Village: *Silwa, Province of Aswan. 336 pp.*
Brandel-Syrier, Mia. Reeftown Elite. *A Study of Social Mobility in a Modern African Community on the Reef. 376 pp.*
Crook, David, and **Isabel.** Revolution in a Chinese Village: *Ten Mile Inn. 230 pp. 8 plates. 1 map.*
Dickie-Clark, H. F. The Marginal Situation. *A Sociological Study of a Coloured Group. 236 pp.*
Dube, S. C. Indian Village. *Foreword by Morris Edward Opler. 276 pp. 4 plates.*
India's Changing Villages: *Human Factors in Community Development. 260 pp. 8 plates. 1 map.*

Firth, Raymond. Malay Fishermen. *Their Peasant Economy. 420 pp. 17 pp. plates.*

Gulliver, P. H. Social Control in an African Society: a Study of the Arusha, Agricultural Masai of Northern Tanganyika. *320 pp. 8 plates. 10 figures.*

Ishwaran, K. Shivapur. *A South Indian Village. 216 pp.*
Tradition and Economy in Village India: *An Interactionist Approach. Foreword by Conrad Arensburg. 176 pp.*

Jarvie, Ian C. The Revolution in Anthropology. *268 pp.*

Jarvie, Ian C., and **Agassi, Joseph.** Hong Kong. *A Society in Transition. 396 pp. Illustrated with plates and maps.*

Little, Kenneth L. Mende of Sierra Leone. *308 pp. and folder.*
Negroes in Britain. *With a New Introduction and Contemporary Study by Leonard Bloom. 320 pp.*

Lowie, Robert H. Social Organization. *494 pp.*

Mayer, Adrian C. Caste and Kinship in Central India: *A Village and its Region. 328 pp. 16 plates. 15 figures. 16 tables.*

Smith, Raymond T. The Negro Family in British Guiana: *Family Structure and Social Status in the Villages. With a Foreword by Meyer Fortes. 314 pp. 8 plates. 1 figure. 4 maps.*

SOCIOLOGY AND PHILOSOPHY

Barnsley, John H. The Social Reality of Ethics. *A Comparative Analysis of Moral Codes. 448 pp.*

Diesing, Paul. Patterns of Discovery in the Social Sciences. *362 pp.*

Douglas, Jack D. (Ed.). Understanding Everyday Life. *Toward the Reconstruction of Sociological Knowledge. Contributions by Alan F. Blum. Aaron W. Cicourel, Norman K. Denzin, Jack D. Douglas, John Heeren, Peter McHugh, Peter K. Manning, Melvin Power, Matthew Speier, Roy Turner, D. Lawrence Wieder, Thomas P. Wilson and Don H. Zimmerman. 370 pp.*

Jarvie, Ian C. Concepts and Society. *216 pp.*

Roche, Maurice. Phenomenology, Language and the Social Sciences. *About 400 pp.*

Sahay, Arun. Sociological Analysis.

Sklair, Leslie. The Sociology of Progress. *320 pp.*

International Library of Anthropology
General Editor Adam Kuper

Brown, Paula. The Chimbu. *A Study of Change in the New Guinea Highlands.*
Van Den Berghe, Pierre L. Power and Privilege at an African University.

International Library of Social Policy

General Editor Kathleen Jones

Holman, Robert. Trading in Children. *A Study of Private Fostering.*
Jones, Kathleen. History of the Mental Health Services. *428 pp.*
Thomas, J. E. The English Prison Officer since 1850: *A Study in Conflict.*
  258 pp.

Primary Socialization, Language and Education

General Editor Basil Bernstein

Bernstein, Basil. Class, Codes and Control. *2 volumes.*
  1. *Theoretical Studies Towards a Sociology of Language. 254 pp.*
  2. *Applied Studies Towards a Sociology of Language. About 400 pp.*
Brandis, Walter, and **Henderson, Dorothy.** Social Class, Language and Communication. *288 pp.*
Cook-Gumperz, Jenny. Social Control and Socialization. *A Study of Class Differences in the Language of Maternal Control.*
Gahagan, D. M., and **G. A.** Talk Reform. *Exploration in Language for Infant School Children. 160 pp.*
Robinson, W. P., and **Rackstraw, Susan, D. A.** A Question of Answers. *2 volumes. 192 pp. and 180 pp.*
Turner, Geoffrey, J., and **Mohan, Bernard, A.** A Linguistic Description and Computer Programme for Children's Speech. *208 pp.*

Reports of the Institute of Community Studies

Cartwright, Ann. Human Relations and Hospital Care. *272 pp.*
  Parents and Family Planning Services. *306 pp.*
  Patients and their Doctors. *A Study of General Practice. 304 pp.*
● **Jackson, Brian.** Streaming: *an Education System in Miniature. 168 pp.*
Jackson, Brian, and **Marsden, Dennis.** Education and the Working Class: *Some General Themes raised by a Study of 88 Working-class Children in a Northern Industrial City. 268 pp. 2 folders.*
Marris, Peter. The Experience of Higher Education. *232 pp. 27 tables.*
Marris, Peter, and **Rein, Martin.** Dilemmas of Social Reform. *Poverty and Community Action in the United States. 256 pp.*
Marris, Peter, and **Somerset, Anthony.** African Businessmen. *A Study of Entrepreneurship and Development in Kenya. 256 pp.*
Mills, Richard. Young Outsiders: *a Study in Alternative Communities.*

Runciman, W. G. Relative Deprivation and Social Justice. *A Study of Attitudes to Social Inequality in Twentieth Century England. 352 pp.*
Townsend, Peter. The Family Life of Old People: *An Inquiry in East London. Foreword by J. H. Sheldon. 300 pp. 3 figures. 63 tables.*
Willmott, Peter. Adolescent Boys in East London. *230 pp.*
The Evolution of a Community: *a study of Dagenham after forty years. 168 pp. 2 maps.*
Willmott, Peter, and **Young, Michael.** Family and Class in a London Suburb. *202 pp. 47 tables.*
Young, Michael. Innovation and Research in Education. *192 pp.*
● **Young, Michael,** and **McGeeney, Patrick.** Learning Begins at Home. *A Study of a Junior School and its Parents. 128 pp.*
Young, Michael, and **Willmott, Peter.** Family and Kinship in East London. *Foreword by Richard M. Titmuss. 252 pp. 39 tables.*
The Symmetrical Family.

Reports of the Institute for Social Studies in Medical Care

Cartwright, Ann, Hockey, Lisbeth, and **Anderson, John L.** Life Before Death.
Dunnell, Karen, and **Cartwright, Ann.** Medicine Takers, Prescribers and Hoarders. *190 pp.*

Medicine, Illness and Society
General Editor W. M. Williams

Robinson, David. The Process of Becoming Ill.
Stacey, Margaret. *et al.* Hospitals, Children and Their Families. *The Report of a Pilot Study. 202 pp.*

Monographs in Social Theory
General Editor Arthur Brittan

Bauman, Zygmunt. Culture as Praxis.
Dixon, Keith. Sociological Theory. *Pretence and Possibility.*
Smith, Anthony D. The Concept of Social Change. *A Critique of the Functionalist Theory of Social Change.*

Routledge Social Science Journals

The British Journal of Sociology. *Edited by Terence P. Morris. Vol. 1, No. 1, March 1950 and Quarterly. Roy. 8vo. Back numbers available. An international journal with articles on all aspects of sociology.*

Economy and Society. *Vol. 1, No. 1. February 1972 and Quarterly. Metric Roy. 8vo. A journal for all social scientists covering sociology, philosophy, anthropology, economics and history. Back numbers available.*

Year Book of Social Policy in Britain, The. *Edited by Kathleen Jones. 1971. Published Annually.*

Printed in Great Britain by Lewis Reprints Limited
Brown Knight & Truscott Group, London and Tonbridge

1373

14